The
Strategic Pricing
of Pharmaceuticals

E.M. (Mick) Kolassa, Ph.D.

The PondHouse Press

Book design by:
Arbor Books, Inc.
www.arborbooks.com

Printed in the United States of America

The Strategic Pricing of Pharmaceuticals
E.M. (Mick) Kolassa, Ph.D.

1. Title 2. Author 3. Business/Marketing/Pharmaceutical Industry

Library of Congress Control Number: 2009923346

ISBN 10: 0-9823715-0-0
ISBN 13: 978-0-9823715-0-3

About the Contributors

E.M. (Mick) Kolassa is Chairman and Managing Partner of Medical Marketing Economics, a global firm that develops value based strategies for pharmaceutical and biotechnology companies. Mick is recognized internationally as the leading expert on pharmaceutical pricing and value-based strategies. He also serves as Adjunct Professor at the University of Mississippi and the University of the Sciences in Philadelphia, and is former Associate Professor of Pharmacy Administration and Marketing at the University of Mississippi. He was editor of the Journal of Pharmaceutical Marketing & Management and authored several articles and book chapters on pharmaceutical marketing and pricing issues. He is coauthor of the book Pharmaceutical Marketing: Principles, Environment, and Practice. Dr. Kolassa's first book on pharmaceutical pricing, Elements of Pharmaceutical Pricing, was published in 1997. Mick also served as Director of Pricing and Economic Policy at Sandoz, and has held positions at The Upjohn Company, the Strategic Pricing Group, and Hastings Healthcare. Mick holds an MBA from Eastern Washington University and a PhD from the University of Mississippi.

Jack Mycka is President, Global CEO and Partner at MME. Since 2001 Jack has provided critical support for strategic marketing and pricing decisions in the biotech and pharmaceutical industries in many product classes and therapeutic areas centered on value and its interaction with pricing, payers, reimbursement, and marketing in general. His expertise in pharmaceutical pricing was first developed while serving as the Director of Pharmaceutical Pricing and Contracting at Roche Laboratories Inc., in Nutley, NJ. Previously, Jack spent ten years as a commercial banker. Jack received a BS in Finance from Lehigh University.

William Lobb is a Vice President & Partner at MME, where he heads up the firm's quantitative marketing and pricing research arm. His community pharmacy experience includes management at several levels. Bill has been a leader in state and national pharmacy associations, including the American College of Apothecaries, where he developed and finalized products to improve the profitability of independent pharmacy practice. He graduated from the University of Texas, College of Pharmacy and holds both an MS and Ph.D.in pharmaceutical marketing from the University of Mississippi.

Kevin Patterson is a Vice President & Partner at MME, whose background is in finance and health systems management. He was Director of Finance for Ambulatory Operations for a major hospital system, and Director of Healthcare Strategies for a large accounting firm. Kevin holds a Masters in Accountancy from the University of Mississippi and is a certified public accountant.

Doug Paul is a Vice President & Partner at MME, where he focuses on market assessments and orphan drug issues. He has been active at the national level with various pharmacy associations and played a key role in the development of the American College of Veterinary Pharmacists. Doug earned his PharmD and an MS in pharmaceutical marketing from the University of Mississippi.

Brian Reisetter is a Vice President & Partner at MME. A former hospital pharmacy director and pharmaceutical sales representative, Brian is a recognized leader in researching community pharmacy. He has a Bachelor of Science in Pharmacy and an MBA, both from Drake University, and a PhD with an emphasis in pharmaceutical marketing from the University of Mississippi.

Renato Dellamano President of MME Europe. Dr. Dellamano, who founded ValueVector, a strategic pricing consultancy, was also Head of Strategic Pricing at the global Headquarters of the Swiss pharmaceutical giant Hoffmann-La Roche, and served as Global Controller of the Pharma Division of the same company. A Health Economist and a former professor of Hospital Management, Renato received his Doctorate from Bocconi University of Milan, and specialized in health economics at the CERGAS - Center for Research on Health Care Management

Table of Contents

Acknowledgments

Where to begin? As with any endeavor, the credit for this book belongs to many people: colleagues, mentors, and others. Taking them in that order I must first thank my partners (in alphabetical order), Bill Lobb, Brian Reisetter, Doug Paul, Jack Mycka, and Kevin Patterson. They have contributed not only to this book, which explains the frequent use of the pronoun "we," but also to the richness of my life. Other colleagues upon whom I have come to depend for this and other efforts are Curt Friehs, Larry Poli, Renato Dellamano, Bill Little, and Jonathan Peck. Thanks guys. I also want to thank Tom Nagle, Reed Holden, Jerry Smith, Kent Monroe, Mike Marne, Gene Zelek, and Dick Harmer for working so hard to innovate in the field of pricing, for making it more important, and for making me a better pricer.

I have also been blessed to have two wonderful mentors who are also friends and colleagues. Dan Nimer, the Jedi Master of pricing, and Mickey Smith, upon whose shoulders I stand, have provided me with support, encouragement, and some of the best lessons I've ever learned.

A special note of thanks goes to Julie Fisher, documatrix extraordinaire, the finest editor on earth, and perennial guy of the year.

Finally, but certainly not least, thanks to Peg Powers for her editorial and proofing work, which vastly improved this book.

Foreword

Mastering the art of pricing draws on multiple disciplines and perspectives. Essentially, pricing is a top management responsibility encompassing financial, marketing, and legal considerations. In the pharmaceutical industry, decision makers must also factor in medical, biological, ethical, and regulatory issues. Dr. Kolassa carefully develops and explains these very complex issues and offers some very important counsel for understanding the complications of pricing pharmaceutical products.

Because pricing is the lone marketing decision variable that directly affects a firm's revenues and, therefore, profits, it is a vital area of business management. Unfortunately, neither businesses nor business schools provide sufficient guidance and training for employees or students to be effective pricing managers. This concern definitely extends to the pharmaceutical industry as well as public policy officials involved in oversight of the industry. It seems that both business managers and business faculty accept the myth that anyone can set prices. Sadly, this myth is false, and we consistently have situations where good decision makers make bad pricing decisions.

Thus, there is great need for Mick Kolassa's book *The Strategic Pricing of Pharmaceuticals*. He appropriately takes a strategic perspective to pricing while at the same time recognizing the need to understand the differences among pricing strategy, pricing tactics, and pricing policies. His chapter on "The Role of Value in the Pricing of Pharmaceuticals" is important and a must-read for the various constituents of the pharmaceuticals world. The way people form value judgments in the very complicated area of medicines and drugs does not necessarily correspond to what is generally assumed in economic theory or perhaps what has been assumed by those involved in the pharmaceutical industry. Consequently, one important reason why managers make bad pricing decisions is that they do not understand how the various decision makers in the purchase of pharmaceuticals perceive prices and judge value.

Overall, this is a very insightful and highly informative book and one that must be read by anyone involved in the pharmaceutical industry.

—Kent B. Monroe
Author of *Pricing: Making Profitable Decisions*

Chapter 1

Why Is Pharmaceutical Pricing Different?

What is a cynic? A man who knows the price of
everything and the value of nothing.
—Oscar Wilde

Few things are as maligned, misunderstood, and mischaracterized as the pricing of pharmaceuticals. Economists, when applying basic economic theory to pharmaceutical markets, are either thwarted or develop spurious models of questionable value. Lawmakers, eager for a populist soapbox, criticize pharmaceutical pricing, and pass laws that complicate it, without understanding the issues and forces that drive prices in this unique market.

The market for prescription pharmaceutical products differs substantially from most other markets in a number of important ways. Typically, markets operate in response to consumer demand, which often can be affected to a great extent by marketing activities undertaken and prices charged by manufacturers and others. Customers, either businesses or consumers, often desire products that are heavily marketed for a number of reasons, not all of which might be considered rational. Pharmaceutical markets, on the other hand, exist only in response to the initial medical need for the relief

1

provided by the product; they are prescribed by an individual not involved in the financial transaction of the actual sale; and they are consumed by another individual who, all things considered, would rather not need the product in the first place and may have no idea why it has been prescribed. This individual, the patient, may or may not have a direct role in the actual purchase of the product. This dynamic is in stark contrast to most markets, and therefore the role that price plays is decidedly different and traditional marketing and economic approaches to pricing cannot be relied upon.

To differentiate the pharmaceutical market from other markets, we must understand three key points:

1. Prescription medicines are subject to derived demand. Products are demanded and sold in response to medical need. Their use is affected greatly by recognized standards of care, and an essential decision maker for prescription medicines is the physician, who neither consumes nor pays for the product.
2. Prescription medicines are considered to be "negative goods," in that those who purchase or consume them would prefer not to do so.
3. Prescription medicines are experience goods, which means that their actual utility cannot be determined until they have been used, and their continued use depends on satisfactory experience.

A PARALLEL EXAMPLE: COLLEGE TEXTBOOKS

Prescription medicines are used in response to medical need, and the choice of medicine is made primarily by physicians. Another product that is subject to such "derived demand" and is selected by an agent working on behalf of the consumer is a college textbook. The professor determines what book or books will be best for the student in a particular course and then instructs the student to make the purchase. Usually, the professor has no idea of the price of the text, only its value. The text itself is selected based on the standards of the subject matter and the institution. The student has no choice in the selection of the text; he or she simply buys it and uses it as directed—or not.

The process described for textbooks is almost identical to that for most prescription drugs with the caveat that the decision is made for each individual patient, not an entire class. In the same way that an instructor chooses college texts primarily on the basis of content, physicians decide which drug to use primarily on the basis of standards of treatment and medical principles, with price seldom affecting the initial product decision. Price, either the full price or the patient co-payment, may play a role in the patient's decision to have the prescription filled, just as the cost of a textbook may cause a student to fail to purchase that requirement, but it does not affect the initial decision to prescribe use or require purchase. And, as just mentioned, it may not be the price of the medicine itself that affects product use, but the price of the co-payment, over which the manufacturer has little or no control. Attempts to apply basic economic and marketing theories to such a complex transaction are destined to fail.

SOME MORE EXAMPLES: TOW TRUCKS AND PEST CONTROL

Unlike most products with which we are familiar, pharmaceuticals are "negative goods," which can be defined as "products or services seen by customers as an unpleasant necessity bought to avoid some disutility." In other words, negative goods are products that people would rather not buy. Pest control, tow trucks, and even gasoline are examples of other negative goods—we buy them because we need them, not because we want them. The primary benefit of negative goods is that they remove an unpleasant condition.[1] A customer purchases a negative good (or fills a prescription) to overcome or reduce an underlying problem, not to add pleasure or enhance personal image. The difference in the reasons for the continued purchase of positive and negative goods can be summed up as follows:

> Positive reinforcement occurs when the subject's positive utility increases. For example, the purchase behavior of ice cream is reinforced by pleasant consumption. On the other hand, negative reinforcement causes an increased probability of a behavior through disutility reduction. The subject is under some pain or discomfort, and the action that reduces that discomfort is reinforced.[2]

Because of this negative nature of pharmaceuticals, the prices of most medicines will always be considered "too high" because people would rather not have to buy them at all. Most people will never look at a price for a medicine and say, "I got a great deal." On the contrary, they will either complain that the price was far too high or that it was okay but could have been lower simply because they didn't want it in the first place.

WINE AND EXPERT ADVICE

Like wine and expert advice, the quality and usefulness of a medicine cannot be judged until it has been tried. An "experience" good is distinguished by the fact that its quality, and therefore its value or usefulness to a customer, cannot be precisely determined at or before the time of purchase. To be distinguished from buying situations in which product quality is known, with "experience" goods customers cannot know until after their use whether they will have positive outcomes. Customers who experience less than satisfactory effects cannot automatically infer that the producer has cheated them, but only that the desired effect was not achieved, as in, "I don't like the taste of this wine." This problem arises from the nature of the product; regardless of the search for information undertaken before the purchase, the customer cannot know whether the desired outcome will be achieved until he or she has had experience with the product. Dr. David Dranove, a noted health economist, in his book, *The Economic Evolution of American Health Care: From Marcus Welby to Managed Care*, notes that health care may be "the quintessential experience good."[3]

A person evaluating a new medicine can't judge the appropriateness, or fairness, of a price until after the product has been used. This makes price comparisons almost meaningless during the initial decision-making process, which, in turn, makes pharmaceutical pricing much more complicated than pricing for many other products.

With these three issues in mind, one must admit that the chance of setting a price that is "optimal" is nearly impossible. Prescribers don't know the price of the medicine that the patients would rather not take, and nobody knows if it is the right medicine until after it has been purchased and consumed.[4, 5] That structure doesn't fit nicely into any marketing or economic model, no matter how hard we try to force it. For this reason, it is much easier to set a bad price than a good one.

But what constitutes a "bad" price? To answer this question, we must look first at the roles that the price plays in the marketplace. For all practical purposes, the price should serve two distinct roles:

1. A clear signal of the quality and utility of the product to the marketplace
2. The mechanism through which the marketer captures a portion of that value and uses it for ongoing enterprise.

PRICE AS A QUALITY SIGNAL

At the core of the concept of value-based pricing is the need for the price of the product to be aligned with its value. Even when firms use some mechanism other than value to set their price, the market will soon use the price to "frame" the value of the product. When members of the market, such as physicians, don't know the price, they ascribe a price based on their perceptions of the value of the product. Over the years, this has led to some interesting situations. Xanax® (alprazolam), a mild tranquilizer, entered the market at a 25% discount to Valium® (diazepam), the market leader. Studies of prescribers found that they believed Xanax was priced much higher than Valium because they perceived it to be a better drug. A similar situation occurred when Lipitor® (atorvastatin) was launched. The bulk of Lipitor prescribers believed it was the most expensive statin because it was viewed as clearly better than the other statins.

In consumer markets, we are taught that price is often used as a surrogate indicator of quality—customers will use price as a cue about the quality of a product. Physicians, generally, use quality (or utility) as a surrogate indicator of price. When the price of a product is set well below its perceived quality, the company is "leaving money on the table."

PRICE AS A VALUE-CAPTURING MECHANISM

Underpricing a pharmaceutical product is perhaps the costliest mistake a firm can make. We disagree with those who claim that pharmaceutical prices are set, in part, to recapture research and development costs because it is almost impossible to know those costs precisely at the time a price is set. However, capturing the value of the product through appropriate prices allows firms to fund future research, which provides these businesses and the market with valuable new products. With R&D costs for a single drug estimated at nearly $1 billion, it is vital that a sufficient proportion of the value of the product is captured by the price charged to provide for reinvestment in R&D.[6] The company that consistently sets low prices for valuable products is inadvertently restricting its future pipeline and shortchanging its investors and patients.

Yet, the internal structures of many pharmaceutical companies allow underpricing to occur regularly. Those behind these decisions may believe that lower prices will help spur higher sales (a myth we deal with in the next chapter) or at least making selling easier and therefore default to lower prices. If discounts or price concessions were seen as direct costs, perhaps it wouldn't be so easy to make this mistake.

Consider the difficulty within a company of acquiring an additional $50 million to support the launch of a new product. The product team will be provided a budget for launch based on the firm's available resources. If the team believes an additional $50 million in initial promotional spending is warranted, most would have difficulty in securing those additional funds. But a decision to set the price of the product 10% below that of the major competitor usually requires little justification; managers throughout the organization will approve it. If that product can reasonably be expected to sell $500 million per year, the 10% discount "costs" the company the equivalent of the $50 million in launch promotion spending...but *every* year, not just during launch. We will argue that it is a much better decision to set the price at the higher level *and* spend the additional money to support the launch.

IT'S THE PRODUCT...

With few exceptions, we have found that the specific price charged for a medicine has little effect on its unit sales. Because the demand for prescription pharmaceuticals is driven by the underlying epidemiology of the disease and the utility of the product in treating it, far too much time and money is spent on fine-tuning the price to fit with traditional demand models (which actually bear little resemblance to actual market dynamics), while far too little time is spent selecting a pricing strategy that allows the product to be used in all appropriate settings and provides the firm with the profits it needs to prosper in the future. This book has been written, in part, to help firms move in the right direction and to help others understand why the prices for medicines are fair and appropriate.

Because the principal determinant of the success of a medicine is its clinical usefulness, in most instances there is little that can be done with price to drive demand higher. We will admit that it is theoretically possible to set a price that is too high. This has occurred often in European and Canadian markets, where the "social contract" between the health care system and the citizens differs drastically from that in the US. However, we have yet to identify such a situation in the US market. In the end, we have yet to find a "pricing problem" that is caused by price or can be corrected by changing price. When customers do not understand the value of a product, their first reaction is to claim the price is too high. A lower price will not "fix" the problem inherent in a product that has no value in the pharmaceutical marketplace. For a product with high value, price objections will have two sources:

- The value of the product has not been communicated and thus is poorly understood by the customers.
- The price objections stem from customers attempting to negotiate a lower price.

If the problem is that the company itself has done a poor job of communicating the value of the product—a situation that happens often in pharmaceutical markets, where the promotional message will focus on the science of the medicine and not the outcomes it provides—the solution is for the firm to better understand and communicate that value. A lower price will not help a product without perceived value. If the value of the product is not recognized, why would a clinician use it? Conversely, if the value is clear, a clinician will use it willingly.

The following chapters further develop this relationship between pricing and value in the pharmaceuticals marketplace and explore as well the myriad other factors and forces that will affect pharmaceutical products' commercial success. To put it succinctly, profitable and purposeful pricing is no big thing—it's a whole lot of little things.

REFERENCES

1. Hawkins DI, Best RJ, Coney KA. Consumer behavior: Implications for marketing strategy. Chicago: Irwin; 1995.
2. Widrick S, Fram E. Identifying negative products: Do customers like to purchase your products? *J Product Brand Manage.* 1992; 1(1):43.
3. Dranove D. The economic evolution of American health care: From Marcus Welby to managed care. Princeton, NJ: Princeton University Press; 2000.
4. Kolassa EM. Physicians' perceptions of pharmaceutical prices: Their accuracy and effect on the prescribing decision. *J Res Pharm Econ.* 1995; 6(1):23-37.
5. Reisetter BC, Bentley JP, Wilkin NE. Relationship between psychosocial physician characteristics and physician price awareness. *J Pharm Market Manage.* 2005; 17(1):51-76.
6. DiMasi JA, Hansen RW, Grabowski HG. The price of innovation: New estimates of drug development costs. *J Health Econ.* 2003; 22:151-85.

Chapter 2

Basic Pricing Principles

*It cannot be too strongly emphasized that the
deciding factor in price setting is the price which
the consumer is willing, or can be induced, to pay.*
—R. Edwards, Economica, 1945

When discussing pharmaceutical pricing, it is best first to consider the basics of pricing, regardless of industry. Economists and others often treat pricing as a simple process of estimating costs and measuring demand, then setting the profit-maximizing price. As the remaining chapters of this book will point out, there is much more to setting and managing the prices of pharmaceutical products than doing some research and identifying the optimal price. But then, there is much more to setting the price of any innovative product than "finding" it through marketing research.

The calculation-driven pricing favored by economic theory, which assumes and relies on the measurement of elasticity, is very different from the concept of value-based pricing, which is consistent with marketing theory. Value-based pricing involves setting a price that reflects and captures the value of the product, as opposed to discovering, through some process, how changes in price will cause changes in unit sales. Before addressing value-based pricing, however, let us put the concept of elasticity to rest.

Price elasticity, as a measurable and useful tool for pricing, leaves a great deal to be desired in practical terms. That the price of a product can and will affect sales is unquestionable, but the ability to measure precisely the trade-off between price and volume must be questioned. The law of demand states: *All things equal, as prices increase, unit sales will decrease, and as prices decrease, unit sales will increase.* The concept behind this law is sound but not simple. Often overlooked is the qualifying statement "all things equal," or, in Latin, *ceteris paribus.* The "things" that are held equal (or constant) are called the determinants of demand, which define the location and slope of the demand curve. The determinants of demand are:

- Prices of other goods or services that can be purchased
- Income or buying power of the customers
- Number of customers
- Customers' tastes and preferences
- Customers' expectations.

If one of these factors changes, the demand curve also changes. One must question the likelihood of *any*, much less all, of the determinants remaining constant for a useful period of time. The ephemeral nature of the demand curve, then, severely limits its practical use.

More important, from a strategic perspective, is that people tend to accept the demand curve as a fixed phenomenon in the market. Studies that purport to measure this curve, even if they could do so with any certainty, simply deliver to decision makers a model that implies they are helpless victims of this curve and must resign themselves to the implied limits rather than seek ways to stimulate demand. Consider the typical conjoint market research study, which finds that, at a particular price and with a particular set of attributes, unit sales will be X or market share will be Y. You then build forecasts and marketing plans around this number.

You are held hostage by this number. In the quest for precision, we generate numbers that are precisely wrong. A huge logical flaw of this approach is the unspoken assumption of conjoint analysis—and most other pricing research methods—that marketing efforts and positive experiences with a new technology will not change demand elasticity. Is it correct to assume that the sales of a product will not change if more selling effort is put behind it? The quotation by Edwards that opens this chapter contains a very important clause: it mentions the price that customers can be *induced* to pay, not just what they are *willing* to pay. Customers are induced when the value of the product is clearly communicated and they understand what it is they are buying. This communication of value is essential with a new technology.

This means not that customers can be induced to accept any price, but that they will accept prices that can be supported through appropriate communications and demonstrations of value. Now, they may continue to be price sensitive. Even when customers understand the value of a product, they are likely to seek a lower price. Such behavior is not price elasticity: it is simply prudent buying. Most customers will be sensitive to the prices they pay, and all of us would prefer to pay less for what we buy. The concept of price sensitivity, as opposed to elasticity, is a more qualitative idea—detectable and describable but not measurable to any degree of precision. Price sensitivity can be driven by several forces, including:

- Failure of customers to understand the value of the product (and/or failure of the firm to establish this value)
- Situational issues that affect the desirability or utility of the product
- Simple gaming by customers, who are attempting to secure even lower prices than those they would be willing to pay.

Each of these factors can affect price sensitivity and a customer's willingness to trade money for your product. Each has a different root and a different "solution."

FAILURE TO UNDERSTAND THE VALUE OF THE PRODUCT

Failing to understand and establish the value of a product is perhaps the single most serious marketing and pricing mistake. When the value of a product is clearly established and understood by both the customer and the marketer, price is seldom a problem. In our experience, and that of most who work in the field of pricing, most "pricing problems" have little to do with the price being charged. The problems tend to lie in the failure of the marketer to understand, establish, promote, and explain the value of the product. This problem manifests itself in every market and has led us to adopt the following rule: *If the value of the product is not clear to the customer, the price will always be perceived as too high.*

It is the marketer's responsibility to let the customer know why the product has value and what that value is. When clearly communicated, value decreases or overcomes price sensitivity, making the sale easier and the customer happier. Every good sales representative knows that when a customer says, "Your price is too high," the real message is, "I don't understand the value of your product." Lowering the price of a product for which the customer doesn't understand the value will not generate more sales—it just generates lower prices.

SITUATIONAL ISSUES

Perhaps no aspect of buyer behavior is less studied, understood, and acknowledged as important than the effect of the situations in which buyers finds themselves. A fair body of academic research has demonstrated that choices vary greatly according to situational differences and that the situation itself is often a better predictor of an individual's behavior than the traits and intentions of the individual. Budget issues provide a classic example of this problem. Customers may believe that a price is fair and appropriate for a product but, because of immediate budget limitations or other constraints, may not be able to afford the purchase at a specific time. A customer may be toward the end of a budget cycle where funds available for any new purchase are limited, but the new budget for the next period will allow the purchase shortly. There are several solutions to this problem that do not involve a price decrease, even though the customer may tell you "the price is too high." Financing, extended dating, or simply putting off the purchase until the new budget cycle are effective ways of making the sale without resorting to a price cut.

A pharmaceutical example of this type of price sensitivity involves patient insurance, which affects patients and physicians alike, although in different ways. Patients may believe that a prescription for a $200 product is too costly during January, when they must satisfy an annual deductible, but not be bothered by the same price tag later in the year when they are responsible only for a co-payment of, say, $20. A physician may freely prescribe a product for patients with third-party coverage but choose not to prescribe it for patients lacking such coverage. Although it is the same product for the same use, the situation affects the physician's decision.

Failing to consider such issues when performing pricing research can lead to some very bad decisions, a problem that will be addressed fully in Chapter 11.

SIMPLE GAMING BY CUSTOMERS

As mentioned previously, even customers who believe the price charged is appropriate will often seek a better deal. For some people, negotiating a lower price is not just their job but a matter of pride or duty. Purchasing agents and institutional buyers, especially, will almost always tell you the price is too high because it is either their nature or their job to minimize the price they pay. Rather than simply accepting a statement that "the price is too high" or "you'll have to give me a discount," marketers should determine first whether they are being "gamed." In certain industries—such as automobiles, appliances, and pharmaceuticals—many customers know discounts are commonly used and feel obligated to seek them. How many of us would be ashamed of ourselves if we paid full sticker price for a car?

This discount-seeking behavior is compounded by the fact that, according to studies, many marketers believe customers' claims that their prices are too high compared with competitors and do not recognize customer bargaining or gaming tactics. A firm's failure to establish and communicate the value of its product *internally and externally* is vital to the protection and enhancement of the bottom line.

PRICING "STRATEGIES"

In any discussion of a price, it is important to examine general pricing considerations and commonly used strategies. The fundamental question in pricing is whether a product's price will be set at:

- A discount
- Parity with current treatments
- A premium over current therapies.

These three price positions are often presented as the three funda-mental pricing "strategies." Although we disagree that these are, in fact, *strategies*, the price position is a very important point to consider, and addressing these questions appropriately is the key to profitable pricing.

There are some general observations and standard questions that prove useful when addressing these issues. First, let us define these pricing positions. Many people define these positions in a simplistic manner: they consider any price higher than the reference to be a premium price, any price lower than the reference to be a discount, and only a price identical to the reference to be a parity price. As shown in Figure 2.1, however, from a value-based perspective, a price can be higher than the reference and still be a discount or lower than the reference and still be a premium if one considers value in the "equation."

Accepting these definitions of pricing positions requires the marketer and the customer to understand the value of the product. Without objective and substantial proof of additional value, a customer may see any price above the reference price as a premium or any price below the reference price as a discount. This is not a problem in a market where the value differences in products are well accepted, but in developing markets customers may have little experience in assessing, understanding, and accepting differences in value and may misinterpret the implication of the pricing position chosen.

FIGURE 2.1 Value-Based Pricing Perspectives

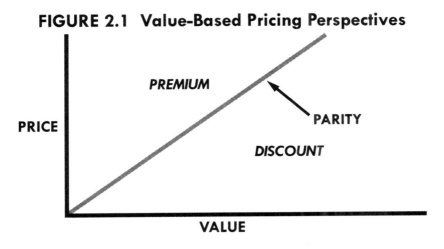

FIGURE 2.2 Value-Based Pricing Diagonal

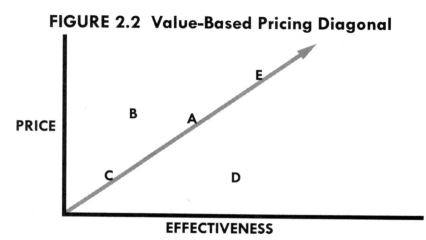

Consider a market with five competitors and three price points, as shown in Figure 2.2. By definition, the current market leader (Product A) has a relationship between price (or cost) and effectiveness (or quality) that lies on the diagonal line. Product A and Product B are priced identically, although Product A is more effective and thus has higher value. Some would consider the price of Product B to be at parity with Product A; others would consider it to be a premium. Product C has a lower cost and lower effectiveness than Product A, which can be interpreted as either a discount or a parity price. Product D possesses a lower price and greater effectiveness than Product A and thus provides the greatest value—this is a discount by most standards.

Prices are a little less clear than Figure 2.2 suggests, however. Figure 2.3 reflects the fact that values, like prices, are fuzzy—imprecise and not conducive to accurate measurement and reporting. This is true, in part, because different parties will value aspects of the product differently and also because not all value is economic. Some value is derived from functional, clinical, and emotional aspects or outcomes of a product to which it is impossible to ascribe a specific numeric value. Because of the difficulty of setting a firm

FIGURE 2.3 "Fuzzy" Value

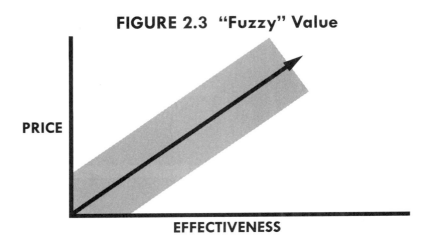

value on some aspects of the product, the value of a product is not a precise figure but a value range. If Product A, the currently available product, sits on the diagonal, its value lies roughly in the area around its point on the diagonal.

The conceptual model in Figure 2.3 can be used to test various pricing scenarios before deciding on a product's launch price. Once the relative value of a company's product, compared with Product A, has been determined, several potential prices can be tested by comparing their position on the graph with that of Product A. A price that reflects parity will place the product on (or near) the diagonal. In this case, the pricer will have decided to retain all of the economic and noneconomic value of the product and not "share" with the marketplace through a discount price. A price that places a product to the left of the diagonal would result in increased costs to the consumer for the same relative value. Neither of these scenarios is wrong, per se, because it may be appropriate to charge a higher or equal price. However, it must be acknowledged that such a price/value position may act to slow the adoption of the product in the marketplace and to limit its use.

A major difference among the three common price positions

is their very purpose. When one considers it, each of these prices makes a statement about the product and the firm's strategy for it. A premium price signals value to customers and competitors with the expectation that customers will interpret the price as an indication of higher quality. A discount price, on the other hand, signals clearly that the seller wants the buyer to consider price first, as the distinguishing feature of the product, and to disregard or reconsider any other issue of product differentiation. Parity pricing signals either that the product is not too different from the competition or that the firm wishes to avoid price competition with similar products.

In the end, price positions are chosen with a certain appraisal of the value of a product. No matter what position is chosen, the marketer must have as complete an understanding of that value as possible.

PHARMACEUTICAL PRICING BASICS

Like any product, the price of a pharmaceutical should reflect its value. But the market for pharmaceuticals, especially in the US, is as complex and ambiguous as a market can be. Many intermediaries can exist between the manufacturer and the eventual user of the product, including a decider (the physician), a buyer (the payer), and a distributor (both wholesale and retail—the pharmacist). Intermediaries define value and set prices according to their own wants and needs, virtually guaranteeing that simple price comparisons for pharmaceuticals will be wrong. That said, how can we apply the labels of premium, parity, and discount to the prices of a medicine? Because the price of a product to the patient or eventual payer can vary considerably, it is possible that a manufacturer could set its price at a discount to a major competitor but actually cost a patient more than the competitor's product because of co-payment or contracting differences. This means that the precise labels of discount and premium require a little elasticity.

Physicians are notoriously unaware of, and thus unresponsive to, price differences among medicines. Fifty years of research into the area has shown repeatedly that physicians are unaware of the prices of products they routinely prescribe.[1,2,3] This, together with the previously discussed vagaries of markups, has led many in the industry to believe that any price difference of less than 15% for a branded product is not a sufficient difference to guarantee a market response. A difference of at least 35% is needed to get the market to really respond. Although we are not aware of any research that has demonstrated this common wisdom, the experience of pharmaceutical marketers has been enough to support it. The 15% minimum threshold seems to have held true for many years, as products that were priced within that range (+/- 15%) have usually been seen as being priced essentially the same, and no price advantage has been measurable, in terms of market performance, for products in that range. Additionally, because price increases in this industry have been a regular phenomenon, price changes among brands and shifting price positions within the limits of those increases make precise placement of a product's price, relative to its competitors, a nearly impossible task. This, too, indicates that minor price differences have no effect on the sales of a pharmaceutical product.

The belief that a 35% price difference is needed to generate a market response seems to be a carryover from the late 1980s, when generic products routinely launched at prices that were 35% below those of the brands. During the infancy of the generic industry, it appeared to take large differences in price for patients to accept the generic products. By the early 1990s, however, public and private payers were putting in place mandatory generic substitution systems, which often paid no attention to the actual price differences. As the public has become more accustomed to and accepting of generics and payers have essentially forced pharmacists to fill prescriptions with these products, the launch prices of the generics have tended to be set much higher in relation to the prices of the brands.

One may also doubt the effect of a specific price difference between two products because of the qualitative differences among most pharmaceuticals. Because different patients require different doses of different products to obtain an equal effect, it is often difficult to compare the prices of two or more drugs in any meaningful way. Differences in efficacy, tolerability, drug interactions, and patient metabolism all render precise comparisons impossible. Attempting to evaluate price difference is always problematic. Among the various methods we have seen are comparisons based on:

- Average daily dose
- Cost per milligram
- Cost per tablet
- Cost per course of therapy
- Cost per most common dose
- Total cost of care.

Although each of these methods may have some validity, it should be obvious that each could result in a different degree and direction of price difference. A product that has a superior safety profile may be used at much higher doses than a similar product that, when used at high doses, causes problems. The price per milligram of these products could be identical, but the average price of the safer drug would be higher because of the higher normal dosage. The total cost of care comparison, however, could make the less safe drug more costly because of the addition of other types of care to compensate for the medicine's side effects.

Thus, while it may be easy in consumer markets to compare, for example, the cost of 12 ounces of Coca-Cola® with 12 ounces of Pepsi®, most price comparisons for pharmaceuticals are problematic. Although comparisons will always be made, for a number of reasons we advise that caution be used when making them, and we believe that it would be wise to follow the general rules that price differences of less than 15% aren't differences at all.

A PHARMACEUTICAL PRICING PHILOSOPHY

The prices charged for pharmaceuticals have been the subject of public policy scrutiny for decades. Politicians wishing to demonstrate their concern for the welfare of citizens have periodically determined that the prices charged for medications provide a relatively risk-free platform to show that concern. The pharmaceutical industry, in turn, goes into a defensive posture and pleads the need for research as its only defense for prices. The net result inevitably is that the industry loses ground, either through a damaged public image or through the loss of some pricing freedom.

Although research is the heart of the branded pharmaceutical industry, the public has not shown willingness to accept that as an argument for what seem to them to be "high prices." The problem lies in the failure of the industry to establish (and hence the public's failure to understand) the value of pharmaceuticals relative to other health care goods and services. Until that relationship is established and communicated in a credible and understandable manner, pharmaceutical firms will have continuous public policy problems with their prices.

Rather than listing exhaustively the litany of reasons for the poor reception of pharmaceutical prices or the elements that make the pharmaceutical industry such a wonderful target for critics, let us consider the general aspects of the problem and seek solutions. To begin, pharmaceuticals are "negative goods." As products used to correct an already existing problem (and this applies to prophylactic medications as well), they are intended to lessen the negative effects of a condition as opposed to adding positive effects. Gasoline is a classic negative good. We don't purchase it because we want to but because we must. Like medications, gasoline is considered a necessity for a normal life, but it is not positively desired. More importantly, although the individual consumer can decide when to buy gasoline and can make decisions about the purchase, the consumer has little control over medication purchases, which tend to be directed purchases. For this reason, pharmaceuticals will always be viewed negatively.

What can companies do to at least moderate the criticism? As already mentioned, pleading the need to generate research funding is not the answer. Perhaps, as with the case of gasoline and other negative goods, the answer lies in communicating some positive aspects of the products while acknowledging that a sizable proportion of the market will never admit to the value of the products. Premium-grade gasolines are positioned to enhance the performance of a car and to protect an investment, and pharmaceuticals can be positioned similarly.

The unique nature of pharmaceuticals—the product of profit-seeking corporations but considered by many to be a public good—has resulted in major differences between pharmaceutical markets and the so-called free markets. That most pharmaceutical purchases are directed purchases and that few patients can correctly be considered well-informed consumers are just two of the reasons pharmaceutical markets are unlikely to be truly free markets. This is not to say that the development and marketing of pharmaceuticals will not continue to be a profitable (and noble) endeavor; it simply means that many of the tools and techniques for pricing and market analysis developed for free consumer markets will not have direct applicability in the market for medications. The discussion of pharmaceutical pricing research presented in Chapter 11 considers this in depth and from a market perspective, but we must reach an understanding on some key issues before that discussion.

WILLINGNESS TO PAY

Pharmaceutical companies should rightly expect to be rewarded for providing value to the health care marketplace. Even most critics will agree with this statement. The problem arises when the industry's rewards and the value provided appear to be out of balance.

This is more a problem of poor communication of value than over-pricing, although the latter is the impression held by many.

Pharmaceutical companies could apply tools developed for other purposes to define and demonstrate the value of their products. Economists specializing in public policy have developed a set of tests to determine the value of a program. These tests are based on the amount taxpayers or consumers state they would be willing to pay for a particular benefit from the program. For example, to measure the value of improved air quality in an area, researchers would ask residents to estimate the amount residents would be willing to pay to achieve cleaner air. The responses would then be averaged to compute the value consumers place on air quality and to evaluate the fairness and acceptability of a tax levy to bring about this quality.

These tests have been transferred into the realm of health care and are widely used in pharmacoeconomic studies in Europe. They have also been used in the United States, both for pharmacoeco-nomics and for pharmaceutical pricing research. However, the concept of willingness to pay—as compelling as it seems—may be not only impractical but misleading when applied to the pharma-ceutical market, where payer systems and patients' lack of direct decision-making authority may distort these measures.

Take, for example, the case of a treatment for Alzheimer's disease. The individual caring for the patient (the caregiver) could be asked, "What would you be willing to pay for a medication that stops the progress of the disease? A typical response may be, "I would pay anything to help my wife (husband, mother, or father)." When pressed for a dollar amount, respondents may give unrealis-tic figures because they cannot make a fully informed assessment of the value of the medication and may simply be grasping at straws, desperate for a cure. Such reactions are not uncommon in terminal, debilitating diseases and, in our opinion, this measurement strategy provides little information of value in setting an appropriate price.

YOUR MONEY OR YOUR LIFE!

Beyond the practical issues of trying to measure accurately willingness to pay, ethical considerations also constrain pricing according to patient need. In health care markets, pharmaceutical manufacturers are granted the unique authority, by virtue of the products they develop, to charge whatever they wish. Because pharmaceuticals are a directed purchase, often reimbursed by a third party, companies have the peculiar ability to say to a patient, "It's your money or your life." The prices charged for medications can, in fact, become a barrier that will deny some patients access to them, and we must keep this in mind. When establishing prices and programs, companies must balance their needs with patient needs and abilities to ensure as near universal access as is practicable.

UNDERSTANDING THE SITUATION

A number of other factors unique to the pharmaceutical marketplace complicate the situation further. Let's consider each of these individually.

Polypharmacy

The term polypharmacy describes the use of multiple medications by an individual patient, sometimes for the same disease but often for multiple comorbidities. Polypharmacy is especially common in an aging population with multiple chronic conditions. There are several medications on the market for which patients and payers willingly pay several dollars per day. But the prospect of polypharmacy for many patients and the fact that the additive effect of several products at such prices can be prohibitive should give us pause before we attempt to charge similar prices for every product we develop. Parkinson's disease provides a very good example of this situation.

It is not uncommon for a Parkinson's patient, who is likely to be retired and a Medicare beneficiary, to take two or more medications for this condition: a dopamine product costing $2 to $3 per day and a dopamine agonist or other agent costing from $3 to $5 per day. In addition, these patients often require antidepressants ($3 per day), antiarthritics ($3 to $4 per day), and perhaps medications for hypertension and/or high cholesterol that add another $2.50 to $5 per day. It is not exceptional for Parkinson's patients to spend between $15 and $30 per day for medication.

Although each of these medications may be priced appropriately by itself, when the additive effect of polypharmacy is considered, do patients really receive this value? Must every new drug for Parkinson's cost $3 to $5 per day, especially if it will be used as an adjunct to current therapy and not as a replacement? Replacing a $3 drug with another $3 drug has no net financial impact on the patient, while adding a new $3 drug to a regimen that already costs $15 per day may force the patient into choices that benefit no one: foregoing one medication to afford another and compromising health or skipping every other dose in an increasing common form of self-imposed rationing. We don't know how many patients ration their medications, but this practice should be measured and evaluated before the prices of new drugs in this and other therapeutic areas are set.

Reimbursement Status

Differences in reimbursement status dramatically alter the levels of price sensitivity for and the economic effects of a product. For seniors, lack of Medicare coverage for outpatient prescriptions before 2006 meant that injectable medicines administered in a physician's office, which were covered, were far less costly than oral agents. This and other examples point to the logical flaws in the payer system, flaws that must be considered in pricing decisions.

A new drug that replaces a surgical or other mechanical procedure may offer significant savings, but the cost of the drug is born by the pharmacy budget while the cost of the procedure is born by the medical budget. Replacing evulsion or debridement (common procedures for nail fungus, decubitus ulcers, and other topical maladies) with a new medication can trigger two major issues: shifting the cost of the disease to another budget area and shifting the financial reward of treatment from one entity to another. During the Watergate scandal of the early 1970s, Deep Throat, the anonymous inside informant, told reporters to "follow the money." That advice applies as well to those establishing prices for new pharmaceutical products. The shifting of financial responsibility from the medical to the pharmacy budget means the pharmacy will see an increase in its costs, perhaps without credit for savings elsewhere. Moreover, the physician who must prescribe the new agent may find that his or her income has been dramatically reduced because the drug has replaced procedures that were a major source of income. In such circumstances, it is foolhardy to assume that the savings provided by your new drug will be welcomed by everyone in the system.

Mandatory Discounts

Federal legislation introduced over the past 20 years has dramatically increased the complexity of pricing decisions. Discounts to favored customers must be evaluated in light of mandatory rebates to the Medicaid system and other federal government entities. Ongoing pricing litigation in federal courts will also alter the pricing landscape. Any pricing decision must now be made in light of these forces.

The Law of Unintended Consequences

The Omnibus Budget Reconciliation Act of 1990 (OBRA 90) effectively penalized companies for providing discounts by requiring them to offer similar savings to state Medicaid programs. The government's attempt to share in those discounts had the effect of changing the economics of discounting, reducing the value of many customers when Medicaid rebates were calculated. The net result was a significant reduction of discounting activities in the pharmaceutical market, which reduced the revenue expected to be generated by the rebates.[4]

The Medicare Modernization Act of 2003 set reimbursement for office-administered drugs at the average selling price (ASP) + 6%, which brings about 3 very important changes to pricing, none of which was anticipated. First, because the difference between the ASP and reimbursement is only 6%, customers who purchase products at prices above the average will be penalized. This means that, in the long run, discounts will shrink as companies seek to ensure that none of their customers loses money when administering their products. Second, because provider reimbursement is now based on a fixed percentage above cost, providers have an incentive to use higher cost medicines, which will generate larger absolute dollar differences between cost and reimbursement. Finally, by setting the rate at ASP + 6%, the government has established an upper limit (of about 5%) for price increases on physician-administered drugs because the lag time between price changes and reimbursement changes would mean that price increases higher than 5% could cause providers to lose money when administering the drugs.

We should remember this lesson of unintended consequences. Just as the federal government's expectations of savings are often thwarted by the industry's response to the imposition of mandatory rebates or changes in reimbursement, so, too, are marketing plans often foiled by the unintended consequences of their pricing actions. Pricing must be seen as a unified strategy that reflects careful consideration of all the factors—and more—that we have discussed.

STRATEGIC PRICING

Many of the problems encountered in the domain of pharmaceutical pricing have occurred because those involved in the decision were not proficient in the field of pharmaceutical pricing and because erroneous, but often logical, assumptions were made concerning the role and effects of price in the market. Pricing mistakes result from failure to consider all the potential consequences of pricing actions—failing to "price on purpose."

Strategic pricing means that each potential price has been evaluated for its effect on the health care system and members of that system and realistically assessed in terms of the willingness and ability of those members to pay or to take action against the price. As the cost of pricing mistakes for the industry increases, the need for strategic pricing grows.

REFERENCES

1. Zelnio R, Gagnon J. The effects of price information on physician prescribing patterns—literature review. *Drug Intell Clin Pharm.* 1979; 13:156-69.
2. Kolassa EM. Physicians' perceptions of pharmaceutical prices: Their accuracy and effect on the prescribing decision. *J Res Pharm Econ.* 1995; 6(1):23-37.
3. Reisetter BC, Bentley JP, Wilkin NE. Relationship between psychosocial physician characteristics and physician price awareness. *J Pharm Market Manage.* 2005; 17(1):51-76.
4. General Accounting Office. Medicaid: Changes in best prices for outpatient drugs purchased by HMOs and hospitals. GAO/HEHS-94-194FS. Washington, DC: United States General Accounting Office; 1994.

Chapter 3

Pricing Flow and Terminology

"When I use a word," Humpty Dumpty said
in rather a scornful tone, "it means just
what I choose it to mean—neither more nor less."
"The question is," said Alice, "whether you CAN
make words mean so many different things."
"The question is," said Humpty Dumpty,
"which is to be master—that's all."
—Lewis Carroll, *Through the Looking-Glass*

As discussed in the previous chapter, the pharmaceutical market operates very differently from other markets. The pharmaceutical market involves distribution and financial chains that are unlike those of any other industry. Whereas in other markets consumers typically buy a product from the manufacturer itself or a distributor for the manufacturer (i.e., a retail store), consumers *cannot* purchase a prescription drug directly from the manufacturer. Instead, they must purchase the drug from a retail pharmacy, and only then with a valid prescription from a licensed physician.

Pharmaceutical firms usually sell to wholesalers and sometimes directly to retail pharmacies or other customers. Wholesalers act as intermediaries between the manufacturer and hospitals or retail pharmacies and comprise a very substantial part of the market—at least 85% of the pharmaceutical industry's sales. In most cases, each firm charges the wholesaler the "catalog price," also referred to as the wholesale acquisition cost (WAC), minus a 2% offset to customers who pay promptly for purchases.

Once the manufacturer sells a product to a customer, there can be any number of intermediary purchases and sales before the product gets to the pharmacy. Each stage in the process involves decisions made by companies and other entities who have pricing, marketing, and profit strategies of their own and respond to economic forces specific to the pharmaceutical industry that are beyond the pharmaceutical company's control. All of these strategies and forces influence the amount that a consumer pays for the product at the retail end. In fact, these factors are often counterintuitive to standard economic theories of supply and demand. For example, products that are far less successful commercially will often receive significantly higher retail markups (for cash-paying patients) than their more successful counterparts.

The financial chain adds even more complexity. Unlike the purchase of a product in any other industry, the purchase of a prescription drug is affected drastically by health insurance and managed care. The vast majority of purchasers of prescription drugs in the United States (approximately 85%) participate in some form of health insurance program that provides prescription drug coverage. These individuals do not pay the full retail amount charged by the pharmacy, but a portion of the retail price known as a co-pay. The remainder is paid to the pharmacy by a third party, such as a health maintenance organization (HMO) or pharmacy benefit manager (PBM).

This chapter introduces the various terms and "buzzwords" of pharmaceutical pricing and addresses the different pharmaceutical prices that exist in the market. Although the term "pharmaceutical market" has often been used, there are, in fact, several pharmaceutical markets, each with its own set of prices and pricing methods. There are retail, hospital, and managed care markets, branded and generic markets, and chronic and acute markets. Each is approached somewhat differently. Before examining these various markets, we must define the common terms used in pharmaceutical pricing.

IMPORTANT TERMS IN PHARMACEUTICAL PRICING

As with all specialized areas, pharmaceutical pricing has its own vocabulary, complete with acronyms. The following is a list of common pharmaceutical pricing terms and their definitions.

- *Actual Acquisition Cost (AAC).* AAC is the provider's true cost to buy drugs from wholesalers or directly from manufacturers, net of all discounts.
- *Average Manufacturer's Price (AMP).* This term was developed by the drafters of OBRA 90 and is used to describe the average price received by a manufacturer, after discounts, for products sold to the retail class of trade. AMP is the average price paid to a manufacturer by retail pharmacies or wholesalers for drugs distributed to the retail pharmacies. AMP is based on sales to the retail sector, which generally pays higher prices than other purchasing sectors. AMP is used to compute rebates paid to state Medicaid programs.
- *Average Sales Price (ASP).* Section 303(c) of the Medicare Modernization Act of 2003 (MMA) revised the payment methodology for Part B-covered drugs that are not paid on a cost or prospective payment basis. (Medicare Part B covers services and products generally delivered on an outpatient basis, such as x-rays, transfusions, dialysis, flu and pneumonia vaccinations, or chemotherapy.) This law established a new average sales price (ASP) drug payment system. Now, drugs and biologicals are reimbursed based

33

on the ASP methodology, specifically, 106% of the ASP. The ASP methodology uses quarterly drug pricing data submitted to the Centers for Medicare & Medicaid Services (CMS) by drug manufacturers. Administrative fees, incentives, promotional fees, chargebacks, and all discounts or rebates—other than those under the Medicaid drug program and endorsed discount card programs—are included in the calculation of ASP if those sales are to an entity whose sales are included in the calculation of ASP and if they ultimately affect the price actually realized by the manufacturer.

- *Average Wholesale Price (AWP).* Neither an average price nor a price charged by wholesalers, this figure is a vestige of earlier times. Few, if any, wholesalers even consider AWP today when pricing their prescription products. It is, however, commonly used by retailers and others who dispense medications as the basis for many pricing decisions. Because of its availability from many sources, AWP is often used as a surrogate for actual prices when studying prescription price trends. (A full discussion of AWP appears later in this chapter.)
- *Best Price (BP).* Best price is the lowest price available from the manufacturer to any wholesaler, retailer, provider, managed care organization (MCO), nonprofit entity, or nonfederal government customer.
- *Cash Discount.* Most pharmaceutical firms offer incentives to their customers for rapid payment of invoices. The most common terms offered are a 2% discount if the full bill is paid within 10 days

of receiving the invoice. Thus a wholesaler that pays the regular ex-factory price actually pays only 98% of that price if it pays within 10 days. The wholesaler that sells at "cost plus 3%," then, is actually charging a markup of roughly 5%.

- *Chargeback.* A chargeback is the difference between the price a wholesaler pays a manufacturer (see WAC) and a lower contract price that has been negotiated by a hospital or managed care organization. Because of the complexities of tracking products and some legal limitations, the chargeback system was developed as a means for discounted products to be sold through wholesalers. The wholesaler purchases the product at the normal list price and sells the product to hospitals or other contract customers at the discount price. The difference is then paid as a rebate to the wholesaler by the manufacturer. This rebate is called the chargeback.

- *Class of Trade.* Under federal law, all businesses that sell to the same customer type must be eligible to receive equal pricing consideration, such as discounts and special offers. To ensure compliance with this law, most pharmaceutical companies have developed lists of similar customers and grouped them into different classes of trade. Pricing schedules and tactics are then developed for each class of trade.

- *Direct Price.* The direct price is that paid by retailers, before discounts, for products from those manufacturers who sell directly to non-wholesale accounts, such as retailers, hospitals, private practice physicians, and public health clinics is the direct price.

- *Disproportionate Share Hospitals.* Disproportionate share hospitals, also known as "safety
  net hospitals" or "340B hospitals," serve predominantly low-income communities and
  have substantial caseloads of Medicaid patients.
  Often, these hospitals are the principal source
  of care for uninsured patients in their communities, but their actual cost of care is frequently
  not covered by Medicaid reimbursement rates.
  The 340B Drug Pricing Program resulted from
  the enactment of Public Law 102-585, the Veterans Health Care Act of 1992. Section 340B of the
  act limits the cost of covered outpatient drugs
  to certain federal entities and qualified disproportionate share hospitals. For branded drugs,
  the 340B ceiling price is the lower of BP or AMP
  minus 15.1%. For generic drugs, the ceiling price
  is the lower of BP or AMP minus 11 %. These
  are the same prices Medicaid receives.
- *Estimated Acquisition Cost (EAC).* EAC is a
  state Medicaid agency's "best" estimate of the
  price generally paid by pharmacies for a drug.
  Although EAC is meant to represent a calculation across all pharmacies of actual acquisition
  cost, the federal government does not spec-
  ify any particular method for calculating EAC.
  Consequently, states have developed their own
  methods for estimating acquisition cost, typically using one of two methods. The "cost plus"
  method calculates the pharmacy's cost based
  upon the wholesale acquisition cost (WAC)
  plus a markup percent. The "list less" method
  relies upon the average wholesale price (AWP)
  less a discount percentage. EAC for most states

is calculated by using the "list less" method, which renders the "estimate" less than accurate.

- *Ex-Factory Price.* The actual selling price, after cash discounts but before other discounts, charged by the manufacturer is the ex-factory price (see also manufacturer's list price and wholesale acquisition cost defined below). The use of the term "ex-factory price" in pharmaceutical markets differs from the accepted use in other industries, where ex-factory prices generally *include* all discounts. This difference demonstrates the problem with assuming that knowing pricing issues in other industries translates into knowing pricing within the pharmaceutical industry.

- *Federal Supply Schedule (FSS) Price.* All direct federal purchasers of pharmaceuticals can purchase drugs at prices listed in the Federal Supply Schedule (FSS) for pharmaceuticals. The Department of Veterans Affairs (VA) negotiates FSS prices with manufacturers based on the prices manufacturers charge their most-favored commercial customers under comparable terms and conditions. During a multi-year contract period, those FSS prices may not increase faster than inflation.

- *Gross Profit (Margin).* Gross profit margin is the difference between the acquisition or production cost of a product and its selling price. Gross profit margin does not include other costs of doing business.

- *Maximum Allowable Cost (MAC).* MAC is a payer's estimate of the appropriate reimbursement for a generic drug. Because list prices for most generics rarely reflect actual prices, payers have used MAC instead. Each pharmacy serving a payer's patients is reimbursed at the MAC price regardless of the acquisition cost of the drug. The federal MAC is also called the Federal Financial Participation (FFP) or the Federal Upper Limit (FUL). It is generally set at 150% of the lowest generally available price for generics.

* *Manufacturer's List Price.* As the name implies, the list price is that published by a manufacturer. Many manufacturers make actual list prices available only to wholesalers, providing a catalog that contains AWPs to the nonwholesale trade (see also ex-factory price and wholesale acquisition cost).

* *Net Price.* Also known as the "landed price," net price is the price, or revenue, realized by a manufacturer after all discounts have been granted.

* *Net Profit (Margin).* Net profit margin is the difference between selling price and all costs associated with doing business, allocated on a per-unit basis.

* *OBRA 90.* The Omnibus Budget Reconciliation Act of 1990 (OBRA 90) is a law drafted by the Senate Committee on Aging that requires manufacturers to pay rebates to state and federal governments for products used by Medicaid recipients. This law set the stage for many of the pricing regulations and mandatory discounts that are now imposed on the pharmaceutical industry.

* *Rebate.* A rebate is a retroactive discount that is paid to a customer after that customer has purchased the product from a wholesaler or retailer. The rebate allows the manufacturer to offer a

lower price to some customers without taking on the burden of special distribution mechanisms.

- *Standard Cost.* The product costing system used by most pharmaceutical firms is called "standard costing" or "fully absorbed cost." This system allocates to each product and package a portion of fixed cost (overhead) in addition to variable costs such as ingredients, packaging, and direct labor. Allocations are based on forecasts made at the beginning of the fiscal year. Such a system ensures that when unit volume increases, the incremental cost of a unit will decline; however, it also ensures that when sales decline the incremental cost of a product will increase significantly. It is not uncommon for half or more of a product's "standard cost" to consist of this fixed-cost allocation.

- *Usual and Customary Price (U&C).* U&C is the pharmacy's selling price to individual consumers. The price includes the cost of the drug and the pharmacy's markup. The markup includes allowances for business operating costs (e.g., rent, utilities, and employee wages/benefits, and dispensing services).

- *Wholesale Acquisition Cost (WAC).* This term is used by some publishers of pricing data, as well as some payers, to represent the ex-factory charge, before discounts, to the wholesaler. This is what wholesalers pay manufacturers for drugs— *before* cash discounts or other allowances. Unlike the AWP, federal regulations—specifically, the MMA, section 3(6)(B)—define the WAC as follows:

The term "wholesale acquisition cost" means, with respect to a covered out-patient drug, the manufacturer's list price for the drug to wholesalers or direct purchasers in the United States, not including prompt pay or other discounts, rebates or reductions in price, for the most recent month for which the information is available, as reported in wholesale price guides or other publications of drug pricing data.

WHAT IS A PHARMACEUTICAL PRICE?

The number of sources of drug pricing information might suggest that comparing or computing the prices of drugs is straightforward, but that is far from true. Differences in the manner in which various prices are set and used render many comparisons virtually meaningless.

Different prices are charged to and by different members of the distribution channels used for pharmaceuticals. Some prices are set using traditional methods, while others are set according to competitive conditions. Even within the same pharmacy, several different pricing methods will be used, depending on a number of factors. Figure 3.1 outlines typical approaches to pricing both branded and generic products in a retail pharmacy. These and other retail pricing tactics will be discussed later in this chapter. In the hospital setting, different rules and methods are used. The "flow" of prices within hospitals is presented in Figure 3.2.

As Figures 3.1 and 3.2 demonstrate, the price of a pharmaceutical product depends on a number of factors, such as the location of drug administration, the relative commercial success of the agent, and the type of manufacturer supplying the drug.

FIGURE 3.1 Typical Approach to Retail Pharmacy Pricing

	BRANDED PRODUCT	GENERIC (NO MAC)	GENERIC (MAC)
List price	$50.00	$10.00	$10.00
AWP	$60.00	$40.00	$40.00
Wholesale cost after cash discount	$49.00	$5.00	$5.00
Wholesaler price	$51.50	$5.15	$5.15
Retail Price (or Reimbursement)			
Cash price (AWP plus $10 fee)	$70.00	$50.00	$50.00
PBM price (AWP - 18% (or MAC) + $2 fee)	$51.20	$34.80	$9.50
Medicaid price (AWP - 10% (or MAC) + $4 fee)	$58.00	$40.00	$11.50
Cost to patient			
Uninsured patient	$70.00	$50.00	$50.00
Private insurance (PBM)	$25 to $50	$5 to $10	$5 to $10
Medicaid	$0 to $5	$0 to $5	$0 to $5

NOTE: *The price paid by individual patients depends on their plan design and the degree of coverage for the product. The figures used in this figure are illustrative only and do not include all the possible prices or costs, even for a single product.*

START WITH A PROBLEMATIC NUMBER—AWP...

The AWP is the most common figure used for drug price comparisons and reimbursement, although it has long been known that AWP does not reflect the true prices charged for all products. AWP,

FIGURE 3.2 Flow of Hospital Pricing

	BRAND	BRAND	GENERIC
Contracted discout	(-0)%	(-15)%	
List price, package of 100	$50.00	$50.00	$10.00
AWP	$60.00	$60.00	$25.00
Wholesale cost after cash discount	$49.00	$49.00	$9.80
Net wholesale cost (with cash discount and chargeback)	$49.00	$41.50	$9.80
GPO admin fee	$1.00	$1.00	N/A
Wholesaler price (2% markup)	$51.00	$43.35	$10.20
Uninsured patient	$250.00	$250.00	$250.00
NET TO COMPANY	$48.00	$40.50	$9.80

as a price representation, was developed by consultants to the California Medicaid program in 1969 in an effort to find a standard method to calculate reimbursement rates for medicines.[1] At the time, according to those responsible, the lack of a standard meant that providers (specifically retail pharmacists) could report—irresponsibly—that their costs were "whatever [pharmacists] decided." The "average wholesale price" was established as the "cost" definition of what wholesalers normally charged for drugs. These figures were soon reported in the price compendia *Blue Book* and *Red Book*. Because manufacturers had no control over the prices charged by wholesalers, they simply accepted the AWP levels published by the compendia. Soon, some manufacturers began to publish catalogs and price lists that included the AWPs reported by *Blue Book* and *Red Book*, and because they had no role or responsibility in the development and establishment of this figure, they simply accepted it. What began as a "better than nothing" approximation of cost soon became the standard. It was created by government, published by compendia, adopted by public and private payers, and imposed on the pharmaceutical industry. There are no established guidelines or statutory definitions of the figure—it just "is."

Through the mid to late 1970s, this definition of cost was a fair—but never true—representation of wholesalers' charges to many retail pharmacies. Until then, there were several hundred small, independent drug wholesalers, each operating regionally. Due to the inefficiencies of such a fragmented system, the operating costs were quite high. The average markup above cost by wholesalers to their retail customers (primarily pharmacies) was 20% to 25%, depending on the manufacturer. Although most pharmaceutical manufacturers used a wholesaler-only method of distribution to the retail class of trade, a significant number of large firms, including Upjohn, Merck, and Squibb, had invested in their own distribution networks and preferred direct sales over the use of wholesalers. Because they wanted to encourage retail pharmacies to "invest" in inventory, the developers of the AWP (MediCal) added 20% to the price of products from companies following a wholesaler-only policy, while adding 25% to the prices of products from those companies who distributed directly.

In the late 1970s and early 1980s, several wholesale drug companies began to acquire smaller competitors. Two companies in particular, Bergen Brunswig Corporation and McKesson Drug, expanded significantly and became national presences during this period. Today there are fewer than 90 wholesale drug companies in the United States. The expansion of major wholesale firms also concentrated competition. Before consolidation, most wholesalers had little or no competition within their trade areas, so there was little pressure to reduce their markups. As consolidation in the industry increased, major companies began competing for the same business, resulting in price competition.

Additionally, during the 1980s, prices charged by manufacturers began to increase. This allowed the wholesalers to practice arbitrage—buying drugs in anticipation of price increases and then selling the inventory at the new, higher prices. Together, these trends lowered the average wholesale markup in the early 1990s to roughly 2.5%, significantly lower than the markup inferred by the published AWP. The original intent and relative accuracy of the AWP was undermined by the failure of reporting services to reflect true prices that payers were being charged by wholesalers.

Through the mid-1980s, wholesalers had two different methods of pricing to the retailers: AWP minus and cost plus. As the names imply, one method used the published AWP while the other ignored it. In recent years, cost-plus pricing has become the norm for wholesalers. Price reporting services, however, still rely upon the AWP because, contrary to their claims, they do not survey wholesalers to determine their prices.

So, despite being published in various reports, the AWP is not a satisfactory starting point for pricing. The figure was developed by government and imposed on the pharmaceutical industry, and it was designed for a much simpler pharmaceutical market in which branded outpatient drugs were the norm—a market that no longer exists.

ADD DIFFERENTIAL PRICING...

The pharmaceutical industry, like most industries, has routinely charged different prices to different customers. Government agencies receive discounts, many of which are required by law. Besides hospitals (both nonprofit and for-profit), MCOs, and government agencies, discounts are also available to pharmacy benefit managers (PBMs), home health care providers (HHC), and nursing homes, which are also called long-term care (LTC) or skilled nursing facilities (SNFs). One reason these buyers receive special pricing is that they can support or impede the sales goals of firms because of the degree of control they may have over product use. MCOs and hospitals often use drug formularies to limit the number of similar products they reimburse or stock. This provides some consistency in treatment and some level of economy. Because of this practice, customers have a fair amount of bargaining power with pharmaceutical companies: they can extract discounts because they may be able to preclude the use of one or more products when there are other appropriate choices. Manufacturers wishing to generate sales to these customers are often compelled to offer their products at lower prices to secure their business. We must emphasize, however, that these special prices do not eliminate the need for firms to promote their products to these or other customers, who still need to be informed about the products and their uses.

Companies will usually offer discounts on their brand-name, patent-protected products only when they believe that those discounts will result in higher levels of sales—that is, the sales to these customers with the discount will be higher than sales without the discount. The more products in a given category that customers have to choose from, the more likely it is that customers will be able to negotiate deep discounts. If a manufacturer has a necessary product with no competitors, discounts are unlikely because the customer has no choice but to use the product. However, if there are five similar products in the market, the business will go to those manufacturers most willing to offer competitive discounts. Because the degree of price competition in a market usually depends on the number of competitors and because new pioneering products have fewer competitors than products that have been on the market for a longer time, discounts tend to be concentrated more in older categories and categories that have several competitive entrants.

AND THE EFFECTS OF BUYING GROUPS AND CHARGEBACKS...

Until the early 1980s, individual drug companies would have separate agreements with each hospital or other institution to which they provided discounts. Companies that shipped products directly to their customers would simply reflect the discounted price on their invoices, and those firms shipping only through wholesalers would provide the discounts directly to their customers in the form of rebates after the products had been purchased through a wholesaler.

Over the years, some hospitals combined their bargaining power by forming buying groups. By forming these groups, the institutions, at first almost exclusively hospitals, could extract even deeper discounts from the drug companies. In the early 1980s, to facilitate administration of the buying group agreement and to use their bargaining power in other ways, some buying groups asked wholesalers to bid on exclusive contracts to deliver products and administer the agreement. A wholesaler who could "tie up" several larger hospital accounts had an incentive to greatly reduce its own markups on products, saving the institutions even more money. The wholesaler selected by the buying group is called the "prime vendor."

The addition of the prime vendor system to the distribution mix required manufacturers to develop a new relationship with wholesalers. Because most wholesalers serve retail as well as institutional customers and because different institutions and buying groups will have negotiated different prices, the system would require that wholesalers charge different prices to reflect the various prices contracted with buying groups and other customers. Indeed, even before the advent of the prime vendor system, some attempts had been made to allow wholesalers to purchase products from manufacturers at prices negotiated by hospitals, with assurances that the goods purchased at discount would be used only for fulfilling orders by hospitals authorized to receive the lower prices.

This system did not work then for two reasons. First, it would have required wholesalers to maintain separate inventories for each hospital, at substantial wholesaler expense. Second, manufacturers were not convinced that wholesalers would indeed keep this inventory segregated but would instead move these discounted goods into regular circulation and profit at their expense. The same problems would have occurred in the prime vendor system.

The solution was the chargeback. Instead of receiving discounts upfront, wholesalers purchase products from the drug companies at full price, and adjustments are made after the wholesalers have delivered products to their customers. The adjustments paid by the manufacturer to the wholesaler are called "chargebacks." A chargeback is, in effect, a retroactive discount. When a wholesaler sells a product to a hospital or other party that receives discounts under an agreement with a pharmaceutical company, it sells at the contract price, which is below the price the wholesaler pays. To correct for this, the wholesaler sends a notice to the pharmaceutical company that the sale has been made, and the company issues a payment to the wholesaler (usually by way of a "credit memo" applied to future sales). For example, if a product is usually sold for $25 and the

FIGURE 3.3 Pharmaceutical Chargeback

HOSPITAL OR NURSING HOME	$21* Price	

MANUFACTURER
$25 Price — $5 Chargeback

PRIMARY WHOLESALER
$26* Price

RETAIL PHARMACY

* In this example, the wholesaler charges each customer a $1 markup.
Product ——▶
Price ·····▶
Chargeback ‑ ‑ ‑▶

hospital has negotiated a contract price of $20, the wholesaler, who paid $25, will sell to the hospital for a price of $20 (plus the whole-saler's markup, usually about 2%) and notify the pharmaceutical company of the sale. The pharmaceutical company will then credit the wholesaler for the $5 difference. Schematically, the chargeback transaction and the way it differs from the typical sale to a retail pharmacy are shown in Figure 3.3.

For brand-name pharmaceuticals, the chargeback is used almost exclusively to adjust the prices charged by wholesalers to their insti-tutional customers. Retail pharmacy sales do not ordinarily qualify for chargebacks on branded products because discounts by brand-name companies on patent-protected products are not generally made available to that class of trade. The chargeback system has been adapted by wholesalers and generic companies to provide discounts on those products to retail pharmacies, which do have discretion over which generic product they dispense.

...NOW, WHAT WAS THE PRICE OF THAT DRUG?

The complexities of pharmaceutical pricing—with their conditions, discounts, and tactical schemes—render simple analyses useless. When discussing the prices of pharmaceuticals, then, it is impor-tant to ask, "Which price do you mean?"

REFERENCES

1. Pennebaker G. The rest of the AWP story. *Computer-Talk for the Pharmacist.* 1998; (Jan/Feb):6-7.

Chapter 4

The Role of Value in the Pricing of Pharmaceuticals
with William Lobb

Price is what you pay. Value is what you get.
—Warren Buffett

It cannot be stated more plainly than this: in general, pharmaceuticals are the most valuable health care intervention available. This statement is true in spite of all the claims that pharmaceuticals are excessively priced. As will be discussed later, it is the lack of third-party coverage for pharmaceuticals that has generated and perpetuated the myth that prescription medicines are overpriced.

Studies have demonstrated the value of pharmaceuticals individually and in aggregate. Lichtenberg found that for each incremental dollar spent on newer pharmaceuticals, the health care system saved between $4 and $8 in overall costs.[1] Pharmacoeconomic studies have also consistently demonstrated individual products' value to the system.

The benefits of pharmaceuticals cannot be overestimated. My grandmother passed away from complications of ulcer surgery. Today H$_2$ antagonists, such as Zantac® and Pepcid®, and proton pump inhibitors (PPIs), such as Prilosec® and Prevacid®, have all but eliminated the need for such surgery. It is not difficult to identify

49

changes in health care that have been driven by pharmaceuticals. Antibiotics have eliminated bacterial infection as a common cause of death. Thirty years ago, if a patient had cancer, the person was very likely to die in a short time. Second, treatment would make the person uncontrollably nauseated. Third, the patient's hair was likely to fall out. Fourth, the patient would feel excessive pain and fatigue. Since that time, improvements in chemotherapy have enabled more targeted treatment with much higher success rates and fewer side effects, such as hair loss. Lance Armstrong, seven-time winner of the Tour de France, had testicular and brain cancer with a poor prognosis. Yet he fully recovered and became the greatest cyclist of his or any age. Improvements have been made in the treatments for chemotherapy-induced nausea and vomiting (CINV). Products such as the 5-HT3 antagonists (Zofran® and Anzemet®) have revolutionized the treatment of CINV, and Merck's Emend® has recently extended the ability to control CINV. Procrit® and Aranesp® have enabled patients to avoid the fatigue associated with cancer and chemotherapy. Finally, significant advances in pain recognition, management, and treatment have been driven by advances in the therapies available, including Duragesic®, OxyContin®, and Actiq®.

The ability of health care providers and patients to control other diseases has also significantly increased. The asthma market, once dominated by short-acting inhalers and theophylline, is now controlled by long-acting corticosteroids (Flovent®), long-acting agonists (Serevent®), combinations of the two (Advair®), and response modifiers (Singulair®). The list goes on and on. Diabetes, hypertension, erectile dysfunction, overactive bladder, restless leg syndrome, allergy, epilepsy, depression, and schizophrenia have all seen light-year leaps in therapeutic improvement because of pharmaceuticals.

It should be clear that the value of pharmaceuticals is, in most cases, significant. Why then does the myth of overpricing continue to plague the pharmaceutical industry? Probably because consumers' (including prescribers and payers) evaluation of a product's price rests on the perception of value and the industry has not done as well in assessing and communicating the value of its innovations as it has in developing them. In examining the history of pharmaceutical pricing, we cannot find an example of "overpricing," in terms of identifying a product whose market failure could be blamed on the high price. There are plenty of situations in which poor assessment or inadequate communication of value has led to a misinterpretation of the value-price relationship (e.g., FluMist,® BiDil®, and Exubera®), but it was the products themselves or the misunderstanding of their value that led to the lack of commercial success, not the prices.

Before delving deeper into the various aspects of value, we must first understand that the term "value," as used in this book, is not a simple translation of the benefits of a medicine into a number. Value cannot be reflected totally in dollars and cents, despite what an economist might claim. Attempts to calculate value solely in monetary terms ignore important aspects of human behavior, as well as the various ways price influences purchases, regardless of value. The total lifetime cost of Nexium® therapy cannot reflect the value of not losing a loved one to the complications of ulcer surgery. The value of allowing a granddaughter to enjoy the company of her grandfather (and vice versa) is incalculable and thus impossible to apply to a pricing decision.

Robert Heilbroner once noted: "Mathematics has given economics rigor, but alas, also mortis." The economist, or pharmacoeconomist, who believes that value can be understood through mere mathematical calculation and the manipulation of sets of numbers misses the subtlety of value by foregoing the rigor of investigation and relying on the mortis.

PHARMACEUTICAL VALUE-BASED PRICING

As discussed in Chapter 1, pharmaceuticals are negative goods: patients would rather not use them. Unlike consumer electronics, which are positive goods, pharmaceuticals are a necessary evil, even in cases of real symptomatic relief.[2] Pharmaceuticals are also largely experience goods. It is only through the trial of these products that physicians and patients can determine and understand their value. The value of pharmaceuticals comes from what people want to occur, not what they want to buy. This is entirely distinct from consumer goods, in which the outcome is predetermined, such as with a television, and it explains a good portion of issues such as patient noncompliance and nonpersistence.

Pharmaceutical pricers are forced to price based on value in a unique situation. Value to the physician, the patient, the insurance provider, and the health care system are all key components of the value determination, and the value differs according to the audience. The most important questions the pricer can ask are, "What problem does my product solve, and who (in the system) owns that problem?" Answering those questions is the first step in understanding and clarifying value.

Value-based pricing of pharmaceuticals is more a philosophy than a discipline because pricing based only on an objective measure of economic value will invariably lead to poor pricing. Value, as we will discuss, is much more than a simple economic concept, and attempting to apply elementary economic principles to pharmaceutical pricing is not advisable if a firm wishes to remain in business.

CUSTOMERS AND THE PERCEPTION OF VALUE

When thinking about the value any pharmaceutical product offers, we must first answer the question: Who benefits from this product? There are myriad "customers" for pharmaceuticals; chief among them are patients, payers, and prescribers. In addition to these three "*P*'s" of health care markets, we must also consider society as a customer for pharmaceutical products.

Society

It is easy to claim that in the US system, unlike those in other countries, society does not enter into the decision-making process. In the UK or Canada, for example, the government-run health care systems are based on a series of "value" checks for the national system. These checks often result in the government failing to make available to its citizens new medicines that are widely available, and valuable, in other nations. However, society is a significant customer in the US system as well, as illustrated by national vaccination programs and recent government and social responses to potential national "pandemics." The calls for the elimination of the patent on Cipro® during the post-9/11 "anthrax scare" or for increased supply of Tamiflu® for a potential bird flu outbreak are evidence of societal-level determination of the value of pharmaceuticals.[3]

Health policy expert Glenna Crooks points out that societal-level determinations of "capturable value," or value that can be defined by monetary measures, are likely to decrease as the absolute importance of the product increases. The willingness to consider the elimination of the Cipro patent is a perfect example of this phenomenon—and a testament to the fact that "value" and "economic value" are not the same. As depicted in Figure 4.1, as the societal value increases, the price that is socially acceptable increases—to a point. At some level of value, society demands that the product become a virtual right and, as such, that it should be lower in price. Vaccines are a perfect example of these societal goods. We expect every member of the US system to be vaccinated, and we thus demand a price much lower than the absolute value of the vaccine.

Patients

Patients are the ultimate consumers for pharmaceuticals. However, unlike the situation for typical consumer goods, the knowledge of

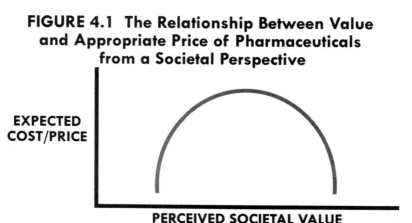

FIGURE 4.1 The Relationship Between Value and Appropriate Price of Pharmaceuticals from a Societal Perspective

EXPECTED
COST/PRICE

PERCEIVED SOCIETAL VALUE

pharmaceuticals and their value often resides not in the patient but in health care professionals, such as pharmacists and physicians. This typically leaves the consumer, who is often the most exposed to the cost, the least informed as to the clinical merits of the product. Thus, experience with the product is very important in determining its value to the patient because it is the utility of the product that predominantly determines the patient's perception of value.

Physicians

In the US, it is largely physicians who determine what products are to be prescribed for patients. Physicians are "learned interme-diaries," meaning that they control the treatment decision because patients are not expected to have the same level of knowledge as a physician. It is the physician's assumed role to judge products on their clinical merits and expected outcomes.

Other influences, such as the "hassle factor," can affect the prescriber's perception of the product's value. For example, if a product is subjected to a prior authorization process that requires the prescriber to complete forms prior to payment for the prescription or service, the physician may perceive that the product's value is less because of the extra effort required to place the product in a patient's hands. Conversely, if the product solves a problem that often drives patient phone calls or excessive visits to the practice, the reduction in man-hours on the phone or in person with those patients may drive the perception of value above and beyond the product's clinical effects.

Payers

Payers determine pharmaceutical value in a manner similar to that used by society, with one notable exception: while society determines the value of a limited number of products, payers are in a position to evaluate the relative value of each product. Payers, through their pharmacy and therapeutics (P&T) committees, assess the value of pharmaceuticals to their collective memberships by balancing the clinical merits and cost of a product. The clinical merits must be realized across a large proportion of the membership of the payer, and the costs are judged on a per-member basis. Often these costs, following rebates and discounts, are calculated in a "per member per year" (PMPY) cost. The determination of value becomes a complex function of the incremental value offered by the pharmaceutical product and the PMPY cost that results from its use.

Other Customers

Certain customers are not singular customers, but combinations of decision makers, each of whom has a part in the purchase decision. Hospitals are perfect examples of this phenomenon. In most hospitals, P&T committees set the formulary, pharmacists order products and evaluate product costs, and physicians write the orders for specific products. In addition, risk management, finance, and even waste management may play a role in determining a product's value and deciding its purchase.

Products that will be used primarily on an inpatient basis will be subjected to significant price scrutiny because the institutional market is perhaps the most price sensitive of pharmaceutical markets. Because of the influence of multiple decision makers, including pharmacy directors and hospital administrators (commonly known as a "buying center"), the cost of any new agent will be considered carefully before the agent is adopted.[4] The buying center involves other roles in the decision-making process as well, including initiators. influencers, gatekeepers, deciders, users, and buyers. The purchase dynamics of each market entity are unique. For any institution, the final decision maker may not be the end user or initiator. Figure 4.2 illustrates the buying center concept.

FIGURE 4.2 The Buying Center Concept

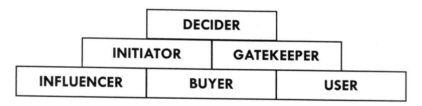

The initiator of a purchase recognizes the need for a new solution to a problem. In the case of a new medication, this could be a physician or a clinical pharmacist. Influencers are parties who have a "say" in the decision to purchase; P&T Committee members and several others will play this role. Gatekeepers are those who control the flow of information. Often the pharmacy director or other head of the P&T Committee will play this role. The deciders are those who decide to purchase the product or include it on the formulary. Users are the individuals who use, order, or administer the product, and the buyer is the one whose budget pays for the product. For hospitals, the pharmacist is often a gatekeeper, a buyer, and an influencer. Physicians are deciders, users, and initiators. Nurses can be users and initiators. Risk management and finance can serve in the influencer roles and perhaps as gatekeepers. This means that the determination of value by customers like hospitals depends on multiple players.

DETERMINATION OF VALUE

For pharmaceuticals, the value determination will be in the context of current therapeutic alternatives, or, in the absence of alternatives, the value determination will be relative to no treatment. As with the decision to purchase or not purchase any product, the value determination will often be a judgment of price versus value.

J. D. Kleinke, medical economist, author, and health information technology entrepreneur, proposed six kinds of value propositions for pharmaceutical products and some examples of each.[5] As Figure 4.3 shows, Kleinke categorizes the market according to who receives the value and how long it takes to realize that value.

This taxonomy focuses on the direct and indirect economic value the product delivers to the health care system. It is very important to note that products have more than economic value. Issues that are often not quantifiable in economic terms, such as quality of life, can drive significant value. This is probably most clearly evident in the "No Pay" category. The PDE5 inhibitors, such as Viagra®, were considered by many payers to be lifestyle drugs. Yet these products significantly improved the treatment of erectile dysfunction. Previous treatments had included intracavernosal injections of Caverject®, urethral suppositories (Muse®), and relatively ineffective yohimbine (Yocon®). Pfizer was able to capture this value in $10 per dose prices that were eagerly paid out of pocket by many patients and eventually covered by many payers. It is therefore important not only to use the quantifiable economic value in the determination of a product's value but also to conduct a systematic evaluation of all value drivers and retarders, regardless of the ability to calculate and place a number on the concept.

FIGURE 4.3 Value Propositions for Pharmaceutical Products

VALUE PROPOSITION	EXAMPLE
Fast Pays	Protease inhibitors, atypical antipsychotics. These drugs lower short-term costs almost immediately, bringing great economic value by reducing the cost of care.
Slow Pays	Selective estrogen receptor modulators, statins. These drugs have recognized benefits, but the benefits come several years after therapy begins. The economic value is not recognized for several years, and many insurers believe the patients will be long gone before the benefit is realized, so why should they pay for it?
Narrow Pays	COX-2 inhibitors, vaccines. These agents provide great benefit to a portion of the patients who receive them, but not to everyone. Payers try to direct these products only to high-risk groups because the benefit is only narrowly received.
Diffuse Pay	Nonsedating antihistamines are the classic example here. The direct medical costs of seasonal allergy are not that high, but while the use of these products actually increases health care costs, it also increases employee productivity. The employer receives a great benefit but has trouble linking that benefit to health insurance spending.
Pay Me Later	HIV drugs, cystic fibrosis and multiple sclerosis medications. These agents reduce short-term costs but guarantee higher costs in the long run by extending life and delaying costly interventions. Anything short of a cure in these areas will fall into this category.
No Pay	Lifestyle drugs. These products don't reduce economic costs and impart only minor economic benefit.

Pharmaceutical value is comprised of multiple components. These components include both negative aspects (e.g., risk, effort, and uncertainty) and positive aspects (e.g., unmet need, criticality of the disease or condition, benefit, and utility). The price charged can also affect the determination of the value of the product. The dynamic between these positive and negative aspects and value is depicted in the Figure 4.4.

Sources of Negative Value

There are many sources of negative value—aspects or features of a product that reduce its inherent value. These aspects are often over-looked by marketers but greatly influence acceptance of a product

FIGURE 4.4 General Model of Value

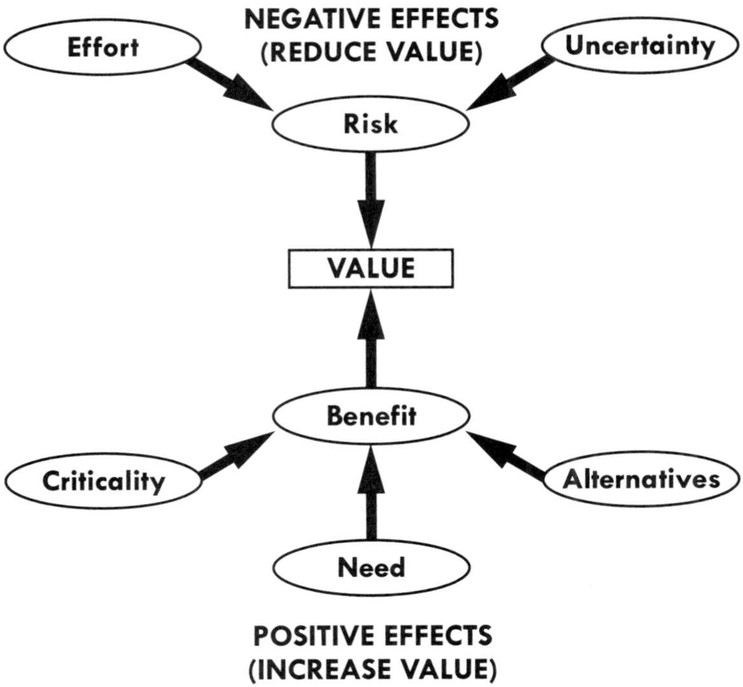

in the marketplace. The degree to which these negative aspects of value affect the eventual pricing of the product will vary. The presence of negative aspects of value does not necessarily mean the price should be lower; it simply means the market will value the product less than some alternatives. Let's consider the three most common negative aspects: effort, uncertainty, and risk (which attempts to quantify uncertainty).

Effort. Effort can be viewed as obstacles to use of the product. Products that reduce effort compared with their competitive predecessors have higher levels of value. Products that increase effort have a reduced value relative to other products. For example, since Betaseron® was launched, the multiple sclerosis market has historically been dominated by products that are self-administered by the patient. A new product that requires physician infusion of an intravenous admixed solution increases the effort associated with MS treatment, which would reduce the product's overall value to the market. On the other hand, Migranal® reduced the effort associated with dihydroergotamine administration for migraine by replacing DHE injection with delivery via a nasal spray. Reduced patient effort increased the overall value of the product. Other types of effort can include insurance obstacles such as prior authorization, doses per day, means of acquisition (retail versus specialty distributors), and maintenance requirements.

Uncertainty. Products that reduce uncertainty increase the overall value of the product. Uncertainty can be associated with a disease. For example, the cure rates for cancer have continued to increase. Newer chemotherapies and chemotherapeutic cocktails reduce the uncertainty of disease progression. The same reduction in uncertainty has occurred in HIV/AIDS treatment, where improvements in regimens have reduced the likelihood of disease progression. These improvements in the probability of positive outcomes over previous treatments reduced the uncertainty of the disease and drove value.

Uncertainty can also be associated with a treatment. The rapid adoption of the COX-2 inhibitors Celebrex® and Vioxx® can be attributed to a reduction in the uncertainty associated with the development of ulcers in nonsteroidal anti-inflammatory drug (NSAID) treatment. Prior to the advent of the COX-2s, many NSAID-naïve patients were concomitantly prescribed an NSAID and an H_2 antagonist or proton pump inhibitor (PPI). This reduction in uncertainty drove the value of the COX-2s.

Similarly, Clozaril® was an atypical antipsychotic that greatly improved the treatment of treatment-resistant schizophrenia. Clozaril had the down side of causing potentially fatal blood dyscrasias, such as megaloblastic anemia, that necessitated a patient registry and regular blood work. Later agents such as Risperdal® and Zyprexa® did not have blood dyscrasia issues and thus reduced the uncertainty of treatment (as well as the effort of treatment because monitoring of adverse effects was no longer necessary). This led to a significant reduction in the risk of treatment compared with Clozaril. Note that this value decreased after the subsequent discovery that Risperdal and Zyprexa use sometimes resulted in increased metabolic problems.

All drugs are controlled doses of poison and are called dangerous drugs by the FDA for a reason; however, the chance of harm from rare causes cannot be appropriately assessed in a clinical trial. In recent years, recalls and withdrawals such as those associated with Baycol for hyperlipidemia and Vioxx for pain have increased the uncertainty associated with any new treatment, and thus any new treatment has some element of risk associated with it.

Risk. Risk can be thought of as the probability that the expected (or hoped for) outcome of product use will not be realized. It is, in essence, a composite of uncertainty and effort, combining the ambiguity over the eventual effects of the product and the amount of work that goes into its use. Higher certainty of effect and ease of use reduces risk. Risk is a huge value driver in that a reduction or increase in the risk for the physician, patient, or payer will greatly influence the value of the product. Products that eliminate a large portion of the current risk of treatment or nontreatment will be adopted at almost any price, and products that are too risky will not be used just because of a low price. In fact, hoping to increase the use of a dangerous product by using the appeal of a low price can be considered unethical marketing.

The introduction or elimination of risk in the treatment of a disease or condition is vital in determining the ultimate value of the product. As a result of experiences with Rezulin and Baycol, any elevation in liver enzymes is perceived as risky and will likely limit the use of the product. For example, the sales of later statins such as Crestor® were impeded by such concerns. AstraZeneca's antithrombolytic Exanta® was pulled from global markets and removed from consideration by the US FDA because of its potential liver issues, despite the fact that its main therapeutic alternative is Coumadin®, the main component of many rat poisons.

Positive Sources of Value

The value of a new pharmaceutical product is judged along three positive dimensions: current unmet needs, the criticality of the disorder for which the product will be used, and the particular benefits the product offers. Each of these factors exerts a different effect on the way the value of a product is perceived. The ability of a product to address currently unmet needs, either clinical or economic, will enhance its value to the market. Products that provide relief from previously untreatable disorders will have a higher perceived value than those that offer little or no new clinical benefits. In these cases, a "performance gap" exists between the level of need and the treatments available.[6] Products narrowing this gap are more readily diffused into and accepted by the medical system; thus, they are more valuable.

Unmet Need. When decision makers examine any new drug to determine where the drug has value, they consciously and unconsciously make comparisons with other treatments and consider the level of satisfaction with current therapies within that disease state. For example, the level of satisfaction with the treatment options available for otitis media is rather high. In other words, there is a low perception of unmet need within the otitis media market. Conversely, there is a much higher level of unmet need in disease states such as Parkinsonism or pancreatic cancer. Unmet need can be thought of as the opposite of satisfaction with current treatments.

Criticality. The other consideration for a decision maker when evaluating a new treatment is the criticality of the disease state itself. For example, sinusitis is perceived to be significantly less critical than stroke. Sinusitis is often not an infection and thus is self-limiting, often heals itself, and is very rarely fatal. Stroke, however, needs immediate attention and is often fatal. Criticality can be thought of as the urgency a physician feels to treat a disorder or the urgency a patient feels to have a disorder alleviated.

Unmet need and criticality cognitively interact to

provide an "imperative to treat" with a new agent. In markets with high levels of unmet need or high criticality, decision makers may be willing to assume more risk and uncertainty in prescribing new drugs. A result of that interaction can be a faster uptake of new drugs into the specified market. The higher the imperative to treat, the higher the price point the market expects and will bear because such products are deemed to be more valuable.

Benefit. A relatively self-explanatory concept, the benefit a product brings to the market is based on its effectiveness. However, the benefits a product can bring can also arise from convenience, compliance, and a reduction in some negative element of value.

Criticality, unmet need, and benefit combine to determine the usefulness, or *utility* of the product relative to alternatives.

The Values Family

So far, it has been established that value can be perceived differently by different decision makers and can be based on multiple criteria. So far, the value that has been discussed is *perceived value* or "the subjective worth of the benefits the buyer believes he or she receives from using the product".[7] There are other forms of value that enter into the determination of value. These are commonly referred to as the *values family* and consist of use, economic, perceived, and expressed values.

Use value is the worth of the benefits received from using the product versus not using the product. **Economic value** is the value in dollars received from using the product rather than the next best competitive alternative.[6] In pharmaceuticals, this value is often partly quantified through pharmacoeconomic analyses. *Perceived value* is the value the customer recognizes from the product. This is perhaps the most important element of the values family because the perception of value is contingent on the way in which the customer understands the product. Marketing that communicates the elements of value to the customer will increase the product's perceived value, placing this aspect partially under the control of the marketer. In other words, helping a customer to understand the value of your product will help you to command a higher price! *Expressed value* is simply a customer's willingness to pay for the product, which is invariably lower than the value the customer perceives. The magnitude of value declines as we move from use to economic to perceived to expressed value. This is one reason that setting prices based on a customer's "willingness to pay" is such a bad idea.

The presence of these different faces of value means that often a decision maker such as a payer recognizes different levels of value based on the value type. The relatively high use and economic values of oral contraceptives can be demonstrated quite easily, but the perceived value and the expressed value could be low, based on the predisposition of the payer. It is critical to be conversant in all of the values and to understand their roles in pricing.

FELE Model

Another method for identifying the value of a product is based on the outcome of the treatment. The functional > economic > lifestyle > emotional (FELE) spectrum identifies the value of a pharmaceutical product based on the end result of use of the therapy. If the therapy improves or enables function—for example, with the atypical antipsychotics Zyprexa, Risperdal, and others—the value afforded is literally *functional*. But functional value can be thought of more broadly as the physical result of the use of the product; in pharmaceuticals, we usually think of this as clinical value. A new product that cures a previously incurable disorder has significant functional value.

Functional values can also offer *economic* value. For example, when the first atypical antipsychotic, Clozaril, launched, it offered significant value to the psychiatric community by reducing the need to institutionalize patients. Sandoz, the maker of Clozaril, estimated that the savings from such changes in the market exceeded the annual cost of Clozaril and thus offset the costs of Clozaril, offering economic value. Although many often believe that "value" and "economic value" are synonymous, it can be seen here that economics is only one aspect of the spectrum of value.

Lifestyle (and work style) value can be derived from a product because it enables a patient to live a more normal life or a clinician to work in a less complicated or constrained manner. Pharmaceutical products that provide lifestyle (or work style) value make a customer's life easier or better, regardless of the clinical or economic aspects of the medicine itself, and therefore bring about a different type of value.

Emotional value is derived from the ability of a product to bring about improvements in a patient's well-being. The most straightforward examples of such value come from many of the so-called "lifestyle" products, which treat conditions where it is often argued that the effects of the condition are not severe. For example, the alopecia therapies, such as Rogaine® and Propecia®, offered reductions in hair loss for balding patients and improved those patients' lifestyles and emotional states. Although many—especially some managed care representatives—argue that such treatments offer no value to society, the demand for products like Rogaine and Viagra shows the power of *lifestyle* and *emotional* value. But other products bring new emotional value as well. "Quality of life" (QoL) is an emotional as well as a lifestyle issue, and many aspects of QoL are purely emotional. Perhaps the best example of a product that provides and communicates emotional value is Procrit, from Johnson & Johnson. In direct-to-consumer (DTC) advertising, J&J points out that Procrit enables a patient to "dance at [his] granddaughter's wedding" or "open [a] bed and breakfast this season." These examples of emotional value are powerful, and patients appreciate Procrit not for the money it saves but for the life experiences it allows.

The Challenges to Measuring Value

For pharmaceuticals, there are multiple methods for measuring value, and health economic or pharmacoeconomic models have become common in the effort to measure a treatment's "value." However, it is important first to identify what values are prized by the market and which can be measured with any accuracy. The quantification of a product's value in cancer is uniquely different from the quantification for insomnia, despite what believers in cost-utility models may believe.

Second, we must recognize that pharmacoeconomic models have been used on both sides of an argument—both in support of and against a therapy. This stems, in part, from the fact that it is far too easy to justify the inclusion or exclusion of costs in any pharmacoeconomic model. Although authorities and experts can arbitrarily decide what should be included and how, this simply sets limits. It does not provide a solution to the problem of measuring value. For example, if one were to perform a pharmacoeconomic model in support of a new migraine therapy, including the cost of employee productivity and lost work time is justifiable and will drive the model to support the therapy. However, excluding those costs is similarly justifiable and may tip the model in the other direction.

Third, we must accept that some values resist quantification. Traditional pharmacoeconomic analyses, such as cost-benefit and cost-effectiveness analyses, examine "hard" values—costs that are directly or indirectly related to the condition(s) and the therapy. Examples of such costs include those associated with hospitalizations, medication use, etc. But pharmaceuticals offer so much more value than what can be directly quantified. For example, while it may be possible to quantify the cost of lost work days for a patient suffering from migraine, it is difficult or impossible to quantify in dollars and cents the quality of life benefits of effective migraine therapy. Similarly, how can we quantify the value of a life saved? Although models provided by cost-utility analysis attempt to quantify the value not only of life, but that life's quality, these efforts do not truly accomplish their goals; rather, they simply satisfy a particular economist's rules and expectations. What is your mother's life worth? To whom is it worth that? The answers to questions like these are so variable that they help explain products that defy pharmacoeconomic models. Erbitux®, a treatment for colon cancer, offered an average increase in life expectancy of only 5 months—and not months with high quality of life—and cost over $40,000 for treatment when launched (in new uses, the cost is higher). The quantification of Erbitux's value in a pharmacoeconomic model has been irrelevant to its use in the US because the assessment of its true value, to patients and others, has not been based on dollars and cents.

Often, it is "soft" values, like the quality and even quantity of life, that drive the true valuation and use of pharmaceuticals—much more so than any economic value. However, for some products, pharmacoeconomic models are very useful and appropriate. As mentioned previously, Sandoz demonstrated that the economic value of Clozaril therapy was a reduction in hospitalizations and associated costs in excess of $25,000, while the drug had an average annual cost of roughly $10,000. In such a situation, the quantified "hard" value drove use as much as the "soft" quality of life value.

Too often those examining pharmaceutical pricing confuse the concepts or "value," "price," and "cost," using the terms interchangeably, or assuming there is a direct relationship among them. The price charged for a medicine is the monetary exchange component of a business transaction, which may or may not be related to the value of the product or the actual cost of acquiring and using the product. Assuming that a change in value for a product would result in a change in its price, or its cost to acquire, indicates a fundamental misunderstanding of the pharmaceutical market and the role of pharmaceuticals in health care. Understanding the value of a product is important, but this does not translate directly into the price that should be charged.

Can Willingness to Pay Be Used to Quantify Value?

Willingness to pay assessments do not focus on the direct or indirect costs or "soft" values. Instead, ultimate purchasers of the product are asked whether they would buy the product at different prices. The trouble with performing such an analysis for pharmaceuticals is that, unlike the end user in consumer markets, the end user in the pharmaceutical market is often neither the decision maker nor the purchaser, and in most situations a person's assessment of his or her willingness to pay is often incorrect.

For pharmaceuticals, the physician decides which therapy is appropriate, and often managed care entities and the patient split the costs of the treatment to differing degrees based on formulary assignment. Because of these issues, willingness to pay for pharmaceuticals becomes less important. When we also consider the fact that the expressed willingness to pay often understates or misstates the person's true willingness to pay, the direct assessment of willingness to pay is practically irrelevant to pharmaceuticals...and to most other goods, for that matter.

PRICING PHARMACEUTICALS BASED ON VALUE

The economist's ideal would be to review the material presented, determine what type of value is being considered (use, economic, perceived, or expressed), and then perform a simple calculation:

Positive Value – Negative Value = Price

However, the pricing of pharmaceuticals based on value is contextual at best, and determining "the price" in this manner is next to impossible. The different faces and types of value, as well as the different types of customers, prevent us from using such a neat and clean, formulaic approach to pricing. Moreover, because several considerations beyond value can and should affect the final price, it is naïve to believe that this mechanical approach could ever render appropriate prices.

In the end, when it comes to a pharmaceutical product's value, there are several key questions that must be asked and answered:

- In lieu of or in addition to which therapies will this product be used?
- What are the cost and value of the current therapies?
- What is the incremental benefit of this product?
- Are there segments where the product is more or less beneficial?
- Which value(s) should I focus on?
- Who receives value from this product?
- Finally, what problem does this product solve and who owns that problem?

Every player in the market will assess the value of a product differently, and in situations where a pharmaceutical product offers significant incremental value over the current therapies, price is often a non-issue. In situations where a pharmaceutical product offers no discernible value over existing therapies, no price, however low, can salvage the product. How does value relate to price? The answer is that it helps move you closer to the final decision, but it doesn't get you all the way there.

REFERENCES

1. Lichtenberg F. Benefits and costs of newer drugs: An update. National Bureau of Economic Research Working Paper 8996. Available at www.nber.org/papers/w8996. Accessed 10 Mar 2008.
2. Widrick S, Fram E. Identifying negative products: Do customers like to purchase your products? *J Product Brand Manage.* 1992; 1(1):43-50.
3. US Department of Health and Human Services. Pandemic planning update II: A report from Secretary Michael O. Leavitt. June 29, 2006. Available at www.pandemicflu.gov/plan/pdf/panflureport2.pdf. Accessed 27 Mar 2007.
4. Bonoma TV. Major sales: Who really does the buying? *Harvard Bus Rev.* 1982; 60(May-June):111-19.
5. Kleinke JD, The Price Of Progress: Prescription Drugs In The Health Care Market, Health Affairs 20(5) 2001, 43-60
6. Greer AL. The state of the art versus the state of the science: The diffusion of new medical technologies in practice. *Int J Technol Assess Health Care.* 1988; 4:5-26.
7. Smith GE, Nagle TT. How much are customers willing to pay? *Marketing Res.* 2002; 14(4):20-5. Available at: www.marketingpower.com/content16236C5033S5.php. Accessed 27 Mar 2006.

Chapter 5

The Role of Price in Medical Decision Making
with Kevin Patterson and Brian Reisetter

From the physician immersed in patient care practicing front line medicine in the trenches, to the professors in our medical schools...the same dictum must be followed—primum non nocere. For the physician, first don't harm the patient but just as importantly for the leaders of the profession, don't harm the profession's ethical code.
—Jerome C. Arnett, Jr., MD, FCCP

Cost containment in health care is a major concern for payers, policy makers, and the public who all frequently call for better cost control. But to what extent do costs play a role in clinical decision making? When pricing a new pharmaceutical product, marketers must ask: What role does price play in the decision to prescribe, use, or dispense products in this category? Understanding how, or even whether, the prices of current therapeutic options affect decisions about their use is instrumental to understanding how to price a new product. The marketer must understand the decision-making process in general and all the influences acting upon various decision makers.

RECENT TRENDS

For the past 30 years, the United States has been engaged in a very public and increasingly nasty social debate on health care costs. A constant pawn in this debate is the price of drugs and its influence on a physician's drug selection. This is not a new issue; several laws have been promulgated or resurrected to address these concerns. These laws, including Stark I and Stark II and other anti-kick-back legislation at both federal and state levels, are all aimed at preventing physician financial factors from affecting medical decision making.

The most significant factors for all decision makers in health care centers are the answers to two questions: Does the product provide the desired benefit? Is Product X the most appropriate therapy for the benefit of the patient and society? In the vast majority of cases, all other factors, including price, play a lesser role. Health care professionals continue to use clinical evidence as the controlling issue in medical decision making. In the world of pharmaceuticals, that means it is "all about the product." If the product is undifferentiated or addresses an issue not considered important by the market, then price may influence the decision.

One of the major complaints of critics of the pharmaceutical industry and pharmaceutical pricing is the lack of pricing transparency and the belief that this lack of transparency results in artificially high prices that inappropriately affect medical decisions. These critics believe that because not all the participants in the market know the prices paid by other participants, companies can charge "artificially inflated" prices of which prescribers are unaware. This causes payers and patients to overpay for therapy or pay for inappropriate or unnecessary therapy. Despite the fact that there is little evidence to support notions of widespread inappropriate prescribing, recent legislative and political agendas have responded to this criticism by attempting to remove any financial incentive from the decision-making process. The result has been an elevated awareness of price in the general marketplace. Is it not ironic that the proposed solution to the detrimental effects of price on decision making is to use price awareness, financial incentives, and penalties as the mechanisms of change? The outstanding question is, for a market that rewards value, does the increased price awareness change the medical decisions in any significant way?

ECONOMICS OF HEALTH CARE DECISION MAKING

In conventional economic theory, the law of demand states: *All things equal, as prices increase, unit sales will decrease, and as prices decrease, unit sales will increase.* Aside from the qualifying statement "all things equal," in general, health care goods and services follow this basic model—although, as we discussed in Chapter 2, "all things equal" is an assumption that simply is not reasonable in the health care market. Social concerns, politics, government regulations, national security, and, more importantly, the multiple decision makers who are not directly affected financially by the decision to purchase all interfere with the caveat "all things equal."

While the law of demand may apply, to some extent, to health care goods and services, it does *not* apply to the incidence of disease, where the selection of treatments is a clinical rather than an economic decision. Attempting to understand medical markets with basic economics can lead only to false conclusions. Demand (or, more appropriately, the quantity of treatment demanded) is driven principally by the incidence of disease, not price levels. A higher price for a therapy does not decrease the incidences of cancer or flu. The inverse is also true for the marketer: a lower price does not generally increase demand. (Would lowering the price of cancer therapy increase the incidence of cancer?) Price differences among treatment options *may* affect clinical decisions, but in what way? The pricing question is: How do differences (or changes) in the price of a medicine affect decision makers?

Rather than using *price elasticity*, the basic measure for the law of demand, to find the "optimal" price for a product, pharmaceutical marketers should be considering *price sensitivity*. In pharmaceutical markets, price elasticity provides what we call a "precisely wrong" measure that often leads the marketer to think in terms of minor price differences rather than in terms of strategy—which should be "roughly right." Price sensitivity, as opposed to elasticity, is a qualitative concept that can be detected and observed in the market but is not precisely measurable. Understanding price sensitivity, its variations, and its sources helps marketers to recognize these influences and actively *manage* them, rather than just *measure and react* to them. Understanding price sensitivity allows you to segment the market by differences in sensitivity, to anticipate the effects of sensitivity on your marketing plans and sales success, and to influence the degree and types of sensitivity.[1]

Price sensitivity, in its various forms, has been described by Nagle and Holden, who delineate ten sources of price sensitivity:

- Unique value effect
- Perceived substitute effect
- Switching cost effect
- Difficult comparison effect
- Price-quality effect
- Expenditure effect
- Shared cost effect
- End benefit effect
- Fairness effect
- Inventory effect.[1]

Each of these determinants may affect the decision to prescribe, purchase, or use a drug. Which determinant most significantly influences price sensitivity depends on various social and economic factors. For a marketer to understand price sensitivity and the role of price in health care decision making, he must first understand these determinants.

Unique Value Effect

Decision makers are less sensitive to price when they value the unique attributes that differentiate a product from its competitors. Orphan drugs are examples of products that have a dominating unique value effect. The epidemiologic realities of orphan diseases argue against investing resources to find new treatments, which results in few treatment options. Patients with these diseases and decision makers are looking for any option for treatment, and orphan drugs may fulfill the need. Even in disease areas where patient populations are much larger, the unique value effect acts to curb price sensitivity when only a single agent is available. When a product is the exclusive source of a desired effect, price sensitivity will be lower.

Perceived Substitute Effect

When decision makers are aware of both a lack of differentiation *and* the prices of similar products, they will become more sensitive to price. The greatest impediment to this determinant is price awareness. Physicians' traditional lack of pricing awareness has acted to prevent this determinant from operating to any great extent in the pharmaceutical marketplace. However, other market participants such as MCOs, patient advocacy groups, and governments are attempting to raise price awareness and encourage therapeutic substitution and restrictive formularies to take advantage of this concept. Restrictive formularies emphasize the existence of substitutes, limit the number of substitutes, and direct decisions toward the MCOs' choice of substitute.

Firms with inferior products have attempted to make the perceived substitute effect work for them by pricing their products below prevailing levels, hoping the low price would result in increased use. The most obvious example of perceived substitute effect is the use of generics. However, capitalizing on this concept is more diffi-cult for branded drugs. This strategy requires a significant investment in promotion to bring about the necessary level of awareness and interest in the price difference. In crowded categories [for example, the proton pump inhibitor (PPI), angiotensin II receptor antago-nist, and angiotensin II receptor blocker (ARB) categories], it is also difficult to use the perceived substitute effect because the multiple competitors reduce the "share of voice" required to communicate effectively. Firms with products that are relatively indistinguishable can sometimes make this effect work for them, but, as discussed in Chapter 3, this requires significant planning and resources.

Pharmacoeconomics can play an important role in managing the perceived substitute effect by comparing the costs and effects of a new agent with those of older treatments. This is particularly true when a new class of drugs appears to compete with an older class of drugs. Clozaril's "high cost" of up to $10,000 per year was overcome by the finding that it reduced cost of care for the treatment-resis-tant schizophrenic patient by over $25,000 per year. By positioning Clozaril as a substitute for inpatient treatment, its manufacturer, Sandoz, moved the debate from the price of the product to its value, using the perceived substitute effect to the company's advantage. This tactic, called "framing," is discussed in Chapters 5 and 11.

The perceived substitute effect can also be invoked through direct-to-consumer (DTC) advertising. When AstraZeneca launched Nexium with a DTC campaign, it informed patients tak-ing Prilosec of a new option (substitute) that could provide more benefit for the same money. AstraZeneca used this strategy to retain current patients and attract new patients by steering them to another company product.

Switching Cost Effect

The cost to change a current or preferred therapy to a new therapy is the switching cost. When users have "sunk investment" into a product, the switching cost effect is in operation. This is a major reason for the difficulty in moving patients using chronic medications between agents. There are three "costs" to switching products: efficacy or utility, economy, and loyalty. The effort required to retitrate and reestablish control (or the risk of losing control, in the case of antiepileptics and anticoagulants) acts as a major deterrent to price appeals. In the hospital market, "switching cost" can be financial in nature because switching products may involve purchasing new equipment, retraining, or revising data systems and protocols.

Product loyalty also brings about switching cost problems for new competitors. Physician and patient decision makers are most prone to loyalty. A physician who is satisfied with the performance of a particular agent will resist adopting a competitive agent for two reasons: the "cost" of learning about the new agent and the "cost" in admitting that the trusted agent may not be the best choice. By training, most physicians are conservative; they rely on a specific set of drugs to meet most of their needs. These are referred to as an "evoked set," and adding or deleting products in that set requires a commitment of time, memory, and new learning.[2] The less specialized the physician, the more conservative he or she is in practice. For example, an internal medicine physician will adopt changes for the treatment of cardiac issues much more slowly than a cardiologist.

In consumers, the switching cost effect accounts for consumer tendencies to block competitive messages when those messages create cognitive dissonance—i.e., when the message conflicts with current behavior.

Difficult Comparison Effect

The difficult comparison effect lessens price sensitivity by making straightforward price comparisons difficult. The introduction of a new class of drugs or a different dosing regimen may trigger this effect. A new class of drugs for treating a condition presently served by another class has the difficult comparison effect in its favor. When Prilosec, the proton pump inhibitor by Astra Merck (now Astra-Zeneca), entered the market, its mechanism of action and eventual effectiveness differed greatly from those of the H_2 inhibitors (e.g., Pepcid) dominating the market at that time. Although Prilosec's price, which was significantly higher than those of the H_2s, raised some early concern, decision makers could not simply dismiss this new class of drugs because it could not be directly compared with the older agents.

Similarly, branded products within a chemical class benefit from this effect when a major competitor loses patent protection. Although it is relatively easy to compare a branded drug with new generic competitors and to make the purchase decision on the basis of price difference, choosing a generic of one brand over another branded competitor is not as straightforward, regardless of the price difference. In a relatively free market, the difficult comparison effect argues against the large-scale loss of sales for a brand when a competitor loses patent protection.

Complicated dosing regimens also induce the difficult comparison effect. Oral agents used in the antipsychotic market benefit from difficult comparisons, as the dosing must be individualized. Comparing the prices of the atypical antipsychotic agents Zyprexa and Risperdal is difficult because doses for each vary so widely.

Price-Quality Effect

The price-quality effect manifests the traditional use of price as a surrogate indicator of quality. Lacking other means of assessing quality, consumers often use the price as a measure of quality. Luxury automobiles are a classic example of this effect. For pharmaceuticals, this effect, we believe, works in reverse: physicians often assume that the prices of products they deem superior are higher than those of competitors. Research at the University of Mississippi found that the majority of high-volume prescribers of Lipitor believed it to be the costliest statin on the market, even though it was priced below Zocor® and Pravachol®. The perceived quality of Lipitor caused them to assume that it was priced higher. This was also true for Xanax, Motrin®, and a number of other products that were launched with pricing "advantages" that offered the marketers no true advantage.

Expenditure Effect

The expenditure effect argues that the higher the expenditure, the more likely it is that people will seek alternatives. Even though a product may be worth $50,000 or more, in economic terms, the sheer size of the expenditure causes many to question the value of the product and seek alternatives.

When trying to reduce overall expenditures, large-volume purchasers like hospital buying groups, the Department of Veterans Affairs, or large MCOs will target expenditures that account for a large proportion of total spending. It is not uncommon for these groups to speak of products coming up on their "radar screen," meaning that expenditures on these items have reached the point where the payers feel obliged to take some action to reduce them. Because of the sheer magnitude of money they spent on statins, payers worked to steer new patients away from Lipitor to Zocor as Zocor's patent ran out. The expenditure effect also explains why antibiotics are a constant focus of cost control in hospitals. It is not that any one agent is so costly, but that the total amount spent on antibiotics is so large that payers feel compelled to take some steps to reduce it.

Companies launching new products into markets where the expenditure effect is operative may be able to exploit the effect by positioning the new product in a way that allows a reduction in total spending. For categories that do not yet show up on the radar screen, marketers need not be unduly concerned that their price will be scrutinized to the point where its sales potential will be severely reduced. This is the reason many orphan drugs are allowed prices that seem inordinately high. Their limited use keeps them off the radar screen of decision makers.

Shared Cost Effect

The concept of shared cost is important because the smaller the proportion of an individual's responsibility for the total cost for a product, the less price sensitive this person will be. The shared cost effect is probably the single greatest reason for the paradoxical effect of managed care on the sale of pharmaceuticals. Despite fears that managed care would restrict access to pharmaceuticals and force prices down, there is ample evidence that managed care has resulted in major increases in the use of higher cost agents. The effect of third-party prescription plans was to reduce patient price sensitivity because patients saw only a portion of the total cost—their co-pay. The growth of these third-party plans and the introduction of Medicare Part D have further encouraged the shift of patients' focus from total cost to co-pay. However, the use of coinsurance, in which patients agree to pay a percentage of cost rather than a fixed co-pay, leads to patients paying a higher proportion of the total cost, thus increasing patient price sensitivity.

End Benefit Effect

The end benefit effect simply uses the total value of a product to frame its price. Pharmacoeconomics was intended to help establish this effect in pharmaceutical markets but has not yet been successful. (A noted economist recently remarked, "Pharmacoeconomics is like teen sex—everybody is doing it, just not very well.") In practice, by having customers focus on the end result of treatment rather than the price of the treatment, price sensitivity should be reduced. Perhaps the finest example of this was the communication of the value of Neupogen®, the colony-stimulating factor. When customers balked at the price, roughly $1,400 for a course of therapy, Amgen responded with data demonstrating that the product saved nearly $6,000 and produced better patient outcomes. That was the end benefit. A less quantified example is Johnson & Johnson's marketing of Procrit, in which J&J described the end benefit to the patient as being able to live, and enjoy, a normal life.

Fairness Effect

The fairness effect is perhaps the biggest reason for the criticism of pharmaceutical products in recent years. Buyers will be more sensitive to and critical of prices that are higher than those to which they are accustomed. The criticism of the price of Cerezyme® was due in large part to the extraordinarily high price compared with that of any other drug in the market at the time. (Eventually, the price was found to be justified due to its manufacturing cost.) Similarly, advances in the technology used to derive and purify insulins brought about significant advances over the older animal insulins. The newer, short-acting insulins more closely mimic the actual performance of native insulin in the patient. They were not immediately accepted and were unable to garner the premiums they should have commanded, however, because of the fairness effect. The "price of insulin" had been established by the older products, and the companies producing the new forms were unable (or unwilling) to fight for a new price level.

Lacking any other cues, buyers will often use a reference price (not to be confused with the price-control tool used by many governments) to assess the fairness of a price. Many believe that BiDil, a new combination agent for congestive heart failure in African-Americans, has not achieved the desired sales levels partly because customers have compared its price to the prices of other agents for CHF, as well as to the prices of the individual components of the drug itself, and decided that the price was unfair. Many new agents suffer from such comparisons, and marketers should consider supporting their prices with more appropriate frames of reference.

Inventory Effect

The inventory effect was responsible for the greater part of drug wholesaler profits during the late 1980s and throughout the 1990s. When buyers can store quantities of a product for later use, they are likely to make larger purchases when a low price is available or when they anticipate a price increase. Drug wholesalers learned to anticipate price increases for major pharmaceutical brands and bought heavily prior to the increases. This allowed them to hold the inventory until the price increases and profit significantly from the increases. The introduction of the Medicare Modernization Act of 2003 and the Deficit Reduction Act of 2005, as well as the inventory management agreements now common in the industry, are likely to lessen this effect in the future.

WHO ARE THE DECISION MAKERS?

One of the key considerations that determine the importance of the ten "pricing effects" is the role and perspective of the decision maker in the buyer center. As discussed in Chapter 4, the concept of the buying center in the health care model is very important in understanding the role of price for the various decision makers. Each of the players in the buying center may define value differently; therefore, their role of price in the decision to purchase, prescribe, or use a pharmaceutical changes.

Additionally, where and how the product will be used changes the role and authority of the decision maker. Products that will be used primarily on an inpatient basis will be subjected to significant price scrutiny because the institutional market is arguably the most price sensitive of pharmaceutical markets. Because of the influence of multiple decision makers, including pharmacy direc-

FIGURE 5.1 Decision for Antibiotic to Treat VAP

ROLE	MD	Nurse	Specialist	Risk Management	Pharmacy	Finance
Initator	X					
User		X				
Influencer			X	X	X	X
Buyer					X	
Gatekeeper					X	
Decider	X					

tors and hospital administrators (commonly known as a "buying center"), the cost of any new agent may be considered carefully before the agent is adopted.[3] In the outpatient setting, however, the practitioner can often choose therapies with little regard to cost. An outpatient drug may still be subject to price sensitivity, though, because the growth of managed care and other initiatives elsewhere may increase the level of price sensitivity over time.

Figure 5.1 illustrates the roles taken by various participants in a hospital setting when deciding what antibiotic to use to treat ventilator-associated pneumonia (VAP). For hospitals, the pharmacist is often a gatekeeper, a buyer, and an influencer. Physicians are deciders, users, and initiators. Nurses can be users and initiators. Risk management and finance may be influencers and perhaps gatekeepers; they may even be initiators, depending on whether risk is created or removed by a therapy. This means that the hospital's determination of a drug's value will involve multiple players, only a few of whom (such as pharmacists, purchasing, or finance officers) may know the cost of the drug.

The complexity of the buying center further removes the simple concept of price elasticity and reinforces the concept of price sensitivity. For the last 15 years—and, it could be argued, since the inception of Medicare—various initiatives have attempted to make the market more price sensitive; however, the resounding conclusion is that these attempts have failed. The market is *value* sensitive. As discussed in the introductory chapter, price is a way of capturing value. In most instances in the pharmaceutical markets, price becomes a significant influencer in the decision-making process only if the *seller* makes it significant.

HOW DOES PRICE SENSITIVITY AFFECT PROVIDER DECISION MAKING?

For physicians and other providers, the decision to prescribe or use a drug may be affected by price knowledge (awareness), reimbursement issues, and organizational economics. Of these influences, only price knowledge is truly a pricing issue. The other two revolve around reimbursement, which may or may not be directly related to the price charged. The price of the product itself is only relevant when there is price knowledge.

Price Knowledge

In most drug classes, physician prescribing is not sensitive to the price of a medicine. The growth of third-party payers has further removed physicians from direct price knowledge for outpatient drugs. Actual price knowledge among physicians is as rare as those proverbial hen's teeth. Physicians, by and large, do not know the prices of the medicines they prescribe. This has been demonstrated repeatedly for over 50 years, and there is little evidence that their price knowledge is increasing.[4, 5, 6] Thus, for the most part, the way the specific price of a product affects prescribing is only indirect.

In a handful of cases, however, physician prescribing actually is affected by incremental differences in the price of a medicine. The introduction of the MMA and its new reimbursement of average sales price plus 6% (ASP + 6%) for physician-administered drugs may increase price knowledge for certain drugs (for example, oncology agents) and therefore increase the potential incentive to prescribe one agent over another. However, when this occurs, the relationship between price awareness and prescribing or use almost always involves thresholds or breakpoints. All prices perceived to be in the range between A and B result in one level of use intentions, and prices between B and C result in a different level of use intentions. Pure price elasticity curves, as described in basic economic theory, simply cannot be found in pharmaceutical markets.

Reimbursement Issues

Providers may be *reimbursement sensitive*—that is, they may be less likely to prescribe a medication if it is not reimbursed directly, if the patient's out-of-pocket cost is seen as too high, if the product is subject to prior authorization or similar restrictions, or if it is simply not covered. Hospital systems tend to be more price sensitive because of the capitated payment systems that make up a significant portion of their reimbursement structure. This is the reason for slower adoption for most new technologies and therapies in the hospital systems. Due to the standard reimbursement rates, reimbursement for new technologies may not reflect costs for months, if ever. The result is that a new drug must demonstrate higher value (social, economic, and preferably both) before hospitals will adopt it. In addition, patient cost sensitivity may occur when a physician is aware of a product being on the plan's third or fourth tier or when a physician is certain the medication is not covered. Patient sensitivity, also called co-pay sensitivity, is becoming more important with the trend of cost shifting from insurance plans to patients through the insurer's use of a "preferred" drug list.

As previously mentioned in the discussion of prescriber price awareness, new reimbursement methods for physician-administered drugs under the MMA and Medicaid outpatient reimbursement (resulting from the Deficit Reduction Act of 2005) could affect the way that providers make decisions in the future. These new reimbursement methods could press providers to make organizational economics a larger part of the decision-making process, even though the intent of those behind these legislative acts was to reduce its importance.

Organizational Economics

The previously mentioned changes in Medicare and Medicaid reimbursement which move away from reimbursement based on AWP to ASP have introduced concerns in most medical practices about the cost and reimbursement of office-administered medications, such as oncology drugs. One of the issues that will need to be monitored is the effect of these reduced reimbursement rates on the corresponding collection or billing rates for the patient's portion of the bill.

Historically, regardless of a patient's ability to pay, the provider has consistently chosen therapy based on clinical appropriateness. Reported collection rates for oncology practices over the last several years have been approximately 50% for the patient portion of physician fees.[7] The profit margins from the drugs allowed providers to be generous when patients were unable to pay their share. The new reimbursement methods, which reduce payments to providers and particularly to physicians, may begin to affect choice of therapy if failure to collect the patient responsibility portion creates a loss for the organization. Assuming a 20% patient co-pay responsibility (the Medicare standard), with the new ASP + 6% reimbursement for Part B office-administered drugs, failure of the provider to collect over 71% of the patient responsibility will result in a financial loss for the provider. For expensive new drugs, the ability of the patient to afford the co-pay will become more important for the provider. The result has been a reevaluation of which drugs will be administered in the office versus alternative sites of administration.

Despite the effect of these recent changes in reimbursement and the desire of payers to raise price awareness, a physician's decision to prescribe, dispense, or use a particular drug rests first on clinical appropriateness and only secondarily on price.

REFERENCES

1. Nagle TT, Holden RK. The strategy and tactics of pricing: A guide to profitable decision making. 3rd ed. New York: Prentice Hall; 2002.
2. Groves KE, Flanagan PS, MacKinnon NJ. Why physicians start or stop prescribing a drug. *Formulary*. 2002; 37(Apr):186-94.
3. Bonoma TV. Major sales: Who really does the buying? *Harvard Bus Rev*. 1982; 60(May-June):111-19.
4. Zelnio RN, Gagnon JP. The effects of price information on prescription drug product selection. *Drug Intell Clin Pharm*. 1979; 13:156-9.
5. Kolassa EM. Physicians' perceptions of pharmaceutical prices: Their accuracy and effect on the prescribing Decision. *J Res Pharm Econ*. 1995; 6(1):23-37.
6. Reisetter BC, Bentley JP, Wilkin NE. Relationship between psychosocial physician characteristics and physician price awareness. *J Pharm Market Manage*. 2005; 17(1):51-76.
7. Johnson KA. New MMA methodology for drug prices is a big change for many payers. *Managed Healthcare Exec*. 2004; (Dec 1). Available at: www.managedhealthcareexecutive.com/mhe/article/articleDetail.jsp?id=136812. Accessed 19 Oct 2007.

Chapter 6

Patient and Disease Characteristics
with Brian Reisetter

Few human experiences have such potent symbolic
overtones as the ordinary acts of
prescribing and ingesting medicines.
Their meaning transcends the pharmacological
properties of the substances.
— Michael Montagne (1)

PATIENTS, DISEASE, AND MEDICINE

One thing that marketers often forget is that behind every drug and every disease is a patient. Not a consumer, but a patient. Disease defines our roles in society and affects everyone, from the very young to the very old. How people react to diseases and how an individual patient reacts to a specific disease will vary, sometimes extensively. From a pricing perspective, it is imperative to understand these variations in how people—patients and others—react to a specific disease. Ignoring patient- and disease-specific characteristics can lead, and has led, to some serious pricing mistakes.

Medicines save lives—there is no doubt about it. Drugs should be welcomed by society then, right? They signify that we have some power over disease. We should be grateful for the technologies that save or extend our lives, but we don't seem to be. Study after study shows that rates of compliance with medication regimens are consistently around 50%-75%, with some variation based on the acute versus chronic or symptomatic nature of the disease. Given that drugs save lives, wouldn't we expect compliance rates to be higher?

Unfortunately, patients' feelings about medicine are very complicated. As we said previously, medicines are negative goods.[2] People don't want to buy them; they pay for medicines only to get well or to stay healthy. A good example of a similar negative good is gasoline. Nobody wants to buy gasoline, but people like and need what gasoline does for them. It powers the cars that transport us to work, take us shopping, and help us accomplish myriad daily chores. But the physical act of purchasing gasoline is not in itself rewarding. Who wants to make an extra stop on the way to work to fill the gas tank?

Cars also supply another analogy regarding medicines and heath care. A car is not just a car. People purchase cars to say something about their personalities, stature, or interests. Just as cars provide freedom and status above and beyond the physical utility of the vehicle, medications also impute meanings to patients above and beyond the physical act of consuming medications. Some medications have even become status symbols. Who would have thought 20 years ago that people would brag about having depression, yet it happened when the act of taking Prozac® became a status symbol several years later.[3] A similar type of phenomenon is happening today with erectile dysfunction drugs, where the stigma associated with the disease has been gradually replaced with acceptance or even pride.

Drugs, in fact, are strong symbols of the relationship between patient and illness. Drugs can symbolize power over a disease by giving patients a way to control their own bodies. In those instances, drugs can be perceived very positively. However, drugs may have the exact opposite effect by validating an illness—a validation that many people don't really want. For example, insulin has saved the lives of hundreds of thousands of people since it was first used to treat diabetes. However, does anyone think that the physical act of taking shots every day is a positive validation of life to most diabetics? Not only is it physically painful, but it is a reminder several times a day that a person is diabetic and is sick. It is a reminder that the person may have complications that will shorten life, and it is a reminder that the person's role in society may be somewhat altered due to the limitations brought on by the disease.

Morphine, an opioid narcotic analgesic, shares a similar stigma. When patients, especially cancer patients, hear that they will be getting morphine, they often see it as a death sentence. They think of morphine as the drug that hospice gives dying patients. So it is no wonder that morphine's negative connotations may limit its use by the patients who may need it most. In fact, this morphine stigma has contributed to the success of the drug OxyContin. Because OxyContin, also an opioid narcotic analgesic, did not have the stigma associated with morphine, physicians began to depend on it when they needed a timed-release product to treat moderate to severe pain. The product allowed for the adequate treatment of pain without the cancer stigma associated with older drugs, such as morphine.

Why all this discussion about patient attitudes toward medications and diseases in a book on pricing pharmaceuticals? Because patients make decisions about their health care that sometimes seem irrational. For example, pharmaceutical companies are constantly looking for the silver bullet that will improve the compliance rates of their drugs. The logic is simple: increase compliance by 10% and increase sales by 10%. Yet few, if any, companies have been successful at dramatically improving patient compliance over time, regardless of the programs they employ.

When patients skip doses of medication, we often assume that it has something to do with forgetfulness. Or, if it is not about forgetfulness, then it must be about saving money. The truth is that it often has nothing to do with either the patients' ability to remember or the cost of the drug. Rather, it is often about proving to themselves and those surrounding them that they are in control of this disease, that they know themselves better than anyone else, and that they will decide how sick they are by taking the drugs they want when they determine they need them. And that is an issue that cannot be fixed with price. Lowering prices will not increase consumption in these instances, and an expectation that it will often leads marketers down a dangerous, less profitable path. However, understanding the patient behavior within the defined disease state(s) of a product will lead to more appropriate, and profitable, pricing decisions.

WHO OWNS THE PROBLEM?

As we mentioned in Chapter 4, the first two questions that any marketer should ask about a new product are: What problem does it solve? Who owns the problem? Answering these questions will quickly reveal the real drivers of product use for any pharmaceutical. For example, consider two new pharmaceutical agents, one to treat severe hemorrhagic stroke and the other to treat children's ear infections. Consider how different the drivers are for each of the products.

Let's apply our two questions stated above to the new drug to treat hemorrhagic stroke. What problem does it solve? It allows for the treatment of a clinically dangerous episodic event that could easily kill the patient. The treatment will likely be provided in emergency rooms, and timing will be critical. We would expect that the patient will be unconscious and will not be participating in the treatment plan, even if he or she understood enough about treatment options to help drive decisions. Nurses would be there as support to the physician but, like the patient, would not likely be involved in any clinical decisions. Who owns the problem, then? In this case, it would be the physician almost exclusively.

Now, let's look at the new drug for otitis media (ear infection) in children. What problem does it solve? It treats sick children who are suffering from an infection. Who owns the problem? The patients, of course, but so do the patients' parents and other caregivers. Often children are not allowed into daycare if they are febrile, so it also affects the coworkers of the sick children's parents. This scenario changes the dynamics of the decision making.

The standard protocol for the treatment of an uncomplicated ear infection is first amoxicillin (an antibiotic that is over 30 years old) and then, if the amoxicillin fails, a cephalosporin or macrolide antibiotic. However, pediatricians will often bypass amoxicillin and move right into more aggressive treatment. Why? Probably because mothers will request more "powerful" or expensive antibiotics sooner in the treatment regimen to make sure that the child gets well "the first time" and the family can go back to a normal routine as quickly as possible.

In this case, the drivers for product selection are both the patient and the caregiver, simply because they own the problem and have some control over the solution. In pricing situations such as this one, it is imperative that one understand fully the patient characteristics driving those decisions before pricing a product within that therapeutic class.

Researching patient acceptance of price ranges or price sensitivities when patients don't own the problem doesn't make much sense, but it happens all the time. Unfortunately, the converse is also true and may actually be more prevalent. It is easy to forget that patients do drive decisions in some markets, and, even though their decisions may not seem rational, it is important to understand what drives that behavior.

For example, right now, two of the largest classes of drugs in the US are the cholesterol-lowering agents (statins) and the drugs used to treat erectile dysfunction. Each of these drug classes has a different level of patient involvement. Patients with high cholesterol are more likely to say, "My doctor wants me to get my cholesterol numbers down," than "I need to lower my cholesterol." The doctor owns this problem, not the patient. Asymptomatic, chronic diseases like hyperlipidemia often suffer from a lack of patient involvement, and the compliance numbers, which are lower in these disease states, support this. Conversely, patients are extremely involved in the diagnosis and treatment of erectile dysfunction. In fact, that is exactly why direct-to-consumer (DTC) advertising has been successful for this drug class. The disease is symptomatic and easy to diagnose, and treatment provides quick therapeutic outcomes that drive patient satisfaction.

Given the differences in patient involvement between these two drug classes, in which class will we probably see less price sensitivity? For which class of drugs would patients be willing to fight their insurance company, PBM, or HMO for access? For which of these classes will patients be willing to pay cash if the drug is not covered by insurers or payers? Understanding these issues is key to understanding any pricing sensitivities that exist within each market.

It is important to understand that price had nothing to do with the ultimate success of drugs to treat erectile dysfunction. These companies did not lower prices to increase use. Instead, they found out who owned the problem and helped those people fight for their drugs. Without understanding these dynamics, though, some companies may have succumbed to pricing pressures—real or imagined—and lowered the price of their products to incentivize sales.

CRITICALITY REVISITED

The interaction between criticality and unmet need was introduced in Chapter 4: a high level of criticality combined with a high level of unmet need can result in less price sensitivity by payers and patients and greater tolerance of risk by prescribers. Because patients are less astutely aware of the therapeutic options that exist for each disease state than their physicians, the concept of unmet need within a therapeutic class is somewhat less relevant within the patient segment. However, patient perceptions of disease criticality are very relevant within most disease states.

When we presented the concept of criticality and unmet need previously, we mentioned that physicians reported moderate levels of criticality and unmet need for Parkinson's disease. Physicians most commonly use dopamine products to treat the disease, which makes intuitive sense to them because they are basically replacing an exact molecule that is missing in the Parkinson's patient. However, exactly replicating human dopamine regulation through oral medications has proven to be extremely difficult, and patients' symptoms often quickly worsen. For example, patients may experience decreased motor control and difficulty walking. Our own research shows that patients attribute higher levels of criticality and unmet need for Parkinson's disease than physicians. Patients, not knowing the science behind the medications, have higher expectations for returning to normal function than trained physicians may have, given the same circumstances.

When the patient "owns" the problem, it could well be in a disease area that physicians pay little attention to because it doesn't really affect them. Our favorite example in recent years is chemotherapy-induced anemia. Most oncologists were unreceptive to Johnson & Johnson's message in support of Procrit because their focus was on treating the tumor, not on the patient-reported problems of anemia and fatigue. Oncologists often argued that Procrit was too expensive for such a minor problem. Fatigue was a patient problem, not a doctor problem. DTC advertising and professional communication with nurses helped raise physicians' awareness of the real problems caused by anemia—problems to which the oncologists were not initially receptive.

In many disease states, therefore, patients will often deem symptoms to be more onerous and current therapies to be less acceptable than their physicians would—particularly for chronic, symptomatic diseases—and will therefore score the disease states with higher levels of criticality and unmet need. In these instances, patients will often assist in driving the acceptance of new treatments that better solve the problems they own. This marketing message can be communicated through word of mouth, discussions with physicians, or talks with advocacy groups.

SYMPTOMATIC VERSUS ASYMPTOMATIC DISEASES

Knowing who is driving decisions can help marketers better understand any pricing sensitivities that may exist in the market. In general, patients with symptomatic diseases are less price sensitive than patients with asymptomatic diseases. The previous Parkinson's disease example helps to illustrate this fact. If patients are provided a new treatment that will improve their motor skills and decrease the peripheral shaking associated with the disease, it is likely that those patients will be less price sensitive than patients being treated for an asymptomatic disease.

Pain is another example where patients are willing to pay more for assurance that their symptoms will be relieved. Eli Lilly and Sandoz were able to stave off the generic erosion of Darvocet-N® 100 and Fiorinal®, respectively, for several additional years after patent expiration because of the higher quality and resultant superior pain relief that patients associated with brand-name products—even in an era when most patients paid cash for their prescriptions.

In contrast, disease states such as hypertension (high blood pressure) and hypercholesterolemia (high cholesterol) are asymptomatic and usually result in markets that are slightly more price sensitive than their symptomatic counterparts. When there is no direct, immediate effect of taking the drug on patients' well-being, they will often be less willing to pay their hard-earned dollars for the medicine. This results in patients more quickly requesting generic alternatives or requesting that other, cheaper branded drugs be used in place of more costly ones.

As mentioned, this phenomenon is documented in the compliance literature when symptomatic and asymptomatic diseases are compared—and that makes sense. The more effective a medication is in treating symptoms, the more patients will see those medications as positive rather than negative goods. The more they desire to take each dose, the more likely they will be to pay for the benefits received from each of those doses.

To take this logic one step further, it must be noted that some drugs make you feel worse—not better—and that has a drastic effect on patient attitudes toward both the medication and the disease. For example, beta-blockers such as propranolol and metoprolol are often used to treat hypertension (admittedly more in the past than recently), and this entire class of drugs has numerous side effects, including fatigue and impotence. In instances such as this, a medication not only moves patients from an asymptomatic state to one of constant and daily reminders of illness but also makes them feel worse than before they started taking the medication. It is no wonder that compliance and persistence are so low in these situations.

ACUTE VERSUS CHRONIC DISEASES

Price sensitivities also differ based on the duration of the illness or treatment. In general, within acute diseases (those in which the patient returns to normal functioning after a short period of time) such as a cold, an ear infection, or a broken bone, patients tend to be less price sensitive than for chronic diseases. For chronic diseases, such as hypertension or diabetes, which persist until death, patients tend to be more price sensitive.

Again, this makes intuitive sense. Patients taking the same medication for the same disease for several years will begin looking for ways to decrease the cost of their therapy. This can be done by shopping different pharmacies to find the best price on existing medications or working with the pharmacist or discussing treatments with the physician to find lower-cost alternatives. The interaction of symptoms and length of therapy provides a way to understand the level of patient price sensitivity, as shown in Figure 6.1.

FIGURE 6.1 Disease Characteristics and Patient Price Sensitivity

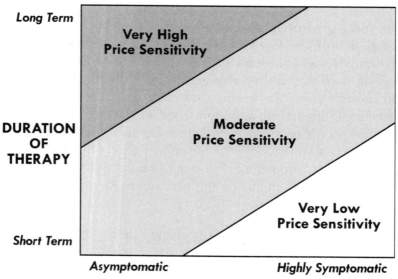

Pharmacies have known about these differences in price sensitivity for decades. It is still not uncommon for pharmacists to have a different cash pricing schedule for products that are used once versus products that are used multiple times. For example, antibiotics used to treat acute infections will often be priced to be more profitable to the pharmacy than medications used to treat chronic diseases like hypertension. In fact, some commonly used medications for chronic diseases have been used by pharmacies as "loss leaders," which are products sold at or near acquisition cost to attract patients to those pharmacies.

If pharmacists know and understand these patient dynamics and resultant pricing sensitivities for our products, doesn't it make sense that we understand these differences as well?

CO-PAY VERSUS PRICE SENSITIVITY

With the advent of Medicare Part D, over 90% of all prescriptions filled in the US are now filled under some third-party payer system. Consequently, most patients are responsible for paying only a portion of their total drug costs—usually either a co-pay or a coinsurance percentage. Co-pays are patient payment amounts for each prescription fixed by a third-party payer. Generics have lower co-pays, in the range of $5 to $10, while branded drugs require higher co-pays, in the range of $20 to $50. Coinsurance, used in Medicare Part D, requires patients to pay a flat percentage of the entire prescription drug price. For example, Medicare Part D participants pay 25% of all prescription drug costs after an initial $250 deductible is met.[4] For this reason, patients are not *directly* price sensitive. Rather, a more accurate term for this type of price sensitivity would be *co-pay* sensitivity. In other words, patients may want to lower their prescription drug costs, but this results from a value determination they have made on the co-pay, not the price.

The fact that patients' behavior is affected by co-pay levels is supported by research which examined how patients act when presented with different co-pay levels for the same drugs. Research has also shown that the same patients may be more or less co-pay sensitive depending on the class of drugs. They tend to be more sensitive to co-pay changes for drugs used to treat asymptomatic diseases than for drugs used to treat symptomatic diseases. To complicate things further, some patients will stop taking a drug deemed to be less important to them when the co-pay for another drug deemed to be more important is increased, even if the co-pay for the first drug stays the same. For example, patients may stop taking their cholesterol drug (for a secondary chronic disease) when the co-pay increases for their diabetes drug (for a primary chronic disease), even if the co-pay for their cholesterol drug stays the same.

Understanding these dynamics is important, but much research still needs to be done to understand patient co-pay and coinsurance sensitivities fully. This is particularly true given the new market dynamics introduced by Medicare Part D. It is likely that the ability of patients under Medicare Part D to change drug providers annually will alter the co-pays for their drugs at least as frequently. Given the previous research findings that patients react readily to changes in co-pays, these potentially annual changes could result in patient behavior that will be important for pricing and marketing managers to understand. Failing to consider these complex interactions of disease state, co-payment, and patient characteristics can lead to poor pricing decisions.

COMORBIDITIES

Many disease states are highly correlated with other disease states, or comorbid diseases. A classic example of this is diabetes. Diabetic patients are also likely to have hypertension, hyperlipidemia, and hypercholesterolemia, as well as other conditions. If these comorbid diseases are not well controlled over time, these patients may also develop renal (kidney) impairment, degenerative eye problems, and neuropathic and circulatory conditions that cause many uncontrolled diabetics to lose limbs.

Fortunately, we live in a world that provides medications to treat each of these conditions. Still, we must understand how these multiple diseases affect the pocketbooks of patients. For example, many of the drugs used to treat these conditions are branded drugs, and branded drugs are either more expensive or have higher co-pays or coinsurance. Imagine a diabetic patient taking 5 branded drugs, each with a monthly $25 co-pay. Although most patients would (or should not) argue the value of each of these drugs individually, combining them results in an annual co-pay bill of $1,500 (12 months at $125 per month). For patients with limited incomes, each additional medication becomes more burdensome than the previous drug, and some patients begin to make dangerous choices.

From our own co-pay research, we have learned that patients are more sensitive to co-pay costs for drugs that are chronic and asymptomatic and that patients are more willing to quit taking this type of product if co-pays increase. As a patient adds new medications to an already costly drug regimen, it is likely that he or she will decide that an older product isn't quite as necessary as it had previously been. This phenomenon adds to the compliance and persistence issues that we discussed earlier.

Understanding where your products might fit into such a scenario becomes important as you make pricing and contracting decisions. Again, such issues cannot be addressed directly by adjusting your ex-factory price, although they may drive your contracting decisions. When is it necessary to discount to managed care to achieve the corporate goals for the product? More importantly, when is it *not* necessary to make such pricing concessions to keep patients on your valuable drugs?

PATIENT GROUPS AND DISEASE STATES

Although understanding patient behavior is imperative for making profitable pricing decisions, it is also necessary to look at the entire group of patients who will ultimately make up your market. You may need to explore several nonbehavioral issues before making final pricing decisions. Typically, companies will look at basic disease state information to understand their customer group better. For example, some fundamental epidemiologic information is necessary to understand the size of the market, the number of new patients coming into the market, and the number of patients leaving the market in any given year.

However, there are also dynamics specific to disease states that may be important from a pricing and marketing perspective. Some disease states skew "old" while others skew "young." For example, most patients with Parkinson's disease are over the age of 50 when they are diagnosed, with a large percentage being over the age of 65 at diagnosis. Conversely, ear infections are primarily a disease of the young. Elderly patients are primarily covered under Medicare, and children are covered under private insurance plans, cash, or state Medicaid plans. Those are considerations that may affect your final pricing decisions.

Even if we have two drugs treating two different disease states and providing the same calculated economic value, the prices we can charge for them may differ just because of the issue of age. Elderly patients live on limited incomes but also have Medicare insurance. However, the rules of reimbursement in the Medicare world are different from those in the private insurance plan world, so knowing and understanding how these differences may affect the price we can charge is critical to making a good pricing decision.

Added to these complexities is the fact that manufacturer discounts and rebates are not isolated events. In fact, discounting or rebating to private payers affects government prices for all drugs sold to them, with some limited exceptions. Medicaid is legislatively entitled to the best price offered to the market for each drug purchased. Overall discounting strategies must take that into consideration. For example, Medicaid pays for a disproportionately large share of prescriptions for atypical antipsychotic medications. Manufacturers offering discounts for these agents to select private insurers must be aware that those discounts to small customers must be shared with Medicaid, which makes up nearly half the market.

The fact that payer mix changes drastically between disease states and patient populations makes it imperative that marketers make these pricing decisions with full demographic and disease state information.

SITE OF CARE

Disease characteristics often drive the location for patient treatment. Although people typically think of oral outpatient products when they think of drugs, medications are administered at several different sites of care. In addition to the medications patients take at home, drugs are used in hospitals, emergency rooms, and physician offices. Each site of care entails different treatment plans, co-therapies, and associated costs that should be taken into consideration when a product is priced.

A recent classic example of how site of care can affect pricing and reimbursement decisions is found within the rheumatoid arthritis market (RA). Remicade®, launched by Centocor in 1998, was the first biologic agent indicated for RA and was significantly more effective than the currently available treatments. One apparent product limitation was that Remicade is intravenously (IV) infused over several hours, most frequently in physician offices. The advantage of such a delivery method, however, is that Medicare will pay for medications administered in physician offices. This became an important factor for Centocor because a significant number of RA patients are over the age of 65.

In 1998, Immunex (now owned by Amgen) and Wyeth developed and launched Enbrel®, another biologic product used to treat RA. Enbrel had the advantage of being a subcutaneous (SQ) injection that, with minimal patient education, could be dispensed by an outpatient pharmacy and administered at home by the patient. However, at the time of the Enbrel launch, Medicare did *not* pay for SQ injections, forcing patients age 65 and older who want to be treated at home to purchase the product themselves on a cash basis. Despite Enbrel's lower price, patients under Medicare were not reimbursed for its use, which meant the market favored the more costly Remicade. (Amgen and Wyeth were later able to work with CMS and get Enbrel an exemption from the reimbursement rule in most instances, thereby removing Remicade's price advantage.)

This is a classic example of how all aspects of a product need to be assessed before an appropriate price can be selected and supported. The added convenience of a patient-administered SQ drug should alone support a price higher than those of office-administered competitors, assuming similar efficacy. However, without reimbursement by the largest payer segment (in this case Medicare), that appropriate price may not be supported, and even a discount cannot overcome the problem.

PATIENT ADVOCACY GROUPS

Some patient groups are highly organized and able to exert political and economic pressure on a company. In the areas of mental health, Parkinson's disease, HIV, and cancer, active support groups play a growing role in therapy selection. The recent CMS formulary guidances developed by the United States Pharmacopeia (USP) show how advocacy groups can affect the treatment of a specific disease. As a result of extensive lobbying on the part of advocacy groups, the Medicare Part D providers must include "all or substantially all" drugs in the immunosuppressant, antidepressant, antipsychotic, anticonvulsant, antiretroviral, and antineoplastic classes of drugs.[5] When setting the price of your product, you must consider how weakened formulary restrictions may affect price.

The degree of patient involvement in therapy decisions appears to be growing across most major therapeutic categories, and the market power of these groups will play an ever-growing role in pricing decisions. Patient considerations are important in pharmaceutical pricing because the degree to which the patient is involved or engaged with the disease and its treatment will affect price sensitivity, as will the presence or absence of organized patient advocacy groups.

SUMMARY

In summary, different patients and different diseases have different issues and associated concerns. These may be age-related, symptom-related, or even reimbursement-related. These characteristics must be considered when developing a successful pricing strategy for any drug or treatment.

REFERENCES

1. Montagne M. The metaphorical nature of drugs and drug taking. *Soc Sci Med.* 1988; 26:417-24.
2. Smith MC, Kolassa EM. Nobody wants your products: They are negative goods. *Product Manage Today.* 2001; (Dec):22-8.
3. Wurtel E. Prozac nation: Young and depressed in America. Boston: Houghton Mifflin; 1994.
4. The Medicare Modernization Act (MMA) resulted in various prescription drug plans by hundreds of different providers, and the plans vary extensively. A full discussion of these plans is beyond the scope of this work. Refer to various CMS or private resources for a full explanation of the Medicare Part D benefit. A starting point is: www.cms.hhs.gov/home/medicare.asp. Accessed 11 Apr 2007.
5. Centers for Medicare & Medicaid Services. Medicare Modernization Act 2007 final guidelines—formularies. CMS strategy for affordable access to comprehensive drug coverage. Guidelines for reviewing prescription

drug plan formularies and procedures. www.cms.hhs. gov/PrescriptionDrugCovContra/Downloads/CY-07FormularyGuidance.pdf. Accessed 11 Apr 2007.

Chapter 7

The Role of Reimbursement in Pricing

with Kevin Patterson and Brian Reisetter

National Health Insurance: the compassion of the IRS,
the efficiency of the Postal Service, all at Pentagon prices!!!!
—Seen on a bumper sticker

Reimbursement is the mechanism by which health care payers compensate providers for services and products used in conjunction with those services. It is influenced, not surprisingly, by many of the same factors that influence drug pricing: the type of payer, site of service, disease characteristics, patient characteristics, managed care, and public policy. Of all the elements to consider when pricing medicines, reimbursement is perhaps the most problematic—not because it is difficult to attain, but because so many people in the industry misunderstand it. The most important thing to remember is that gaining reimbursement will not guarantee sales, and failing to get reimbursed does not doom a product. As with everything else in pharmaceutical pricing, it's never that straightforward.

Confusion caused by a lack of consistency in reimbursement systems for various sites of care and an overreaction to managed care have unfortunately driven many pricing decisions in the recent past—often in the wrong direction. The importance of reimburse-ment on drug pricing is often overestimated and misunderstood and is usually manifested in the statement, "But managed care will not cover the drug at that price." Keep in mind that managed care is in the business of *ensuring* "appropriate care," not *preventing* it. At its core, managed care possesses the power to restrict the use of certain drugs and procedures *only* if there is no clinical value or if the cost of the clinical benefit is so disproportionate that therapy is blocked by arguing "social good." Like pharmaceutical companies trying to set prices, managed care must take into account not only the cost of making the drug available to members but the elements of disease and patient characteristics, public policy, and the organi-zation's ability to control use. However, at the end of the day, if the clinical value is determined to be present by the provider and the patient, managed care can do little to stop a medication's use.

Another misconception about reimbursement is that it is a simple "either/or" process: either payers will cover the product or they won't. It is not at all that simple. More frequently now, medications are partially reimbursed. The trend in reimburse-ment, particularly in private insurance, has been a shift in financial responsibility from the commercial payer to the patient. Although this is more prominently seen in co-pays for drugs, it is happening throughout the entire health care system. The result of cost shifting to patients has heightened the awareness of health care costs and, in particular, drug prices. Unfortunately, the metric used by the public is not based on drug price at all, but on out-of-pocket (OOP) expen-ditures that reflect cost shifting by public and private payers. In many cases, perceived increases in drug prices are actually changes in drug formulary tier structure or drug tier placement that result in higher co-pays, not an actual change in drug pricing.

The most important message about reimbursement is that the reimbursement situation *should not dictate the price of a product.* A payer's decision on how to cover a drug may have little impact on the success and use of the drug. Reimbursement is seldom based on the direct value of the product or service to the health care system, nor should it always be viewed as "the" limiting factor for drug pricing—even in the managed care environment. This chapter aims at removing some of the inaccurate preconceptions about reimbursement and the extent of its influence on the price of a pharmaceutical product.

TYPES OF PAYERS

To understand reimbursement and its influence on price, you must first understand the various players in the market and the numerous systems by which they pay for health care because each payer has a different set of priorities that affects how decisions are made. In some instances, third-party health care plans are more interested in providing open coverage and choice. Other plans may be more focused on decreasing overall costs by more aggressive limitation of services. Other plan types, particularly plans operated with public funds, are more susceptible to political pressures when developing formularies for the constituents they serve. Knowing these differences in advance can help companies tailor their reimbursement tactics to the needs of the client and may even affect the list price selected at launch—particularly when product use will reside predominantly in one segment. For example, drugs for the elderly will be reimbursed primarily through Medicare Part D, while cosmetic drugs will be paid either out of pocket by patients or by commercial plans.

There are essentially three types of payers: public third-party payers, private third-party payers, and patients. Most reimbursement systems involve a combination of at least two of these. Examples of public payers include Medicare, Medicaid, and the Civilian Health and Medical Program of the Department of Veterans Affairs (CHAMVA). These programs are administered through federal and state agencies and now cover most sites of service and forms of health care, including—since the passage of the Medicare Modernization Act (MMA)—outpatient drug coverage. Examples of private payers include the Blue Cross and Blue Shield Association companies, Aetna, Kaiser Permanente, and Humana. Private payers are complex organizations that vary in structure and profit status. For example, Kaiser Permanente is a not-for-profit, staff model HMO, while Aetna is a for-profit insurance company that uses a multitude of plan structures and a hybrid of resources to provide à la carte insurance options for its clients and patients.

Within the commercial plans, there are also different payer types that can affect how products are reimbursed. Some commercial plans, (e.g., MCOs such as Aetna) started as insurance companies that are traditionally more prone to look at overall cost per patient rather than just the drug costs. Pharmacy benefit management companies (PBMs), as a business model, manage drug benefit programs and are therefore more focused on drug costs than overall patient health care costs. PBMs use formulary placement and rebates to incentivize patients and providers to use the less costly regimens they have negotiated for their client plans. For this reason, PBMs may tend to be more focused on rebates while MCOs tend to be more interested in overall costs to the plan. This may seem like a small distinction, but it can have a huge impact on choosing a pricing tactic that emphasizes list price, rebates, or net price to plan.

Understanding these payer types, though, is just the beginning of predicting how any product will be viewed by managed care. Many companies have found, when expanding into new therapeutic areas, that the rules can change completely. What was once a hard and fast rule when negotiating with payers changes completely once the type of product changes. If one company sells injectable cardiac drugs, oral oncolytics, oral antihypertensive agents, and nasal insulin, it will need four different approaches for working with its managed accounts.

FIGURE 7.1 Sites of Care (Administration) for Pharmaceuticals

OUTPATIENT-Administered Drugs	INPATIENT-Administered Drugs
Self-Administered:	• Hospital
• Retail Pharmacy	• LTC/SNF**
• Mail-Order Pharmacy	
• Specialty Pharmacy	
• DME*	
MD/Nurse-Administered:	
• Physician's Office	
• Infusion Center	
• Ambulatory Surgical Center	
• Hospital Outpatient Clinic	
• Home Health Care	
• LTC/SNF**	

*   *Durable medical equipment: Usually self-administered in the patient's home, these products are used in conjunction with a device, such as a nebulizer or pump.*

**   *Long-term care facility or skilled nursing facility: Depending on the medication and the conditions under which it is administered, a product could be considered either inpatient or outpatient.*

SITES OF CARE AND REIMBURSEMENT

Health care is provided in a wide array of settings. At the macro level, the market has historically viewed pharmaceutical sales under three large budgets: hospital, physician office, and retail pharmacy. Common sites of care under these three categories are illustrated in

Figure 7.1. It is important to note that although public and private payers appear vastly different, their reimbursement mechanisms for specific sites of service are essentially the same.

A single patient may receive a given product in multiple sites. The reimbursement for the product will depend upon the site at which the product is administered, but the role of price in the decision to administer the product varies much more widely. For example, Medicaid has traditionally been the principal payer for the Medicaid patient age 65 and over receiving a prescription medicine in a nursing home. However, under the MMA, Medicare Part D has now assumed that responsibility. Regardless of who the payer is, the decision about which product to use typically belongs to the attending physician, not the consultant pharmacist and surely not the nursing home administrator. In such a case, the site of care is irrelevant to the pricing decision. On the other hand, the decision about which antibiotic a patient receives for pre-surgical prophylaxis will depend more on the hospital formulary than on the specific physician who writes the order. In the infusion center, the physician will normally decide which medicine to administer, but the ability of the patient to pay for that medicine, because of insurance reimbursement, may play a much larger role.

The key determinant of the interplay of price and reimbursement, then, is not simply the site of administration, but also the autonomy of the prescriber within that setting.

Hospital-Administered Drugs

Health care services and products are usually reimbursed using one of three conventions: fixed fee, cost-based, or percentage of charges. While there are various formulas and even hybrid reimbursement systems combining two or more conventions, most can be classified into one of these three types. Inpatient services are predominantly reimbursed through prospective fixed-fee systems. Medicare, the largest payer for inpatient services, reimburses according to a predefined schedule based on diagnosis-related groups (DRGs). The exceptions are numerous, but, in general, the hospital providing care is paid a predetermined amount for treating the patient, including complications, regardless of the acuteness of the patient's condition. In these situations, drugs are not considered sources of revenue or reimbursement, but simply a cost center within a much larger reimbursement environment. With hospitals "at risk" for the cost of care provided to patients, the inpatient market is considered the most price sensitive due to the lack of flexibility of the reimbursement system.

When a hospital is reimbursed on a prospective fixed fee for a specific procedure, the hospital must deliver the services at or below its own cost to avoid financial loss. So cost minimization is an important goal for this market segment. If the cost of a new medication exceeds the hospital's reimbursement for the DRG, the hospital must bear the cost overrun. This is an important consideration when pricing hospital products. Expecting a hospital to subsidize the use of a new drug is a bit naïve, to say the least. If the product is substantially differentiated, and can save or preserve lives, most hospitals will take steps to ensure the product's use, but they will also take extraordinary steps to ensure it is used only when truly needed. Should a new product become the standard of care, reimbursement for that procedure is likely to be increased to accommodate use of the new product. This may mean that, until the reimbursement is adjusted, users will lose money—perhaps for several months or years. To avoid this problem with its new Cypher® drug-eluting stent, Cordis took preemptive steps to secure higher reimbursement before launching the product. This allowed much earlier and widespread use of the product. Had the company not taken this step, the adoption of the Cypher stent would likely have been much slower—not because of a "pricing problem," but because of a reimbursement problem.

Not all hospital reimbursement is fixed fee, however. A substantial proportion of private payers still base reimbursement on the "percent of charges" convention, which means the payer will reimburse the hospital at a set discount from the hospital's normal charges. In such cases, the hospital can pass along higher costs driven by new drugs; therefore, understanding which patients will receive a new product and how their hospital stay will be reimbursed is vital in setting prices. Not all hospital-administered medicines are given only, or even mostly, to Medicare patients, and understanding this can make a great difference in the way a price is set.

To control their pharmaceutical costs, hospitals use formularies and clinical guidelines. A formulary, or list of drugs approved for use within a hospital, may limit the number of drugs available for use within therapeutic classes to only a few choices. For example, most hospitals only have one or two third-generation cephalosporin antibiotics or ACE inhibitors on their formularies. The choice of which agent to use is driven by both clinical evidence and price. The more differentiated a product is from other drugs used to treat the same condition, the less likely it is that the product will be restricted from hospital formularies. Clinical guidelines, which are recommended treatment regimens, influence drug choice by driving appropriate use of medications. For example, if a physician attempts to use an expensive agent off-label (outside the approved indication) or without any clinical support for its use, it is likely that hospital pharmacy and administration would step in to prevent the drug from being used.

Because reimbursement is often limited to a DRG-like mechanism, controlling costs is near the top of the agenda for hospital pharmacy departments. Use within the institution can be controlled through formularies. Costs can also be controlled by using products included in contracts that the hospital's group purchasing organization (GPO) has made with manufacturers and distributors. GPOs contract on behalf of hospitals for everything from paper to pacemakers, from bedpans to drugs. Negotiating with the GPO directly to be included in the contract may be imperative to the success of some products but will be totally useless in driving share for other products. Again, product differentiation is the key, but the clinical value (and evidence thereof) is the doorway itself. Discussions with hospital pharmacy directors will help you determine the best pricing strategy.

Outpatient Hospitals and Ambulatory Surgery Centers

Outpatient (O/P) hospital services and ambulatory surgery centers (ASCs) are the bridge between traditional inpatient hospital procedures and physician office procedures. Since June 2007, Medicare reimburses both O/P hospital services and ASCs under the outpatient prospective payment system (OPPS). The OPPS is similar to the inpatient prospective payment system in that procedures are paid on a "reasonable cost" basis. Covered procedures are listed under 11 ambulatory payment classification (APC) groups. As with a DRG, an APC group assigns a predetermined payment rate that includes most supplies, drugs, and biologicals. However, for certain new drugs or biologicals, such as those used in cancer treatment, special payments called "transitional pass-through payments" may be reimbursed in addition to the traditional APC payment for two or three years.

The special transitional pass-through payment rules do make the O/P hospital and ASC market less price sensitive than the inpatient market As a prospective payment system, though, the O/P hospital and ASC market is still more price sensitive than the physician-administered market. What is important to understand is that the price of the new drug or biological is not the only or even the most important factor determining reimbursement coverage or use in this segment. The reimbursement system defined by law requires the consideration of other factors, such as the disease and medical need. In many of these cases, price cannot solve the issue of reimbursement coverage, and any attempt to use it in this way is usually ineffective and comes at the expense of company profits.

Office-Administered Medications

The office-based physician is generally reimbursed under the Resource-Based Relative Value Scale (RBRVS). The RBRVS system assigns relative value units (RVUs) to procedures based on the professional expertise necessary, the cost of providing the service, and the risk associated with providing the service. The RBRVS includes codes for drugs and supplies used or administered as part of the office treatment as well. These alphanumeric codes designate which drugs or supplies are used and can be reported separately to the payer for reimbursement. J-codes (so named because they usually begin with the letter *J*) are designated for most physician-administered pharmaceuticals. Physician-administered means these drugs usually require the oversight of a physician to be properly administered.

Pharmaceuticals administered in the physician office setting are currently reimbursed in several ways. Medicare reimburses physician drugs under a hybrid system. For most single-source drugs the provider is reimbursed at the average sales price (ASP) plus 6%. Multisource drugs can be reimbursed under the ASP method or, depending on the number of drugs on the market, the federal maximum allowable cost limit, which is set quarterly by CMS. Historically, this market has not been price sensitive because reimbursement was previously based on the average wholesale price (AWP). However, reimbursement sensitivity varies according to the category, the cost, and, most importantly, the clinical value of the drug.

Drugs administered and reimbursed by physicians are limited to a few categories, such as cancer, rheumatoid arthritis, multiple sclerosis, and asthma. Because most physicians will own or be part of a large outpatient clinic designed for the administration of these agents, they usually have access to price contracts similar to those negotiated by GPOs. For example, U.S. Oncology provides support for practicing oncologists, including full-service group purchasing for oncolytic agents. Decisions to contract with these specialty group purchasers should be made in a manner similar to decisions to contract with hospital GPOs.

Outpatient Prescriptions

The most familiar and common mode of pharmaceutical administration is in the outpatient setting—patients self-administering medication at home. Until the 1960s, virtually all prescriptions purchased by patients at retail pharmacies were purchased with cash. That has changed dramatically over the last 40 years. Currently, well over 90% of all prescriptions purchased at retail pharmacies are paid for, in some part, by a third party, usually an MCO, PBM, or government entity like Medicaid. (Medicare Part D drug plans are managed by MCOs and PBMs.) Those parties negotiate with local pharmacies to create a "network" of sites where patients can fill their prescriptions. The actual transaction between the pharmacy and the third party is entirely automated (called online adjudication), and the pharmacist is told immediately whether a product is covered by that plan's formulary and how much, if any, the patient is required to pay. For most plans, patients will be required to pay a portion of the total charge—the co-pay.

Payers will often arrange their formularies in tiers with different co-pay levels. Most plans currently have a three-tier structure where generics have the lowest co-payment ($5 to $15), preferred branded formulary drugs have a medium co-payment ($15 to $30), and nonpreferred branded formulary drugs have a higher co-payment ($35 to $50). Preferred drugs sometimes receive that status based on manufacturer net price to the MCO or PBM, particularly when the drug in question belongs to a crowded therapeutic category. For example, most plans have only one or two statins (e.g., Lipitor, Crestor) in the preferred tier. Generic agents are put on the first tier when they become available, but all other branded statins are usually relegated to the third tier, where patients must make higher co-pays to obtain that product through the plan.

It must be noted, however, that tier status alone does not drive sales. If the product is not perceived as valuable by the clinician, the product could be given away and still not be prescribed. Too many times, marketers have tried to solve a problem—like a crowded market or inferior product—by negotiating with managed care for preferential status only to find out that the market yawns when products don't deliver, even when they are less expensive.

Conversely, not every product on second tier required a price concession to achieve that status. In some situations, a product's use (market share) drives formulary placement, not the other way around. Marketers sometimes forget that MCOs and PBMs must compete with each other and will respond to patient and employer demands to maintain their competitiveness.

Of special note within the discussion of co-pays is Medicaid. Each state Medicaid plan differs, but the plans do have one thing in common—very low co-pay levels. Co-pays of $0 to $5 per prescription are not unusual. Because of these low co-pays, it is extremely difficult for Medicaid programs to drive product use from one drug to another through co-pay differentials as the three-tier plans can. Consequently, most Medicaid plans are likely and willing to block a product's use completely within some therapeutic classes unless manufacturers provide rebates that qualify them for the state's preferred drug list. Political pressure, though, can be fierce for Medicaid administrators, so some categories, such as oncolytics, AIDS medications, and drugs used in the treatment of mental illness are usually exempt from this type of restriction.

In addition to understanding the relationship between pharmacies and payers and how these payers use formularies to control costs, it is also important to understand the flow of money within a pharmacy. Reimbursement may or may not drive behavior within a pharmacy setting, and that decision rests directly on the shoulders of the pharmacists filling those prescriptions. Outpatient prescriptions filled under both commercial plans and government-sponsored plans are reimbursed through a two-part formula designed to compensate the pharmacy for both the ingredient and the cost of dispensing plus any other services that may be supplied by the pharmacist. Historically, retail pharmacy reimbursement has been based on AWP plus or minus a percentage or WAC plus a percentage *plus a dispensing fee for single-source branded drugs.* For example, a branded drug may be reimbursed at AWP minus a percentage (usually 15% to 18%) or an estimated acquisition cost plus a percentage (such as EAC plus 15%), plus a dispensing fee (typically $3 to $6). Reimbursement for generic drugs is similar, but an upper limit, a maximum allowable cost (MAC), may be imposed by the plan. The MAC tends to reflect actual pharmacy cost more accurately than the list price. The pharmacy collects part of that negotiated payment from the patient in the form of a co-pay, while the rest of the payment comes in the form of periodic batch payments from the payer.

What is important in this discussion is that pharmacists are intermediaries in this transaction. They are contractually obligated to abide by the payment structure of each plan, but that does not necessarily mean that they will drive use of a preferred agent with a lower co-pay. With the exception of FDA-approved generic drugs, which can be substituted without physician approval, most pharmacists in the retail setting will not proactively encourage the use of one product over another because of cost. If patients ask whether less expensive agents are available, pharmacists will typically have patients call the MCO or PBM number on the back of the card to find out which product is preferred on their plan and then encourage patients to discuss options directly with their physicians.

Specialty Pharmacy

Specialty pharmacy is a relatively new market element that has received quite a bit of attention recently. These pharmacies are increasingly being used to distribute expensive specialty products within limited therapeutic areas. In addition to distributing products, these pharmacies also provide clinical and reimbursement support services for the patients they serve. Therapeutic areas for specialty pharmacies typically involve high-cost injectable drugs and include cancer, multiple sclerosis, rheumatoid arthritis, organ transplant, and hepatitis B. As will be discussed later, reimbursement for products distributed through specialty pharmacies can vary depending on the type of pharmacy. These differences clearly affect pricing decisions.

There are several advantages, both real and perceived, to patients and insurers using specialty pharmacies for these types of products. First, there are some significant inventory advantages of specializing in a limited number of therapeutic areas, particularly when those drugs are expensive. Most retail pharmacies will not stock a product like Betaseron to treat multiple sclerosis because of the cost and the limited patient population. However, if the treatment of many MS patients is centralized to one pharmacy, the pharmacy can realistically carry inventories of Betaseron and other drugs used to treat MS. In addition, the clinical specialty knowledge available from pharmacists specializing in a limited number of therapeutic areas can theoretically improve patient outcomes. Finally, the specialty services of these pharmacies can actually improve patient customer service by quickly providing the product (usually via overnight express) and insuring reimbursement before the therapy is initiated.

Like most categories outlined in this chapter, it must be noted that all specialty pharmacies do not act alike. There are several types of specialty pharmacies, and each will act differently based on its company mission and structure. In general, there are three types of specialty pharmacies, although hybrids of these classifications do exist:

- Some specialty pharmacies contract with manufacturers to provide limited distribution of specific drugs, usually drugs with a very small patient population where clinical follow-up is important.
- Other specialty pharmacies contract with PBMs or MCOs to provide distribution and clinical care for multiple therapeutic areas. For example, a PBM may contract with one or several specialty pharmacies to distribute all the costly self-administered injectable drugs for its plans. Recently, there has been a trend toward the purchasing of specialty pharmacies by MCOs and PBMs to provide these services. In fact, most national payers now have separately run specialty pharmacy divisions.
- Regional specialty pharmacies may specialize in a limited number of therapeutic classes and allow local clinicians in these specialties the ability to provide dispensing, reimbursement support, and clinical expertise. For example, a small regional specialty pharmacy may provide services to the transplant patient population within a geographic region by working directly with the transplant clinics within the area of coverage.

From a pricing or reimbursement perspective, the differences between these pharmacy types are important. For example, a pharmacy that acts as sole distributor for a single product will have little impact on use based on cost or reimbursement issues. However, a pharmacy owned by a PBM or MCO may develop legal mechanisms to support a cost-effective restrictive formulary that may affect reimbursement and, consequently, your pricing. These differences should be explored through qualitative research before final pricing decisions are made for any agent distributed through specialty pharmacies.

MANAGED CARE COST CONTROL MECHANISMS

Because outpatient medications comprise such a large portion of any MCO's budget, these organizations have developed a number of mechanisms to control their use. The most basic mechanism is built into the fabric of the reimbursement system through the tiered pharmacy benefit, which is designed to shift the financial burden to the patient for certain drugs and discourage use of drugs on the second or higher tiers through higher co-pays. However, MCOs do employ other techniques to control drug expenditures.

Prior authorization (PA) requires that clinicians receive authorization from the payer prior to prescribing or administering the drug. Because PAs are expensive to implement, they are usually reserved for drugs for which there is clinical justification. While price can trigger a PA, price is often not the primary issue.

Step therapy prohibits reimbursement for a therapy until alternative, less expensive therapies have proven unsuccessful. This technique is more commonly seen in a mature market with a significant amount of generic competition. The technique is most effective when employed on drugs in which little clinical differentiation is perceived. In such cases, particularly in a generic market, the success of the technique depends not on reimbursement level or drug price but on the lack of clinical differentiation.

Quantity limits are exactly what the name implies. Managed care will limit the amount of therapy that may be received by a patient within a period of time. For example, when news broke about possible cardiovascular effects of long-term use of high doses of Vioxx, the COX-2 inhibitor, several managed care plans placed quantity limits on the 50mg strength of Vioxx, limiting the patient to a single prescription with no refills.

THE IMPACT OF MMA ON REIMBURSEMENT

Until 2004, a lack of Medicare coverage for seniors' outpatient prescriptions meant that injectable medicines received in a physician's office, which were covered by Medicare, were far less costly to patients than self-administered medicines. The MMA reversed the trend of patient cost shifting and potentially reduces the financial burden for many Medicare patients by providing outpatient drug coverage for the first time. While the intention of the MMA was good, as with most legislative initiatives, the unintended consequences could counteract any positive effect for patients, payers, and drug manufacturers.

Under the Deficit Reduction Act of 2005, Medicaid has been given the authority to change reimbursement methods from an AWP- or WAC-based system to an ASP or AMP plus a dispensing fee method. This change may provide more pricing freedom than the AWP model and may reduce the incentive for price discounts and rebates, as evidenced by the historical market reaction to the implementation of OBRA 90.

Both Medicaid and private payers are moving to adopt this method, although most private insurers appear to be adding much more than 6% to the ASP for their reimbursement rates. However, while the methods of reimbursement may change, the influence of reimbursement on pricing in a retail pharmacy setting is negligible.

THE IMPORTANCE OF
UNDERSTANDING REIMBURSEMENT

For most outpatient medications, the reimbursement environment is typified by inconsistent coverage for new products, with systems adopting different products at different rates. For products used primarily on an inpatient basis, prospective payment systems have made it difficult, at best, for innovative new products to be assimilated into the system unless these products offer savings sufficient to offset a major part of their costs.

The pressure of managed care cost control mechanisms may vary. In private insurance plans, some costly physician-administered medications are reimbursed through the medical benefit rather than the pharmacy benefit. In these cases, the overt cost controls typical of pharmacy benefits are absent. However, other agents, especially oral agents in crowded markets, may be subject to extreme scrutiny, with price pressures applied constantly by the payers.

Understanding the idiosyncrasies of the reimbursement environment surrounding the individual product is vital to maximizing not only the profitability but also the market potential of the product. During the Watergate scandal of the early 1970s, Deep Throat, the anonymous inside informant, told reporters to "follow the money." That advice should also be taken by those establishing prices for new pharmaceutical products. For example, replacing evulsion or debridement (common procedures for nail fungus, decubitus ulcers, and other topical maladies) with a new drug therapy may deliver savings to an MCO's bottom line, but the shift of financial responsibility from the medical to the pharmacy budget means the pharmacy will see an increase in its costs, perhaps without credit for savings elsewhere. Moreover, the physicians who must now prescribe the new agent may find their income dramatically reduced because they no longer perform income-generating procedures. In such circumstances it is foolhardy to assume that the savings provided by your new drug will be welcomed by the system.

Chapter 8

Competition

*Focus on competition has always been
a formula for mediocrity.*
—Daniel Burrus

Competitors play two important but distinct roles in setting and managing the prices of pharmaceuticals. First, competitive products provide a starting point and the most logical point of reference for evaluating the price of a product. Second, competitive pricing actions can have a significant effect on the success of a product because competitive price changes affect your value proposition.

Competitive products and competitive actions both play large—sometimes too large—roles in effective pharmaceutical pricing. The key competitive questions in pharmaceutical pricing are:

1. What are the current competitive alternatives?
2. Are new competitors anticipated?
3. Do the competitors have a history of responding to the pricing actions of others?
4. What steps might competitors who feel threatened by this new product take?

The first and second questions focus on the issue of price reference points, while questions two through four address competitive pricing behavior. All are vitally important in setting and managing prices.

COMPETITION AS A REFERENCE POINT

Typically, and logically, the first pieces of information we gather when arriving at an initial price estimate are the prices of competing medicines. If a new product is to be launched into a therapeutic area that is already served by one or more agents, the prices of those agents should provide initial guidance in price selection. Which prices to use for this analysis—whether ex-factory, discounted, per dose, per day of therapy, per package, per course of therapy—will depend upon the perspective of the analysis and the product under study. Generally, list (or ex-factory) prices for a comparable unit of therapy (whether a single day's therapy for a chronic disorder or a complete course of therapy for an acute treatment) is an appropriate place to begin. Discounts and other considerations should not be a starting point because they are tactical in nature, and the first steps in any analysis of initial pricing should be focused on strategy.

In addition to the current prices of competitive agents, the price histories of products in this class should be examined to assess any recent changes in the price positions of the various products and to estimate future prices. Anticipated competitive product launches must also be considered.

The price histories of products *outside* the class should also be investigated to determine whether competitors' pricing in this class reflects an overall company pricing policy or a deliberate pricing strategy for this specific class. If the price for a new entry into the class reflects a departure from a firm's typical approach to pricing, it may be a signal that price sensitivity is at work in this market, or at least that the other company believes that is the case.

FIGURE 8.1 Comparison of the Statin Prices

PRODUCT	STRENGTH	AWP
Crestor	5mg	$4.27
Crestor	10mg	$4.27
Crestor	20mg	$4.27
Lipitor	10mg	$3.51
Lipitor	20mg	$5.01
Lipitor	40mg	$5.01
Lipitor	80mg	$5.01
Zocor	5mg	$2.34
Zocor	10mg	$3.13
Zocor	20mg	$4.60
Zocor	40mg	$4.79
Zocor	80mg	$5.47

Source: Analy$ource, February 2, 2009

Although using the current and anticipated prices of competitive products sounds simple, even this can be problematic. How do you compare prices? Because some firms use flat pricing, where all strengths are priced at the same level, and others use some version of variable pricing for different strengths, it can be impossible to compare prices for all products in the market. Additionally, because most products are available in multiple strengths, determining which strength of each product is the best comparator for each strength of your product is incredibly difficult. In Figure 8.1 we have listed all the strengths and prices (AWP) for three major statins in the

US market. Obviously, one cannot make a clear comparison. If you were making a comparison, what would you do?

Our approach is to use the leading strength of the leading product—in this case, Lipitor 20mg—as a base, which would give us a reference price of $3.75 per dose. If we were to be pricing a new statin, this would be our starting point for comparisons, but only the starting point.

What makes the price of a market leader the "right" price? Nothing! Being the leader doesn't make the price right—it could be very wrong. It is merely the price by which a new product is most likely to be evaluated, by customers and competitors alike, and thus a logical starting point. Although other considerations, such as qualitative product differences, the product position and strategy, and a number of other issues, should go into the final pricing decision, competitive prices are where we begin.

It is important to note that we caution against using the prices of generic products as the starting point or even as a major consideration in price setting. Generics compete on a different level and in a different world than brands, and attempting to set a price for a brand that is competitive with generics is a costly mistake. A brand cannot be supported with the revenue from such a low price.

PRICE COMPETITION

Know your opponent, know yourself,
and your victory will not stand in doubt.
—Sun Tsu

Competitive prices and competitive pricing behavior are two different things. Understanding the pricing behavior of competitors is vital for ongoing management of the prices of products. Some firms respond quickly to the pricing actions of competitors, while others are seemingly oblivious. Some respond to challenges by raising prices, while others respond by offering discounts. (Note that lowering a list price in response to a competitive price is very rare.) Knowing how a competitor is likely to respond to your pricing actions, and how you should respond in return, is a key strategic skill.

Competing on the basis of price, especially with branded pharmaceuticals, is a risky proposition. Of all the competitive advantages upon which a company can compete, price is the easiest to eliminate. A competitor can take away your price advantage in a matter of minutes. In markets where other advantages exist, especially clinical advantages, price difference tends to be of little value. Because of this, we believe that competing on price should be considered only as a last-ditch effort for a company that sells branded pharmaceuticals. But, as not all companies share this belief, price competition is something that must be faced.

If a competitor has a history of responding to challenges with pricing actions, such as deep discounting to MCOs, this behavior must be factored into the pricing strategy you develop. It may be wise in this situation to set a price that is not perceived as threatening to that competitor. If you do plan to enter the market with a low price, you should probably indicate at the time you announce your price your intentions to occupy the lowest rung of the pricing ladder in the category. When SmithKline Beecham announced the price of its antidiabetic agent Avandia® in 1999, its CEO stated that it intended to have the lowest priced glitazone on the market, and it was prepared to make future changes in Avandia's price to maintain that position. Although some may question the wisdom of this price position, none can question the effectiveness of such an announcement in allowing the company to maintain it.

In the mid 1980s, Upjohn's market-leading NSAID Motrin received some unwanted competition. Boots, the British firm from whom Upjohn had licensed ibuprofen, entered the US market with its own brand, Rufen®, which was priced 10% below Motrin. Boots also offered the first consumer coupons to encourage prescriber switching. Rufen's sales grew slowly, so Upjohn continued its policy of regular price increases for Motrin. Over a two-year period, the price difference between Rufen and Motrin grew to 35%, and Motrin's losses mounted. Upjohn's initial response to these losses was to implement a retail deal that provided retail pharmacies access to Motrin at prices equivalent to Rufen's. Taking steps to curtail the losses was prudent, and the deal seemed to be working—it basically stopped the rate of loss. The deal allowed Upjohn flexibility: it could turn its price competition off and on at will. Unfortunately, the company decided to make the price cut permanent and lowered the list price to match Rufen's, thereby totally eliminating Rufen's only competitive advantage. Boots responded within hours by announcing a 35% price decrease of its own, regaining the advantage and, with Upjohn's help, reducing the value of the entire ibuprofen market by 35%. Meanwhile, Motrin's slide resumed.

Entering into price competition without understanding fully the behavior of your competitor is dangerous and costly, as Upjohn learned. Boots had no choice but to match the Motrin price cut with its own. A complete understanding of competitive behavior may have prevented that costly mistake.

Misconstruing the pricing actions of competitors must also be avoided because responding to a misunderstood action can undermine pricing stability in a market. Understanding the difference between a new pricing policy of deep discounts and a "one-off" discount to a specific hospital or MCO can mean the difference between ongoing profitability and a costly and unproductive price war. (For a detailed discussion on managing price competition, see Nagle and Holden, *The Strategy and Tactics of Pricing*, Chapter 5, "Competition: Managing Conflict Thoughtfully.")

The importance of competitive analysis in pricing cannot be overstated. Pricing and the presence of competitors, together with the uniqueness or therapeutic value of a new product, are the major determinants of launch prices for new drugs. W. D. Reekie wrote in 1977 that the price levels of current competitors and the anticipation of future competitors were the driving factors in setting prices for pharmaceuticals.[1] New entrants that offered significant

FIGURE 8.2 Typical, But Flawed, Competitive Consideration in Pricing

NEW PHARMACEUTICAL PRODUCT

Adapted from Reekie WD. Pricing new pharmaceutical products. London: Croom Helm; 1977.

benefits over current competitors were consistently priced above the prevailing prices in their therapeutic classes. Those products offering little or no therapeutic advantage tended to be priced at or below prevailing levels. This process continued into the 1980s and 1990s, and appears to be alive and well today.[2]

An interesting finding of Reekie's study, however, was that, even for unique products offering improvements, those that had close or superior competitors entering the market within two years of launch tended to be priced lower than those that anticipated little or no competition from new products in the near future. The general rule is illustrated in Figure 8.2.

Reekie and others have noted that although it appears that most pharmaceutical markets are not price sensitive, most companies act, and price, as though they believe markets are sensitive. The lack of responsiveness to discounts in many markets in the US implies that:

1. These markets do not respond to price in a significant way.
2. The companies marketing many of the products act as though they believe the markets are responsive to price.

Belief in price sensitivity, as opposed to an objective measurement of price sensitivity, appears to have led many pharmaceutical companies to under price their products. A later entrant in a competitive category that is priced at a 30% discount and achieves a market share of 2% to 5%, which can be expected of most such products regardless of price, implies that the 30% discount represents an opportunity cost to the company of nearly 50%. This means that a price 50% above that charged may have delivered the same level of unit sales as the lower price but with significantly greater dollar sales and profits. That is a very high cost to pay for such timidity.

LIFE CYCLE ISSUES

A meaningful competitive assessment includes an analysis of product life cycle issues because the varying market dynamics of each life cycle stage demand different strategies. The market's response to price differences, as well as competitors' pricing actions and responses to other companies' decisions, will vary over the course of a product's life cycle.

For instance, a newly established market with only one or two competitive products is very unlikely to exhibit any price sensitivity whatsoever because the types of physicians who adopt new technologies early are essentially unconcerned with costs and unlikely to respond to price appeals. In contrast, a well-established category with many competitors often includes segments of prescribers and payers who will be price sensitive, thus increasing the potential appeal of a lower price. We say "more likely" because this is the way a market *should* respond, but it has done so only in a limited number of cases. In two cases, we have found low cost appeals to be effective:

the statin Lescol® and the SSRI Celexa®. In those cases, the categories were mature, and the products were able to find segments to whom the lower costs appealed. Neither of these categories had generic competition at the time those products were launched, allowing them to offer lower prices to a group of patients. In markets where generics are present, however, we believe it is highly unlikely that such an appeal would work, and a firm would be better off setting a parity price and competing on clinical merits alone.

WHO IS YOUR COMPETITOR?

Unlike many markets in which competitive products are obvious (e.g., premium beers competing with each other), competition among pharmaceutical agents is often not so straightforward and easily identified. Because product selection for medicines is based on the health state of the patient (indication) and type of relief or treatment the prescriber prefers or is seeking, products that appear to be direct competitors may not, in fact, truly compete with each other. Before assuming that every product indicated for a specific disorder is a "competitor," it is wise to determine the degree to which it truly competes. This case of similar but noncompeting products arises frequently in pharmaceutical markets and can lead to costly pricing errors.

To understand the often subtle differences, it is best to begin with some definitions, including direct, indirect, and complementary competition.

Direct Competitor

A direct competitor is a product that a physician would choose in lieu of another specific product to attain the same result through the same biological mechanism. This can be thought of as "competition for the same patient." Marketing efforts can help distinguish competitors or keep a product at the "top of mind" of a prescriber who may be indifferent to or unaware of product differences. Price may play a more important role in this type of competition than in others.

The competition within a product class is, for the most part, direct competition. A physician wishing to treat a patient's asthma with an inhaled corticosteroid (ICS) can choose among several different products with confidence that most, if not all, will perform well and provide the patient with relief. The choice of ICS could be driven by the physician's own experience with the drugs in the class, the specific delivery system, patient preference, and the price or formulary status of the product.

Indirect Competitor

An indirect competitor is a product that a physician would choose in lieu of another class or category of medicines to attain a similar result through a different biological mechanism. This can be thought of as "competition for the disorder." Marketing in this regard takes place at the class level, with efforts aimed at "selling" the mechanism of action of one class over another, as opposed to brand-to-brand competition. In these situations, all members of a class will compete collectively against the other class, and price differences between classes are not as important as the clinical differences.

When the first SSRI, Prozac, was launched, it provided physicians with a new and different choice for treating depression. This product relieved depression without the side effects that were common among the older class of drugs used, the tricyclics. Prozac did not compete with any individual tricyclic directly; its mechanism competed with the mechanism of the older products. Similarly, no single tricyclic actually competed with Prozac as a brand, but the entire category competed with the mode of treatment offered by the SSRI category. They were indirect competitors. Once Zoloft and other new SSRIs entered the market, Prozac had its first direct competition. The differences between the prices of Prozac and Zoloft could tell us much more than the differences in prices between SSRIs and tricyclics. The physician treating a patient with depression must first decide which category—not brand—of product to prescribe and only then which brand. The competition between the tricyclics and Prozac ended when prescribers decided to use an SSRI. Then the competition between Prozac and its SSRI competitors began.

There is nothing from a marketing or pricing perspective that an individual product in one class can do to reverse or even forestall the loss of the entire class to a new category. That rests on the clinical merits of the new mechanism of action. In other words, the brand Elavil® (a tricyclic) could not compete against the brand Prozac in the same way it competed with the other tricyclics Pamelor® or Ascendin. The basis and results of the competition would be very different. In cases of indirect competition, the acceptance of the new class of medicine will take business from all agents in the competing class, usually on a relatively equal basis. The market shares of the individual tricyclics did not differ within the category after the launch of the SSRIs, but the tricyclics' share of the total market declined.

Complementor

A complementor is a product that enhances or improves outcome when used in combination with another product. In pharmaceuticals, two products from different therapeutic classes are often used so the patient can benefit from both mechanisms of action. In such cases, the cost of the combination may become an issue, but the costs of the individual products are unlikely to be key determinants of use.

A different situation occurs in cases where the mechanisms of classes of drugs differ sufficiently that they do not compete. Such a case occurred when Johnson & Johnson launched its GI drug Propulsid® (cisapride). This drug, indicated for the treatment of reflux and other gastric disorders, worked by quickly emptying the contents of the stomach, not by reducing acid secretions (like the H_2 antagonists) or inhibiting the body's ability to produce acid (like the PPIs). Although a prudent marketing team for an H_2 antagonist would monitor the use and uptake of Propulsid because it marked an important market development, Propulsid's mechanism of action differed so much that there was little, if any, real competition. Instead, physicians would often prescribe Propulsid along with an H_2 antagonist or a PPI, making Propulsid a complementor to either the PPIs or the H_2 antagonists. A firm or multiple firms in a category hoping to reduce or slow the use of a complementary product would find their efforts to be futile because the result would be a reduction in patient benefit, something prescribers would resist.

In some cases, products that may be indirect competitors can also be complementors, in that physicians may choose to prescribe one class in lieu of another or an agent from two or more different classes. A physician may choose to treat an asthmatic patient with an inhalable product, such as Serevent, or to begin treatment with a leukotriene agonist, such as Singulair. At some point, that same physician may add the other product to the patient's treatment to achieve better results. In the first case there may have been some level of indirect competition, as the physician chose between different mechanisms of action for the initial treatment, but later the products were complementors because treatment required both approaches.

The fact that brands may be both competitive and complementary makes the typical market share measurement imprecise and problematic. If the market consists of 100 patients, 20 of whom receive 1 product and 30 a different product while the remaining 50 receive both, there will be a total of 150 prescriptions. The "leading" product will have a 53% share of total prescriptions (80/150) but will also have an 80% share of patients. In some cases, there may be competition but not in most. This makes the dynamics of prescription drug competition different from many other markets and identification of competitors very problematic.

Because of the different levels of direct and indirect competition and complementarity, the Federal Trade Commission, when evaluating competition in the pharmaceutical industry, has restricted its definitions of markets and competitors to the level of therapeutic class, or mechanism of action. This, for the most part, eliminated the ambiguity of the noncompetition among many products. Even at the class level, however, there can be problems.

DIFFERENCES WITHIN A CATEGORY

Within a class, some products will be approved for different indications because the products actually differ in the effect they have on the patients, because not all manufacturers have sought approval for that indication, or because one or more products in the class are contraindicated in specific patients. Because of this, class or category does not always determine direct competition. Atacand® (candesartan cilexetil), an angiotensin receptor blocker (ARB) developed and sold by AstraZeneca, competes with several other ARBs but is the only agent of its class indicated for the treatment of heart failure in combination with ACE inhibitors (another class of drug). Several other ARBs have been tested in this indication but have failed to prove effectiveness. While all ARBs are indicated for the treatment of hypertension, others cannot be used for the treatment of heart failure. Thus, all ARBs are competitors for the hypertensive patient, but only Atacand, among the ARBs, can be used in heart failure together with ACE inhibitors. ACE inhibitors, which are a different class of drugs, are commonly used for both indications. This means that Atacand competes with all of the ARBs for some patients, competes with the ACE inhibitors for some patients, and complements ACE inhibitors in other patients. The other ARBs compete with the ACE inhibitors for only hypertensive patients and cannot be used with ACE inhibitors. Because the ACE inhibitors are also indicated for the treatment of chronic renal failure but none of the ARBs is so indicated, there is no competition between the classes for these patients. This is quite confusing but common in pharmaceutical markets.

The same problem of defining competitors occurs in the antibiotic market. Although several classes of drugs may be indicated for a specific infectious pathogen, there are commonly differences within the classes as to the specific pathogens against which they are active. As with ARBs and ACE inhibitors, in some cases antibiotics will compete, but in others they will not. And in many cases multiple antibiotics will be used for the same patient if multiple pathogens are present or a specific pathogen has not yet been identified.

It must be asked then, which products compete with which and to what extent? This can be determined only on a case-by-case basis, but we do know that attempts to compete on price with products that are only indirect competitors or complementors are doomed to failure. Clinical needs supersede pricing considerations, and attempting to overcome true clinical differences with price are, at best, futile.

WHAT DIFFERENCE DOES A PRICE DIFFERENCE MAKE?

Because of the vagaries of pharmaceutical pricing (including third parties setting AWPs, others setting various levels of reimbursement, and pharmacies and others using different markup conventions for different products), minor price differences between branded pharmaceuticals are really of no consequence in the marketplace. We have argued for years that price differences of less than 15% constitute no real difference at all in terms of effect on the sales of the products.

This "rule" has held for many years. In the mid 1980s, Upjohn launched Micronase® and Hoechst launched Diaβeta®. Both agents were glyburide, available in identical doses. Micronase was launched first, and Hoechst priced Diaβeta slightly below the Micronase price. Throughout their useful lives, Micronase held a higher market share at a higher price, despite the fact that the products were identical. In the late 1980s and early 1990s, Sandoz's antidepressant Pamelor (nortriptyline) outsold Lilly's Aventyl® (nortriptyline) by several multiples. Throughout those years, Pamelor maintained a 15% premium over Aventyl with no ill effect.

While Pamelor was enjoying its premium price, over in the ACE inhibitor segment, Merck launched Prinivil® (lisinopril) and Zeneca launched Zestril®, its own lisinopril. Merck launched first, establishing a price that was below the price of its other ACE inhibitor, Vasotec®. Two weeks later, Zeneca priced Zestril approximately 10% below Prinivil, prompting Merck to lower its price soon after. Merck apparently was concerned that its brand would be harmed by a price difference. Some months later, Merck implemented a price increase of approximately 6%. Zeneca responded with a 3% price increase, to which Merck responded with a price decrease to bring the two products' prices into equality. Although lisinopril became the most prescribed ACE inhibitor, its price was depressed by the concern of the two firms that there be no list price difference.

Three of the next four ACE inhibitors to enter the market— Altace® (Hoechst), Monopril® (BMS), and Lotensin® (Ciba)—all entered at prices approximately 25% below Vasotec and 15% below Prinivil and Zestril. The fourth new entrant, Parke-Davis's Accupril®, was priced at parity with Vasotec and thus above all the remaining ACE inhibitors. Accupril's share of 13% was substantially higher than the shares of Monopril (8%), Altace (4%), and Lotensin (11%), but its dollar sales were much higher. Price competition cost those other firms a considerable amount of money.

The pharmaceutical market only rarely responds to price competition, so a firm must be positive that competing on price will work and that it can maintain the price advantage.

Two firms that were able to establish successful price competition were Sandoz, with Lescol, and Forrest, with Celexa, but those two succeeded for very different reasons. When Sandoz developed Lescol, it found itself with a statin that was less potent than the products already on the market at a time when more aggressive lipid reduction was gaining popularity. Sandoz, needing to overcome this clinical disadvantage, chose to price Lescol at half the price of Mevacor and then to offer even deeper discounts to MCOs and hospitals.

Lescol's relative success appears to have been due to the large cash-paying segment of the market: the patients who were unable to afford Mevacor and new agents. Lescol's low price enabled Sandoz to tap into an unserved segment of the market. The availability of generic versions of Mevacor, however, eliminated Sandoz' competitive advantage and cut into Lescol's sales.

Sandoz's tactic of discounting to managed care plans, however, did not appear to be as successful because Lescol's share in the noncash segment was quite low. Physicians, when given the choice, will usually opt for a more efficacious agent, and they chose those products for patients with third-party coverage, not Lescol.

When Forrest launched its SSRI Celexa, it entered a crowded market in which some products had already attempted to gain a pricing advantage. Pfizer's Zoloft was priced approximately 15% below Lilly's Prozac, the market leader, and Pfizer's sales representatives often pointed this out in their presentations to physicians. Celexa entered the market priced approximately 35% below Prozac and also contracted aggressively with MCOs. For the first few years, Celexa enjoyed only moderate sales, mainly because physicians appeared to be satisfied with the other SSRIs.

Because Lilly's contracts with MCOs were not aggressive, offering only relatively small discounts, some plans explored limiting patient access to the product, including moving Prozac to third tier or requiring prior authorizations. At first, Prozac's sales were not harmed by these actions because the restrictions had no effect on the clinical demand for the trusted drug. But, as more physicians gained experience and grew comfortable with Celexa, it emerged as a viable alternative to the market leader. When faced with protests by patients over the high co-pay or the prospect of having to obtain prior authorization, many physicians decided that it was easier to prescribe Celexa than to fight for Prozac. In this case, once prescribers were convinced they were not giving up any clinical benefits, they chose to take the path of least resistance. It wasn't the price of Celexa that helped it grow against Prozac: it was the ease of use which was made possible through the combination of lower prices to MCOs, which led to more favorable formulary status for Celexa over Prozac, and the medical community's experience with and confidence in the product. The lower price was one tool, but the success was due to the entire package.

THE DIFFERENCE BETWEEN A PRICE AND A PRICING STRATEGY

Many firms apparently believe that setting prices below their competitors will provide them with a true competitive advantage. As just discussed in the Celexa case, the price was an important element in the success of the product but not the *most* important. Several other products have attempted to use low prices to gain share without similar success because a low price *in and of itself* really doesn't have much value in pharmaceutical markets, which are driven by clinical need more than anything else.

Straightforward price competition is useful only when other product differences are minimal—when customers are not forced to give up something they value (such as efficacy) in exchange for the lower price. Even in nonpharmaceutical markets, most customers will not sacrifice essential aspects of a product just to secure a lower price. For a low price to deliver incremental sales, the product itself must also deliver the essential benefits the customer is seeking. As discussed earlier, Celexa's low price began to deliver sales only when physicians were convinced that, in prescribing it, they were not sacrificing the known efficacy and safety of Prozac. Similarly, Lescol's success was due to the fact that patients who couldn't pay for Mevacor and other more powerful statins were able to get at least some effect from the less potent agent; it was much better than nothing, which was their only alternative. Because the products brought distinctive benefits, augmented or actualized through their use of low price, they became successful. As discussed earlier, other products priced at discounts but lacking a complementary clinical message have not fared as well.

When Roche entered the market for hepatitis C therapy with its own pegylated interferon, Pegasys®, the company knew it was in for a challenge. Schering's PegIntron® was the only product in that arena, and toppling the leader would be difficult. Roche priced its product substantially below the leader and targeted its offering to the most price sensitive segments of the market. The addition of its ribavirin, Copegus®, which competed with Schering's Rebetrol, also at a substantial discount, made Schering's job that much harder.

But Roche had several advantages. First, it conducted several important clinical studies to support its products. Customers also knew they could rely on Roche to support the product and its patients and that they would sacrifice nothing on the clinical side when using Pegasys. Roche displaced Schering as the market leader but not just because of its low price. It was the company's clinical support and commitment to the therapeutic area that allowed the price to deliver sales. Roche employed a strategy, not just a low price.

Setting a low price and hoping to gain additional sales, then, is simply not effective. When we are told by a firm that its "strategy" is to set a low price, we ask it to let us know the rest of the strategy. We are usually met with silence. A pricing strategy that involves a low price must include several other elements, beginning with an understanding of the segments of the market that will respond to a discount and knowledge of what those customers are willing to sacrifice (in terms of clinical or other elements) in exchange. The price for Lescol worked because there was a large group of patients for whom there were no other alternatives, and

Celexa's success was due to its equivalent clinical effects. Both took time to be successful.

Relying on a low price, without an accompanying strategy and rationale, to deliver sales is misguided and lazy, timid, or an act of desperation. There is no other way to describe it. Although every customer favors a lower price, few use it as the exclusive reason for product selection. To be successful, a pricing strategy that includes a low price must be built on sound reasoning, with a clear path to success identified. This includes:

- A clear plan to assure customers that there are no true clinical disadvantages to the product. This requires clinical studies that support the claims and communications of that evidence.
- An understanding of the ways in which the price advantage is best communicated, including identifying the prescribers and patients to whom the advantage even matters
- Securing outside support from payers, thought leaders, and others, to legitimize the medical decision to consider the price
- A competitive plan to manage any situations in which other firms may try to minimize or eliminate your price advantage.

This final point is key because your competitive price is valid only if your competitors allow you to keep it and make it an advantage. When Merck launched its calcium channel blocker Plendil®, it did so at a substantial discount to Norvasc, Pfizer's market leader, and other similar agents. Although Plendil was, and remains, a good product, it had no clear advantages and a few disadvantages when compared with its competitors. This was the first time Merck had attempted to use a low price as an advantage, a fact which its competitors were quick to point out. Clinicians were left wondering if the low price was a signal of Merck's lack of confidence in the drug. Because prescribers were not unhappy with their current choices, it seemed risky to try a new drug that the company itself didn't seem to have faith in, and the product never achieved the significant sales that Merck hoped for.

As discussed earlier, when Zeneca attempted to gain a price advantage with Zestril by pricing it below Merck's Prinivil, Merck responded by lowering its own price. Although we do debate the need for this move, it illustrates the fact that your competitors are capable, and often willing, to remove any price advantage you seek.

Competing on price is, in our view, among the riskiest propositions available to a branded pharmaceutical firm and should be considered only within the context of a comprehensive strategy.

REFERENCES

1. Reekie WD. Pricing new pharmaceutical products. London: Croom Helm; 1977.
2. Kolassa EM. Reductions in pharmaceutical price growth: An assessment of list price changes in the US pharmaceutical market, 1989 to 1992. Technical report. University, MS: Research Institute of Pharmaceutical Sciences, University of Mississippi; 1993.

Chapter 9

Public Relations and Policy
with Brian Reisetter

When it comes down to a choice between
good politics and good policy, which usually wins?
—Bill Schneider, CNN

For the foreseeable future, pharmaceutical companies must consider the response and actions of government officials, the press, and patient advocates when setting prices for their new drugs. Criticism by one of these sectors, no matter how unfounded, can severely limit the success of a new product. The launch of a new agent at what is perceived to be a high or unfair price, no matter how justifiable, can bring a torrent of criticism from public officials and the press. Newspapers and TV news shows keep the issue in the public's mind with feature stories on drug prices. In the past ten years, it has become increasingly fashionable to decry the pricing policies of the pharmaceutical industry. In fact, it was the public policy issues of the early 1990s that elicited voluntary "caps" on price increases by the industry, but they did little good. These caps resulted in no noticeable changes in the public policy environment for the industry. In fact, Al Gore, in a speech to the Democratic National Committee, likened "Big Pharma" to "Big Oil" and "Big Tobacco."

The problem stems from a deep disconnect between the industry and the public. Most pharmaceutical marketers see the relationship between value and appropriate price as purely linear: as value increases, so can the price that is charged. Patients and policy makers, on the other hand, perceive clinical value—but in the context of *social good*. As the social good provided by an agent increases, so does the price that is perceived as "just," but only to a point. As the social value continues to increase, the public begins to see the product as a necessity or entitlement. The public definition of a "just" price decreases, to the point that the clinical and social value becomes a "public good" for which no price should be charged. For example, if the true social value was captured in each vaccine offered, the full-value price would be perceived as unjust. The high social value of vaccines forces a price that is below the economic value. Another market where we see this phenomenon take place is in HIV therapy, where the price of virtually every new therapy is seen as "unfair." The difference between the value perceptions of the public and manufacturers, as described by health policy expert Glenna Crooks, is shown in Figure 9.1.

In *Covenants: Inspiring the Soul of Healing*, a wonderful book on the health care crisis, Crooks has observed that a medicine or other intervention can often be seen as so important and valuable that many in the public believe that it should be provided to all who need it free of charge. This is in stark contrast to the way the pharmaceutical industry thinks and works, but it is part of the human psyche. Because of this situation, pharmaceutical pricers would be prudent to consider not just the business consequences but also the public perception of their pricing actions. Understanding this perception of medicines as a public right and not products of a for-profit industry should cause all involved in the pricing decision to pause and consider the way the price will "play on Main Street."

The current political environment remains distinctly anti-pharma, with drug prices the favorite topic of politicians of both parties. Recent calls for the reimportation of prescription medicines

FIGURE 9.1 Value Perceptions of Manufacturers, Policy Makers and Customers

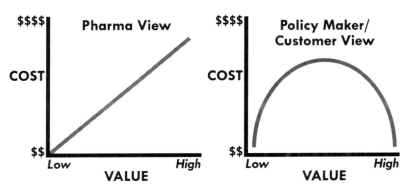

Source: Crooks G. Covenants: Inspiring the soul of healing. Fort Washington, PA: Covenant Matters Press; 2002.

sold in other nations are one tangible result of this atmosphere. Senators who traditionally supported the pharmaceutical industry now complain of having been "abandoned" by the industry and left with little choice but to go along with more radical calls for some level of control. Opportunistic politicians will rush to point out pricing actions they believe to be unfair. This is not new. For example, the former senator David Pryor of Arkansas decried the pricing of Clozaril by Sandoz in 1991 and forced price concessions.[1] Similarly, public pressure forced a price cut for the antiretroviral drug

---

[1] Actually, the effect was to unbundle the product from the Clozaril Patient Management System, which safeguarded patients from a potentially fatal side effect, agranulocytosis. The cost of the safeguard (regular monitoring) was included in the cost of the medication, and Senator Pryor, seeing an opportunity to criticize a pharmaceutical company, accused Sandoz of gouging patients and payers. The end result was that the safeguards were "unbundled" from the product and Sandoz set a new price. Without the cost of the system, the company actually made more money, but the political move by the senator resulted in patients being put at greater risk.

Retrovir® (zidovudine) in 1988. More recently, during the post-9/11 anthrax scare, Bayer had to work hard to dissuade the federal government from breaking the company's patent for Cipro. In the current atmosphere, one should expect critics in the US Congress to scramble for the soapbox and express outrage at ANY action taken by research-based pharmaceutical companies that critics believe can be made into an issue.

It is important to stay abreast of these developments, but it is equally important not to be paralyzed by them. Taking appropriate steps in pricing medicines and being able to articulate clearly and fully the reasons for the price selected can go a long way toward calming the critics. It is the firms that set prices without considering all of the important issues that run into problems. But we must also be aware that, while public policy problems with prices can be problematic, they are seldom fatal. It is indeed a public relations nightmare for a pharmaceutical manufacturer to have to defend or support its price in the face of public complaints, but the reality today is that, in light of other price drivers, price complaints have become not only commonplace but inevitable. The real effect of public policy problems appears to be almost nonexistent on product use, managed care adoption, and a product's price…so far. How long the industry can continue to dodge the bullets remains to be seen.

Let's take a moment to consider who's firing those bullets. It's not just politicians at the federal and state level. It's also the general public, the lay press, and patient advocacy groups.

The General Public

Any pharmaceutical marketer or product manager worth his or her salt will have a story about defending the industry, its products, and its prices to a cab driver, waitress, or other perfect stranger. Public misconceptions about the pharmaceutical industry and its pricing are staggering, both in their errors and in the basic ignorance they betray. For years, the major problem with pharmaceuticals has been lack of coverage, not cost. This was exacerbated by lack of prescription drug coverage under Medicare until 2006, but the MMA has not dispelled the public's complaints. Believing negative press stories that the pharmaceutical industry is profiteering on the public's welfare, the general public is not sympathetic to the pricing rationales offered by pharmaceutical companies—this in spite of the facts that growth in spending in other health care sectors has outstripped the rate of increase in pharmaceutical expenditures and that the practices of managed care contribute as much, and probably more, to increased patient out-of-pocket costs than do the actual prices of pharmaceuticals.

The Lay Press

The "reporting of news" has devolved into just another aspect of the entertainment industry that must compete for audience share, usually by alternately vilifying and deifying different entities nightly. Popular villains, such as large corporations, get return engagements. While the oil and tobacco industries lead the way in the press's stable of villains, the pharmaceutical industry is not far behind. Biased reporting has become the norm in descriptions of pharmaceutical manufacturers and pricing by the press. Unbiased reports and reports that favor the industry are often ignored because these segments do not make "good television." As a recent article in *The Economist* stated, outrage in the press, and the US public at large, has reached epidemic proportions. .Regardless of the behaviors of the industry or the prices charged by the industry, it is highly likely that unfavorable reporting will continue.

Advocacy Groups

Advocacy groups have several missions: first, to increase awareness of the disease or condition; second, to advocate, on behalf of disease sufferers, with the government, the industry, and the press; and, third, to achieve access to necessary treatments and health care for patients suffering from the disease or condition worldwide.

This last objective often leads advocacy groups to align with the pharmaceutical industry, but they can also quite often decry the industry as well. AIDS advocacy groups support initiatives to increase worldwide access to medications while targeting certain manufacturers for their pricing policies. Recently, Abbott, the manufacturer of Norvir®, an anti-retroviral agent for the treatment of HIV and AIDS, came under fire after a sizable price increase. Before Abbott had time to respond with justifications for its pricing, the advocacy groups had already alerted the press and politicians of the price increase and made it a key and urgent issue among the lay press, policy makers, physicians, and the general public.

Policy Makers

"Hot" issues are as popular with policy makers as they are with the lay press. Recent examples of the pharmaceutical industry becoming political fodder and sound bites include threats to Cipro's patent protection as a result of anthrax scares, calls for increased availability of Tamiflu to protect against bird flu, calls for reimportation of pharmaceuticals into the US to deliver cheaper prices for senior citizens, and the biopharmaceutical hearings of the early 1990s which questioned the prices charged for various products.

Some of the biggest threats to the industry arise in "political solutions," including price controls, litigation, and extensions of specific policies into larger populations such as applying Federal Supply Schedule pricing to all government expenditures or USP (United States Pharmacopeia) formulary guidelines to Medicaid. It can be easily argued that none of the well-intentioned political solutions, such as Medicare Part D, has provided all of the benefits or controls that policy makers intended.

IMPACT OF PUBLIC POLICY ON PRICING

History has shown an increased willingness of policy makers, the lay press, the general public, and advocacy groups to vilify the pharmaceutical industry as privateers in the health care market, yet many instances have occurred in diseases with even the most vocal advocacy groups, such as AIDS and oncology, in which products' prices have led to increased scrutiny of manufacturers but with no real effect on sales of these products. What this means is that in situations in which the product offers clinical benefit, policy pressures on price are largely ineffective.

As we have stated several times in this book, pharmaceutical markets are, for the most part, not subject to the same rules of elasticity and price sensitivity as most other markets. This puts the pharmaceutical marketer in a unique position and simultaneously creates a dilemma: although it is true, especially for drugs that treat tragic diseases, that marketers are essentially free to charge any price they want, at what point is the price "too high," and who will tell them so? There have been examples in the past where prices perceived as "too high" brought about public criticism, Congressional hearings, and other scrutiny. Much has been written over the years about the pricing of Clozaril, Ceredase®, Epogen®, and most of the medicines for HIV/AIDS. There have been calls for lower pharmaceutical prices, but these are aimed at the entire market, not a specific agent. New prices or pricing actions by companies often bring about some public attention, but none has resulted in anything but a temporary blip in the press. At what point does the price of a single agent bring about new backlash?

Generally, so long as the price charged for a product does not impede its use, any policy issues will be moot. If firms develop and incorporate insurance assistance and patient assistance programs that ensure coverage and provide free medicines when patients cannot otherwise afford medication, they will generally be shielded from ongoing criticism or any untoward consequences. A pricing problem becomes a real problem only when it affects patient care.

However, it is most likely that some firm, in the near future, will test the limits of price sensitivity by pricing a necessary drug for a severe indication at a level that is several multiples above what the market is prepared to accept without having taken the steps necessary to ensure access for all patients. If this happens, it is unlikely that there will be an immediate backlash, but if the price results in the imposition of restrictions that limit the use of the agent to only the most severely ill patients—in other words, if the medication must be rationed—and if these limits result in undue morbidity or mortality, it is the company, and not the payers, who will be called to task. The consequences for the individual company are impossible to predict, but the fallout will probably affect the entire industry.

Until that happens, public policy issues will continue to be a concern for pharmaceutical manufacturers but, in most cases, should not have a major impact on pricing decisions for individual products. When considering policy issues and their impact on the price (or vice versa), marketers should first ask, "How likely is this price to raise concerns in the public arena?" Taking a premium on a new statin or antibiotic is very unlikely to create a public policy problem. Customers may not like the price but it is highly unlikely that anyone in Congress, or elsewhere, will even notice. The situations that are most likely to elicit a public response from critics are those where products target unique patient populations (e.g., HIV, Alzheimer's) and carry a price that is perceived as too high or out of the ordinary or where a public payer, such as Medicaid, may face budgetary problems because of a very high cost (e.g., antipsychotics, HIV). In such situations, where a public policy problem is likely to occur, the firm should take special precautions, such as developing specific price communications messages explaining (not "justifying") the price. Of course, these messages should be tested prior to their use.

Developing messages that support the price are, in fact, useful for all products, and should be done at an early stage in the pricing process. In this way, anticipating questions the public might ask is the best way to ensure you have considered every perspective and can actually lead to a better pricing decision.

REFERENCES

1. Crooks GM. Covenants: Inspiring the soul of healing. Fort Washington, PA: Covenant Matters Press; 2002.

Chapter 10

Company Needs and Abilities

with Doug Paul

You're messing with a company's DNA
when you change how you do prices.
—Executive in charge of strategic pricing

Perhaps the single most important consideration in determining the appropriate price for a new pharmaceutical product, or in managing the price over time, is the company doing the pricing. The company's overall strategy for the product, what the company needs the product to accomplish, and what the company is willing and able to undertake to support the product and its price have a much greater bearing on the price and its success than any of the other factors discussed in this book. As this chapter's epigram suggests, a company's approach to pricing is integral to the company's past (its corporate culture), its present (the short-term goals the product must accomplish), and its future (the role of this product in the company's long-term strategies).

The ongoing needs of the company, including compliance with overall corporate strategy, the importance of establishing a position in the market for future performance, the need to build morale in the organization, or any of a number of other issues, have a massive effect on—and will be affected by—the price and the pricing strategy selected. A company that wants to establish broad use of a product as a means of gaining competence and credibility in a new market in preparation for the launch of a more significant agent may price the product low to make sales easier. This low price is often seen as a way to enhance the confidence of the sales force and speed the entry of the product into the market. In such a case, the pricing need is to build experience and presence in the market, not to establish and manage a profitable product.

Conversely, a company that has short-term cash needs cannot afford to forgo early profits and may be compelled to set a higher price. There are trade-offs with such a strategy. A high price with no support or justification may generate enough controversy to consume an inordinate amount of management time, but underpricing may mean senior managers must explain the pricing decision to the board of directors or the investment community. The pricing strategy must complement the corporate strategy.

Pricing strategies must also be tempered by the ability and willingness of the company to support them. Many well-reasoned strategies have been thwarted because insufficient resources were made available to support them. Others have failed because groups or factions within the company who may have championed different goals were not consulted in the development or implementation of these pricing strategies. For example, a decision to set a high price and provide no discounts within managed markets is certain to raise objections from the account management function. Even though the strategy is sound, it may result in making the account managers' jobs more difficult—the opposite of what any reasonable person would prefer.

A firm preparing to launch its first product will have a very different set of objectives and pricing considerations than one launching its 100th product. For the new firm, the success of the product could well determine the success of the overall corporation, and certainly the success of current managers. In such a case, the risk tolerance of the management team will become the predominant factor in price setting. Fear of market failure may drive the team to set a price that is lower than may be charged simply to enhance the probability of commercial success. Similarly, even a firm with a track record in the market might have to defer to the expectations of major stockholders for premium pricing, despite management's preferences. Both are rational pricing decisions but lead to very different prices.

It is not uncommon—in fact, it is healthy—that much internal debate is dedicated to the question of high versus low pricing. Often different factions within a firm will hold different views. The polarity is usually driven by the degree to which profits versus unit sales affect their compensation and evaluation. Firms with influential sales or managed markets managers, or those whose senior managers came up through those ranks, will often set lower prices than those dominated by the "business" people in finance or general operations.

In the long run, most companies reveal a pattern in their pricing. It is, in fact, easier and more accurate than any other metric to predict the price of a new product simply by knowing the company's pricing predilections. Some firms always seek premiums, setting their prices above the competition and often above market expectations. Other firms routinely set prices below market expectations. The reasons for these differences are manifold, but these patterns tend to hold true.

Setting prices in a predictable pattern may be easier for a firm, and administrative ease does have economic value, but the financial consequences of choosing to follow only one path to pricing are huge. When a firm manages its prices strategically, these patterns are less likely to emerge. Sadly, strategic pricing appears to be the exception rather than the rule.

When Sandoz set a low price for Lescol, its third-to-market statin, it knew the product had clinical weaknesses in terms of efficacy. The firm had also recently undergone two demoralizing events: the unsuccessful launch of Dynacirc®, a calcium channel blocker, and the loss of patent on Pamelor, its category-leading antidepressant. With these recent events shadowing the company, the prospect of selling a less potent drug into a market that valued potency was very demoralizing. So, Sandoz set the price of Lescol at half the price of Mevacor, the category leader. The firm gave the sales force something to sell—economy. It fired up the sales force and marketing team and beat market expectations. Despite the conjecture that Sandoz could have earned higher profits by accepting a lower share with a higher price, what the firm needed was a success, and low-priced Lescol delivered one.

Although Lescol illustrates using a low price to achieve a strategic goal, some firms set their prices lower in competitive markets deliberately, apparently not to make low price a selling point (because the discount is not that great) but to ensure that the sales force won't have to take time away from the clinical message to handle price objections. Whether the opportunity cost of forgoing a higher price is worth the added benefit of more efficient sales force time is unknown, but the decisions appear to be deliberate.

Other firms elect to set premium prices and let the products speak for themselves. This requires a different approach to sales force management and a readiness on the part of senior management to address any potential pricing issues. These firms, at least those who are successful in this approach, prepare for pricing objections before launch and have the plans at the ready. Those who are unsuccessful have usually not considered the possibility of objections. Their initial reaction to customer resistance is…surprise.

The power of corporate attitude in this regard is substantial. Firms that have routinely set relatively low prices often have this tendency so deeply fixed in their corporate culture that the prospect of setting a premium price for a valuable new agent literally frightens decision makers. Conversely, firms that have traditionally set high prices can easily convince themselves that every product they launch should be priced at a premium. It goes without saying that the more timid firms encounter few pricing problems, but it may come as a surprise to many that those firms that routinely set higher prices also seldom find them to be problematic. Which problem would you rather have: continually avoiding pricing objections by forgoing profit or occasionally missing profit projections?

The fact that different prices may be appropriate for the same product may confuse those who adhere to simplistic economic theories of supply and demand, but it is true. Some firms pride themselves on their pricing restraint, while others celebrate their aggressive stance on price. Both can be successful, although the more aggressive firm may be rewarded with higher profits. In the end, it boils down to the philosophy of the firm. Regardless of the decision to price at a premium or a discount, if managers have thoughtfully approached the question and are confident in their decision, then it is, at least in the short run, the appropriate decision.

Chapter 11

Pharmaceutical Pricing Research

*If scientific reasoning were limited to the logical
processes of arithmetic, we should not get very far
in our understanding of the physical world. One might
as well attempt to grasp the game of poker entirely by
the use of the mathematics of probability.*
—Vannevar Bush

It goes without saying that the pricing decision for anything, especially pharmaceutical products, is filled with uncertainty and ambiguity. The price of a medication may have a substantial effect on its adoption and use in the marketplace, but it is equally, if not more, likely to have no effect whatsoever. Pricing research is a logical and necessary approach to reducing uncertainty and ambiguity in the pricing decision, but no amount of research will eliminate risk completely. This point is crucial to understanding the purpose of pricing research. No matter how comprehensive the research, a large element of risk remains in the pricing decision.

But having the wrong expectations for pricing research is only one potential problem. We advise that, before embarking on any pricing research, you answer two questions: which price are we researching and with whom?

THE BASIC PROBLEM WITH MOST PHARMACEUTICAL PRICING RESEARCH

There are three critical problems with most approaches to pricing research for pharmaceuticals today. First, the research tends to be undertaken by people—internal and external—who often have only a limited understanding of the complexities and dynamics of pharmaceutical pricing. They tend to operate under simplifying assumptions that often result in flawed conclusions. Second, many of the research methodologies that are commonly used in many pharmaceutical firms actually induce price sensitivity in the respondents, resulting in studies that advise setting prices that are lower than could be attained. Finally, the price that is usually tested (AWP or some other measure) often has no bearing on what the various market participants actually pay.

Simplifying Assumptions

As we have described in this book, pharmaceutical pricing is complex and affected by multiple influences. Because of these complexities, the task of pricing requires much more than simply running a large amount of information about a product through a model and solving for the optimal price. As we hope we have established by now, an optimal price is a wonderful ideal but a poor goal for such an important decision. By assuming that a survey of several hundred physicians (and perhaps pharmacy directors) can help derive the ideal price for the product, the firm makes three critical assumptions:

1. Prescribers and other decision makers can precisely predict their own future behavior based on the information presented within the study.
2. These decisions vary quite significantly at slightly different price levels.

3. All of the factors we have outlined as crucial to the pricing decision truly do not matter.

We trust that no reasonable person is willing to accept those three assumptions. We do not imply, however, that pricing research has no value. You just need to be sure that the research is focused on asking the right people the right questions in the right manner. The simplifying assumptions that appear to drive much of the pricing research in the industry just do not comport with the way the market truly works. Researchers want a precise estimate of the relationship between the price charged and the volume sold, but the way that payers, prescribers, and patients decide to use pharmaceutical products precludes obtaining that precision. The precision desired of any study that measures intended use is thwarted by the most basic of the elements of Fishbein's model of behavioral intent: B ≅ BI, or **Behavior** is **approximately** equal to **Behavioral Intent.**[1] Asking research subjects what they *think* they will do provides you only with their estimate of what they *think* they will (or should) do, not what they *will* do. In other words, you are measuring only intent, not behavior or action. In addition, the use of pharmaceuticals is independent of price in some situations. For example, it is hard to imagine that the use of Gemzar®, a treatment for pancreatic cancer, will vary based on price, regardless of what price you use. Many of the pricing research methods currently in use, however, would be likely to "find" price sensitivity simply because of the way the research is designed and implemented.

Methodological Problems

Perhaps the biggest problem we see with pricing research, as practiced by much of the industry, is the use of research methods with known flaws that exaggerate price sensitivity and fail to capture correctly the effects of price on product use. In our experience, the continued use of research techniques that expose respondents to more than one price is a serious mistake. These techniques, called "polyadic" because they work by exposing respondents to more than one price, are predisposed to finding price sensitivity, even where none exists. For detecting price sensitivity that truly exists, as opposed to that induced by the research, we support the use of monadic approaches.

The term "monadic" refers to a research design, not a quantitative analysis technique. A monadic design, in which a respondent is exposed to a single price, is identical to the classic clinical trial study design, in which subjects are assigned randomly to parallel groups. By that measure, a monadic study design should be considered the gold standard by which other sampling approaches are judged.

A polyadic design, in which each respondent is exposed to multiple prices (or, in a clinical study, different treatments), is akin to a multiple crossover design in a clinical trial, the analysis of which is at best difficult and usually not sufficient to gain product approval. Most regulatory authorities do not readily accept such designs because the effect of an individual treatment cannot be easily isolated from those of the other treatments to which the subject is exposed. In a pricing study, exposing respondents to multiple prices introduces the problems of *framing* and *anchoring* to the study. This occurs through the use of either PSM (which stands for "price sensitivity meter" and is also known as the von Westendorp method); other approaches where an array of prices is presented for a single product; or the various conjoint and choice model designs in which a range of prices is presented, each for a different product, within the same research instrument.

Framing, also known as "reference price effects," is a major facet of transaction utility theory, a field of research that suggests people are motivated to purchase more than just "acquisition utility"— what they get from using a product. They are also motivated by the "transaction utility," which is associated with the difference between the price charged and what the buyer considers reasonable. The reasonableness of the price is judged by comparison with an external reference price. It is well established that people evaluate prices relative to their exposure to previous prices, and the more recent the exposure the greater the influence.[2, 3]

Side-by-side comparisons of products with vastly different prices will *force* the issues of price to take on a greater weight in the decision (real or simulated) than would be normal for the respondent. In a classic study of this phenomenon, Simonson and Tversky showed that when consumers were asked to choose between 2 microwave ovens, a Panasonic costing $179.99 and an Emerson costing $109.99, 57% chose the Emerson and 43% the $180 Panasonic. When a different group was shown three microwaves (the third being another Panasonic priced at $199.99), only 27% chose the Emerson, and a full 60% chose the $180 Panasonic.[4] This dramatic difference in choices (the proportion choosing the lower cost product was cut in half with the addition of a higher priced product) defies "rational" economic theory and demonstrates the effect of framing in a pricing test.

Anchoring refers to the effect of the order in which prices are seen. The order creates what are termed "anchors," which also exert a powerful effect on the perception of prices. Della Bitta and Monroe found that when respondents were presented prices for a series of products in descending order, they formed higher reference prices (20% or more higher) than those exposed to prices in ascending order.[5] The conclusion of the researchers was that the first prices to which respondents are exposed exert a larger influence on price perceptions than prices introduced later. Thus, respondents who are exposed first to low prices will evaluate subsequent higher prices as higher than those first exposed to high prices, once again refuting rational economic theory.

Those supporting polyadic designs argue that by rotating or otherwise alternating the order in which prices are presented the bias of the design will be eliminated. This argument rests on the assumption that averaging biased responses will render an unbiased estimate.

Conjoint and discrete choice models (DCM), unlike other polyadic methods, do not expose respondents to multiple prices for the same product, per se. Instead, they present respondents with a series of product abstractions, each representing a different bundle of attributes, including price, either singly (full profile conjoint) or in groups (DCM). Conjoint analysis uses multiple regression techniques to portray a model of choice behavior. The models, which tend to be linear but can take other forms, measure the likelihood of selecting one product over another when there are differences in product attributes.

Discrete choice models use logistic regression, a nonlinear technique that seeks to predict an event that has only two outcomes (e.g., buy/don't buy). Unlike conjoint analysis, which renders a score for each product (the higher the score, the greater the likelihood of purchase), DCM and other logistic regression applications simply predict whether a product is selected.

The goal of choice-based trade-off models such as conjoint and DCM is to determine the relative importance (utility) of each attribute.[6, 7] The methodologies require that every combination of attributes be evaluated. Using fractional factorial designs, a selection of attribute bundles can be derived that presents each level of each attribute together, eliminating the need to present respondents with every permutation of the attributes. In practice, this means that the same respondents must be presented with hypothetical products that include the greatest efficacy with the lowest price and the least efficacy with the highest price. This, by its nature, sensitizes respondents to prices by providing anchors that will affect price perceptions, artificially raising price sensitivity.

Thus, polyadic designs, regardless of the method, risk altering respondents' perceptions of and sensitivity to price, even as they attempt to measure them. It would appear that polyadic approaches could virtually guarantee the effect of Heisenberg's Uncertainty Principle—that by measuring a phenomenon we actually change it.

Polyadic designs also run counter to the decision-making process used by prescribers selecting pharmaceutical products. Physicians are seldom aware of the prices of the products from which they choose, but even if they are aware, they see the prices as fixed as they compare the other attributes of the products.[8] The context in which price is considered (or not considered) differs greatly from the multiple price potentials displayed in a polyadic design.

Similarly, in one of the few academic studies to use the monadic research method, this one with hospital pharmacy directors, the price of a drug was varied from $250 per dose to $3,250 per dose. Researchers found that, in this supposedly price-sensitive segment of the market, price did not achieve significance as a variable. Any variations in product selection were better explained by several other variables.[9]

Based on observations of the minimum noticeable difference for pharmaceuticals at the retail level, prices in research studies should be at least 15% apart. A significant difference, in which little doubt about preference exists, occurs when the price difference is between 25% and 35%. But even this difference does not guarantee that the predicted action will take place in the marketplace because physicians, in general, have shown little interest in prescribing lower cost drugs and pharmacists or others often see no advantage in promoting the use of lower cost agents.

The use of monadic techniques, whether or not they are used in conjunction with multiple regression or other similar methods, allows the identification of an *inflection point* through a process similar to triangulation. The inflection point is the price at which large differences in product use are noted in the research. Wide price bands can be tested to determine differences in intent to prescribe (or support or resist prescribing) at the various price points. If no differences in intent emerge among the prices tested, the point of inflection has not been reached. If the highest price tested is at the upper range of prices deemed acceptable to the company, the most likely launch price has been identified. Should the company wish to evaluate the effects of higher prices or to identify the point of inflection, a set of higher prices can be tested.

In a series of proprietary studies, the subjects of which we will not identify, the monadic technique was used to determine the price-volume relationship, or to identify the point of inflection. The products tested included neurological agents (both for chronic, difficult-to-treat disorders), respiratory therapies, oncolytics, and immune modulators. In each case, the price-volume relationship either proved to be nonexistent (because the inflection point was not reached) or identified the inflection point, indicating the probable upper limit of the price.

The same inflection point was identified for the two neurological agents. In each case, 4 prices, ranging from $2 to $4 per day, were tested. At prices up to $3 per day (cost to patient), there was no difference in intent to use (or allow the use of) the products. At a daily cost of approximately $3.50 per day, intended use fell dramatically. These products have been launched successfully, but an agent similar to one tested was launched before the test product at a price of $4.00, and its sales have proved disappointing to the company and to Wall Street.

For the respiratory agent, prices between $15 and $30 per package (the highest price at which the company would be comfortable) were tested. No differences in intended use emerged, and it was concluded that the product could be safely priced at the company's upper limit. The study of the immune modifier produced similar findings.

The study for the oncolytic agent included patient-specific information, which, due to standardization of patients by stage of disease and age, was relatively straightforward and proved to be quite useful. Price resistance emerged for some patient types at some price levels. The study demonstrated that oncologists, globally, would reserve the product for later-stage disease in younger patients at the highest prices and would readily use the product earlier in the disease at lower prices, although slight improvements in efficacy would have significantly enhanced use.

In the case of the oncolytic agent, a price/volume relationship was attainable because population estimates by disease stage were available. For the other products, where the point of inflection could not be identified or it was concluded that the point had not been reached within the range that was comfortable for the companies, forecasts of sales volume relied on nonprice variables such as promotion, competition, and patient types.

This last point is key to understanding the usefulness of pricing research and the desire to model market potential: *the task of pricing research is to determine at which point pricing interrupts the normal process of product diffusion.* This is because, in almost all circumstances, other variables will likely be much more important in determining product success.

Putting all of this into a single and accurate pricing model is a challenge, to say the least. Because there are so many dimensions to a prescribing or reimbursement decision, all of which must be profiled differently within a study, and pricing may play a different role in each, the complexity of the final model may prove daunting. Those wishing to pursue the development of precise, comprehensive models would be well served to study the concepts underlying chaos theory.

PHYSICIAN PRICING RESEARCH

Despite the fact that over 50 years of scientifically valid studies have shown that the majority of physicians are oblivious to the costs of the products they prescribe every day, countless firms spend huge sums of money to solicit pricing guidance from these same physicians.[8, 10, 11] Why is this?

People within organizations often follow rules, written and unwritten, that they believe govern their jobs, and performing pricing research before a product launch is one of these "rules" in many firms. Organizational behavior is a fascinating area of study and is vital to understanding why certain erroneous actions are repeated over and over. The much maligned economist John Maynard Keynes once noted: "Worldly wisdom teaches that it is better for reputation to fail conventionally than to succeed unconventionally." Because few people, if any, have lost their jobs for doing pricing research, it must be easier to do the study than it is to think about why it might not provide good information after all.

If half a century of academic research demonstrates that physicians, by and large, don't know the prices of the drugs they prescribe, logic dictates that physicians' decisions can't be affected by drug prices. Social science research also tells us that if we ask people a question that they believe should be answered in a particular way—such as, "Doctor, are you concerned about the costs of the drugs you prescribe?"—many will provide what they believe to be the most socially desirable answer. In this case, they would agree: "Certainly I am concerned about the costs of the drugs I prescribe!" If we offer to pay them $150 to participate in a study, they will answer these questions to the best of their ability. Many of the physicians with whom we interact are more than willing to share their opinions with anyone who will ask, especially if they are being paid for it. That is another important aspect of human behavior that must be acknowledged.

But even if prescribers were aware of the prices charged for most drugs, the way in which most pricing research is structured would still render their awareness irrelevant. The price that may be most important to a prescriber is the price the patient pays which, in most cases, is a co-pay, not the full amount and certainly not the average wholesale price (AWP). But the co-pay for an individual drug varies widely according to the health plan and even *within* the health plan. Three different people may each take the same proton pump inhibitor. One pays a $3 co-pay, another pays $25, and the third pays cash for the full amount. What price should be tested with the doctor, and is it the price or complaints or questions that arise from price that are more important to test?

Testing sensitivity to co-pays instead of list price, however, still presents some problems. You still get only the physicians' best guess about the effect of various co-pays on them because they tend to be equally uninformed about the specific co-pays a patient faces. Because most physicians' practices include patients covered by several different health plans, there is no uniform co-pay for a drug within an individual practice. This is not an insurmountable research problem, but one that must be acknowledged and addressed with this audience. Until all physicians use e-prescribing systems that provide formulary and co-pays for individual patients, it is unlikely that a perfect research interface can be built that can test for such decision-making differences.

Because the pharmaceutical marketplace is nebulous, research design must be more sophisticated and thoroughly grounded both in the realities of clinical practice and the principles of marketing. Only then can pricing research predict approximate behavior and avoid confounding issues.

PRICING RESEARCH IN MANAGED CARE

Managed care organizations (MCOs) and Medicaid together pay for more than 85% of all outpatient prescriptions. As a customer group, MCOs are obviously very important. A number of firms do quantitative pricing research with MCOs before selecting a price, but this is as problematic and misleading as pricing research with physicians. The old saying, "If you know one MCO, you know one MCO," has never been truer. A pharmacy director for a major MCO, such as Caremark or one of the Blues (the Blue Cross Blue Shield health insurance companies), cannot provide you with a remotely accurate estimate of the policy that would be in place for a new product in all of the plans the MCO offers. Instead, the pharmacy director is more likely to tell you what the MCO would *like* to do, or *wishes* it could do. We have found that many in the MCO community view pricing research as their opportunity not to provide the firm with any real insight but to begin price negotiations. MCOs, first and foremost, respond to medical demand. So the best way to understand how an MCO will treat your product is to understand whether or not physicians and others see it as a valuable new treatment tool.

Even if the responses of pharmacy and medical directors to pricing research questions were accurate, they still could not be quantified. Because they have different plans and plan sponsors, most large MCOs have dozens, if not hundreds, of medical and pharmacy directors. The majority of these plans are fairly liberal in terms of coverage. In only a minority of plans is reimbursement for prescription drugs tightly and successfully restricted. So, when an MCO says that it would put your product on its third tier, does that mean for 100% of the plans it offers or in just the 20% over which it has most control? Is the MCO referring to *all* the lives covered by it or only the lives that it manages?

There are methods that can be used to quantify the likely formulary status, but they are complex and rarely, if ever, used. The problem is that this quantification requires an understanding of the true roles and influence of those within MCOs and what factors drive their decisions. That is, one needs to understand the organizational behavior issues to predict their behavior. Without in-depth knowledge of MCO organizational behavior, research with this audience will consist of verbatim reporting of what the respondents *think* they should do, or would *like* to do, with your new product. In the majority of cases, this bears no resemblance to the way payers will actually treat your product.

PRICE RESEARCH WITH PATIENTS

If physicians aren't the best source of price guidance and the responses of MCOs are suspect and difficult to quantify, where does that leave you? The answer is with the patient. The patient's actions in response to different levels of co-pay will, in all likelihood, have more impact on the use of a product than any other pricing issue. Because a vast majority of prescriptions are reimbursed through some third party, most of whom use co-pays as a way to control use or lower their costs, it is the area of reimbursement that warrants study.

Asking generic patients (those who do not have the condition treated by the drug) to imagine they have a specific disease and to speculate how a series of different co-pays might affect them ranges from pointless to dangerous. Yet, it is a common exercise in pharmaceutical pricing research, despite several academic studies that have shown people to be, in general, poor predictors of their own behavior—especially people without the disease in question.[12, 13] Asking people with no basis for a response to speculate as to their future behavior under a hypothetical scenario yields unreliable and potentially misleading information

We do know that co-pay differences affect prescription compliance, but what specifically do we know? Although research demonstrates a drop in use when co-pays increase, some studies have shown normal use resumes within a year after the change. This means that the co-pay sensitivity is not to the price but to a *change* in price. After a year, when the new price becomes the norm (also known as a new reference price), use returns to previous levels. If I ask a patient who has a $25 co-pay to estimate use with a $35 co-pay, the patient is almost obliged to respond that use would be lower. The $35 conflicts with the patient's reference price, and thus it seems too high. What good is that information?

Understanding patient compliance behavior under different co-pay scenarios is important for forecasting. However, asking patients to tell us what they *think* their behavior would be is dangerous because it could force a decision to price low or offer discounts to gain better formulary status when these tactics are not really necessary. So, what can we do to fix this problem? First, hundreds of studies have examined co-pay effects on patients, and making sure that you or your research providers are current with this literature is vital. Second, there are several sources of secondary information that can provide great insight into co-pay effects for similar products, and one should turn to those sources before undertaking most primary research into this area.

There are ways to use primary research to identify co-pay effects on patients, but you must begin with patients who are already diagnosed with and are being treated for the disorder instead of asking people to role-play. Moreover, you must limit the number of options they are given. As already mentioned, research shows that exposing people to more than one option in a study like this opens up real potential for anchoring; their reaction to one co-pay would be affected by the first one they are shown. The first co-pay becomes the reference price by which others are judged. Once respondents see a $25 co-pay, they would consider a $35 co-pay unacceptable. If they see the $35 cost first, the $25 co-pay looks like a bargain because of the higher reference price.

Another problem with exposure to multiple options is that when more options are offered, people are less likely to want to make a decision and more likely to look for ways to simplify the task, for example, by preferring the lowest price. This bias can be minimized by testing a single co-pay level with each respondent (monadic sampling).

UNDERSTANDING THE MARKET AND CUSTOMERS

Regardless of the research approach taken, nothing can substitute for an in-depth understanding of the market and the customers. Marketers must know what motivates their customers, what worries them, and what actions they can and will take. There have been dozens, if not hundreds, of well-reasoned studies that failed to take into account the issues raised here. The results were accepted and often implemented and invariably affected the pricing decision negatively. Ultimately pricing research—and even market research that is not focused on price, such as positioning and promotional sensitivity testing—should not be used to discover a magical number that will be the perfect price. Rather, research should help marketers understand more fully their products' *value*, so that they can develop sound pricing strategies.

REFERENCES

1. Fishbein M. An investigation of the relationships between beliefs about an object and the attitude toward that object. *Hum Relations* 1963; 16:233-40.
2. Nwokoye N. Subjective judgments of price: The effects of price parameters on adaptation levels. Proceedings of the American Marketing Association Fall 1975 Educators' Conference.
3. Monroe K, Petroshius SM. Buyers' perceptions of price: An update of the evidence. In: Kassarjian HH, Robertson TS, ed. Perspectives in consumer behavior. 3rd ed. Glenview, IL: Scott-Foresman; 1981.
4. Simonson I, Tversky A. Choice in context: Tradeoff contrast and extremeness aversion. *J Marketing Res.* 1992; 29:281-95.
5. Della Bitta AL, Monroe K. The influence of adaptation levels on subjective price perceptions. *Adv Consumer Res.* Proceedings of the Association for Consumer Research. Vol. 1. Urbana, IL: ACR; 1974.
6. Curry J. Understanding conjoint analysis in 15 minutes. *Quirk's Marketing Res Rev.* 1994; (June/Jul).
7. Struhl S. Discrete choice modeling: Understanding a "better conjoint than conjoint." *Quirk's Marketing Res Rev.* 1994; (June/Jul)..
8. Kolassa EM. Physicians' perceptions of pharmaceutical

prices: Their accuracy and effect on the prescribing decision. *J Res Pharm Econ.* 1995; 6(1):23-37.

9. Kolassa EM, Smith MC, et al. The effects of acquisition cost and budget-based compensation on the attitudes of pharmacy directors toward the adoption of a cost-effective new drug. *PharmacoEconomics.* 1998; 13(2):223-30.

10. Zelnio RN, Gagnon JP. The effects of price information on prescription drug product selection. *Drug Intell Clin Pharm.* 1979; 13:156-9.

11. Reisetter BC, Bentley JP, Wilkin NE. Relationship between psychosocial physician characteristics and physician price awareness. *J Pharm Market Manage.* 2005; 17(1):51-76.

12. Ross L, Nesbitt R. The person and the situation. New York: McGraw Hill; 1991.

13. Schwartz B. The paradox of choice. New York: CCC (Harper Collins); 2004.

Chapter 12

Managing
the Pricing Function

When pricing is everybody's responsibility,
it is nobody's responsibility.
—Dan Nimer

Before describing the ways in which the pricing function can and should be managed, we would like to illustrate what happens when the pricing function is not managed.

A mid-sized pharmaceutical firm had enjoyed two years as the only supplier of a key product for cardiac care. When a competitor with a similar product and a history of aggressive pricing entered the market, the pricing committee, comprising several marketing and finance managers, developed a strategy that was intended to avoid a costly round of price competition. The market was expanding, and distinct segments were beginning to appear. The committee decided that the firm would not contest selling efforts by the new competitor to the most price-sensitive segments, allowing the newcomer to enjoy a relatively high sales volume and avoiding head-to-head confrontations.

The new pricing strategy was approved by senior management, and those who developed it confidently went about their business. Within two months, account managers assigned to accounts in the price-sensitive segments had reduced prices to 10% below those of the new competitors. A price war ensued. When asked why they had ignored the newly formed strategy, the account managers responded that this product line accounted for the majority of their evaluations and compensation and they could not afford to lose the income. Failing to consider the effects of a successful strategy on individuals in other parts of the organization had undermined the strategy and, worst of all, reduced average prices for the entire category.

Was the strategy wrong? No, the overall strategy was sound. Were the account managers wrong? No, they were doing what they were paid to do: sell products to their assigned customers. The problem was in the implementation of the strategy and the pricing committee's failure to consider the ways in which their strategies affect others and others affect their strategies.

In many ways, the prevalent approach to pricing today is like the US health care system. As we are all aware, health care reform has become one of the major public policy issues in the US. The basic problem underlying our health care system is the fact that it is oriented not toward the ongoing process of patient care and health, but toward the episodic treatment of illness. Medical training and practice are focused on curing sick patients, not on maintaining wellness. Such a focus can result only in high—and ever increasing—costs.

Pricing suffers from this same orientation. Most businesses treat pricing as an isolated event or episode rather than as a process. The initial price setting is done within the context of the current business environment, and subsequent pricing actions are often taken in response to real or imagined changes in the competitive or customer environments. For example, a lower price or new product by a competitor brings about a reaction—usually a price cut. When a customer complains that a price is too high or threatens to seek other bids, panic-laden messages from the field bring on consternation at headquarters and lower prices.

Rather than following a well-reasoned strategic pricing plan, each new event in the market triggers a reevaluation of prices...and the pricing doctor (or sales manager) is called upon to do some magic. By recognizing some of the forces that bring about this event-driven pricing, we can begin to manage the process of pricing strategically through the life of the product. But, as our story about the conflict between the pricing committee and the sales force demonstrates, even the soundest strategies can fail if you do not consider factors *both* internal *and* external to your company.

Everyone recognizes the basic equation: *Profit = Revenue - Cost.* And most will agree that a significant amount of corporate time and effort is put into organizational actions like cost control and cost management initiatives. We can further define one element in that equation in this way: *Revenue = Price x Quantity.* Again, most will readily admit that considerable resources are directed at increasing the quantity sold through those actions usually referred to as sales and marketing.

The question we must all ask, then, is: how much effort is put into pricing as an ongoing process? Regardless of the work that goes into the initial pricing decision, failure to properly manage the pricing process in the long run results in poor prices and lower profits in the long run. This often happens without managers even realizing it. Even when managers believe that they have developed an effective pricing strategy, one that has a long-term vision, they often find that strategy tossed aside by someone in their own organization because the strategy failed to take that person's situation and orientation into account.

In many organizations, prices are set without regard to the firm's overall marketing objectives. This is an obvious disconnect that most of us recognize quickly. But how many of us have considered the potential conflicts that may exist between the pricing strategy and the objectives and strategies of other departments—or the personal objectives of key individuals within the organization? Groups and individuals without official pricing authority often exercise a great deal of influence over the pricing of products, both in determining the initial pricing action and in setting the selling price for the product as it reaches the customer.

Whether a firm has a pricing department in place or not, there is a pricing function in operation. The question is whether it is a coordinated function. When firms rely on an informal network and power structure to set pricing policies and implement pricing actions, the results can be costly.

THE PRICING CENTER

In his classic 1982 *Harvard Business Review* article "Major Sales: Who Really Does the Buying?" Thomas Bonoma presented a structured look at "buying centers," the "anonymous kingpins who really make buying decisions".[1] We know that many people are often involved in purchase decisions, frequently individuals who are essentially invisible to us. Although unseen, they may play one of the basic buying center roles: initiator, influencer, purchaser, gatekeeper, decider, and user. Most marketers and salespeople know they must apply the buying center concept externally, when selling to organizations. They must identify buying center members and understand their unique needs and interests. They must also realize that these buying center roles may be played by different groups and individuals according to the purchase and that the actual buying center may differ considerably from the public face presented by a firm.

We propose that this same approach can be applied *internally* to help us identify those individuals and groups who should be involved in the pricing process—those whose needs and interests we must consider when making the pricing decision. These persons and groups constitute the firm's "pricing center." Those involved in pricing must understand the ways in which these participants in the pricing center view the market, the role of price, and the importance of profits. Conflicts between the motivations of these groups

FIGURE 12.1 The Pricing Center

	Initiator	Influencer	Advocate	Gatekeeper	Decider	User
Top Management		X		X		
Strategic Planning	X	X	X			
Pricing	X		X	X		
Marketing	X	X	X			
Finance	X	X	X	X		
Sales	X	X	X			X
Contracting	X	X				X

(e.g., get the deal, increase volume, maintain a minimum margin, maximize commissions) can thwart the soundest strategies. The roles outlined in the buying center have analogous players in the pricing center. Figure 12.1 describes the pricing center roles and players found in most organizations.

Pricing centers exist in virtually all organizations. Some are recognized, even purposefully formed, and incorporated into operations. Most are not. As with buying centers, the key to understanding and managing the pricing center is to identify and understand the motivations of the people involved. But first those individuals must be identified.

UNDERSTANDING AND DESCRIBING THE PRICING CENTER

Because the roles and the individuals involved in the pricing center change as pricing circumstances change, there is no single profile or map of the pricing center. Different individuals and departments are involved with new product pricing decisions than with price changes or price negotiations with customers. These actions, of course, will vary over time. To understand and manage the pricing center, one must:

- *Develop internal case studies.* Conducting a series of internal case studies can be an effective way to describe the pricing center. To create case studies, select products at different stages in their life cycles and assemble a chronology of pricing actions for each. Then, start the "detective work" of determining the reasons behind and persons involved in each of the price changes that took place. Although the exercise is very likely to yield an incomplete picture, the investigation will result in the beginnings of a map and an understanding of the pricing center in your organization.
- *Perform an image study of pricing.* Concurrent with the case study exercise, you should undertake an internal "image study" of pricing. This involves polling personnel in all departments that have input into or are affected by prices and pricing decisions about how they view prices and the firm's pricing policies. Determining the ways in which prices and pricing practices are viewed by others within the firm will identify impediments to good pricing practices. The information gathered should include:

  1. The individual's level of comfort with unilateral price changes by the firm
  2. Attitudes toward the value of certain customers and key accounts
  3. Satisfaction with overall price levels

4. Attitudes toward the firm's prices. Do individuals view the firm's prices as an impediment to their own job performance? For example, sales and contracting personnel often view prices as impediments to sales. When these individuals have some level of pricing authority or a high level of influence in pricing decisions, they will work to reduce this impediment.

- *Identify organizational motivation and orientations that may subvert good pricing practices.* Finally, examine the ways in which organizational motivation, compensation, and orientation systems complement or subvert appropriate pricing practices. This will highlight the areas of greatest danger. During a meeting at a major pharmaceutical company, I watched a vice president of key account management claim credit for $8 million in sales of an older product as proof of the value of his long-term care (nursing home) department to the company. Upon questioning, he acknowledged that nearly $7.5 million in rebates had been paid to customers after their purchases, but his group was evaluated on sales volume at list prices and was not accountable for discounts and allowances. A thorough audit of that operation showed that, of the $40 million in total sales credited to the LTC department, fully $18 million had been rebated back to customers. Moreover, research showed that over $27 million of the total sales could have been achieved at full list price because of the unique value of the products involved. In effect, this operation was incentivized to transfer over $5 million of pure profit from the company to its customers (not including the administrative and other costs of the program). These people were doing what they were paid to do, despite the fact that their activities had a negative impact on the firm's bottom line. This is not the fault of the department. It is the fault of the organization's top management for failing to understand conflicting organizational motivations. Such conflicts are common in most industries: department-specific orientation and evaluation criteria often undermine corporate pricing goals.

We have focused on examples of the way in which the pricing center can lower prices unnecessarily, but forces in the pricing center can also act to move prices too high. In competitive markets where small differences in prices can determine the likelihood of generating any sales at all, finance or accounting departments that insist on maintaining minimum profit margins often act to force prices above appropriate levels in the market and actually reduce the profitability of the firm. Standard accounting procedures that allocate fixed costs to the unit level overstate product costs and often force prices higher than necessary. This occurred recently at a small but growing microelectronics firm. Sales growth led to the need to expand manufacturing capacity and make significant new investments in facilities. Because the firm used a fully allocated costing system, the new fixed costs were factored into the unit cost equation, dramatically increasing the stated cost and unfortunately leading management to believe that a substantial price increase was needed to cover these costs. The price increase was implemented, and unit sales fell sharply, resulting in even higher per-unit cost allocations. This "death spiral" was halted only when the company, near bankruptcy, was sold. The new owners changed the accounting system and "returned" the firm to profitability with appropriate price reductions.

Although there is no single profile of a pricing center, the most common members of the pricing center include:

- Top management
- Strategic Planning
- Finance
- Marketing
- Sales
- Contracting or Account Management
- Pricing

These functions are driven by distinct motivations and perspectives. For example, top management personnel are often charged with making the ultimate pricing decision. They draw upon a number of sources for input but are usually oriented toward two, often conflicting, ends: maximizing the profitability of the firm and ensuring that quarterly performance meets expectations. These different goals are then interpreted by various groups in the organization in a myopic manner, with one group focusing on profit maximization while another looks only at meeting short-term forecasts. Depending on these factions' relative influence, prices can be driven too high or too low. Finance and accounting managers often focus on unit profit margins as desirable endpoints, while sales and customer service managers seek to maximize unit sales and customer satisfaction.

Functions, like individuals, will act out of self-interest. The firm must develop processes and policies that take these differences into account and prevent them from undermining strategic efforts.

FORMAL PRICING DEPARTMENTS

Pricing departments within the pharmaceutical and medical device industry vary in structure, responsibilities, resources, and effectiveness. Research conducted with firms in these industries in the mid-1990s found four types of pricing functions:

- Large, fully integrated pricing departments
- Small strategic pricing departments
- Standing pricing committees
- Ad-hoc pricing committees.

Obviously, only two of these forms are actual pricing departments staffed with personnel dedicated to pricing. The two committee types are simply assemblies of senior managers from various functions who met on a regular basis to set pricing policies and list prices, determine list price changes, and establish discounting and contracting policies. The fully integrated pricing departments contained personnel dedicated to several different aspects of pricing, including strategic pricing guidance, contract administration and negotiation, and compliance with government mandates. Fully integrated departments were staffed with 12 to 75 employees. Smaller strategic pricing departments reported to another function within the firm, ranging from marketing research to the vice president of marketing or sales. These departments ranged in size from a single individual to five employees. Both department types set or recommended pricing policies and list prices for new products, managed list price changes, and either administered or monitored contracting. There was no relationship between company size and pricing function type.

The differences in pricing discipline among these types, as measured by the depth and degree of discounting, was striking. Firms managing prices by committee provided more and deeper discounts than those with dedicated departments. But there were also differences in effectiveness, as measured by success in setting and maintaining prices, among those firms with dedicated departments.

Which organizational approaches were successful? Our work with dozens of firms, both within and outside the industry, has revealed some consistencies in pricing execution. First, the pricing departments have a clear charge: to manage the prices of the firm. More than simply setting list prices and making recommendations, these departments coordinate pricing activities across the firm, interacting with the other departments that affect or implement prices. They not only set or recommend prices and policies but also enforce those policies and, at their best, educate others in the firm on the "how" and "why" of pricing and, in doing so, generate support for and cooperation with the policies and procedures.

Of utmost importance to the success of these departments is the full support of senior management. We have seen several cases in which departments became much more effective after a senior manager, often the CEO, proclaimed the importance of the pricing department and the firm's commitment to the policies that the department develops. This was most notably seen in 1998, when the CEO of a major firm announced that the pricing policies established by the department were *his* policies, and that others, even the managers of foreign affiliates, who disagreed with those policies were free to leave the firm if they disagreed with or did not follow them.

The most effective pricing departments reported to high levels in the organization, often the VP of marketing. Although departments that report elsewhere can be effective, the location of the pricing department within the firm can be vital to the effectiveness of the department. Those pricing departments that were subordinate to other departments and served a more advisory role tended to be less effective.

OVERCOMING THE CONFLICT BETWEEN PROFITABLE PRICING AND FIELD OPERATIONS

The greatest problem in implementing appropriate pricing policies occurs when the goal of strategic pricing—profitability—clashes with the goals of other functions, particularly sales organizations incentivized to achieve market share. An organizational goal focused on market share or unit sales conflicts with the goal of profitability. When the overarching objective of a firm is to achieve unit sales, it is virtually impossible for a pricing department, regardless of the resources committed or the talent of the personnel, to achieve its goals.

To overcome this problem, some firms have developed and implemented policies that reward sales and marketing personnel for achieving specific pricing or margin goals. Armstrong World Industries, maker of building supplies and materials, has developed competitions that reward sales personnel and regions for achieving specific pricing goals. This program has stopped the downward pressure on prices and has even resulted in competitive prices firming up.

In the late 1980s, the US affiliate of a European pharmaceutical firm implemented a policy that required account managers to demonstrate to the firm that any discount offered would generate more profit from the account than the higher prices. When account managers became conversant in break-even analysis and were rewarded based on the profitability of the contracts, the firm realized a substantial increase in net prices—and profitability. A major US pharmaceutical firm recently undertook an initiative to train its sales and account management personnel on the value of its products to its customers' business. This initiative has resulted in a substantial lessening of the internal conflict and negotiating that was thought to be interfering with the efficient operations of the firm.

THE PRICING MANAGEMENT PROCESS

Regardless of the consistency of goals, the most effective pricing functions monitor and understand both their internal and external environments. Personnel are dedicated to the specific processes of:

- *Interacting on a regular basis with sales and marketing teams.* Because pricing is, first and foremost, an element of the marketing mix, it is important that personnel from the pricing function interact routinely with the marketing team. To be effective, the marketing strategy and the pricing strategy must complement each other. The best performing pricing departments have personnel with regular membership on product teams. Some pricing departments assign personnel to business units according to customer type, aligning specialists who focus on hospital or retail markets with product teams to ensure their pricing actions are consistent with marketing plans and with the realities of the market. In several large firms, pricing personnel are assigned to specific product or therapeutic areas. Others develop a matrix approach, with individuals assigned to both therapeutic and customer segment areas. Regardless of the manner in which these people are assigned, their role is to ensure a constant presence of the pricing department in marketing team activities and decisions.
- *Interacting with other departments as needed.* Other departments, including finance and legal, should be regular "touch points" for pricing personnel. To remain in touch with customers and

the dynamics of the marketplace, the pricing function must interact with the sales function, including making customer visits with sales representatives.

- *Monitoring compliance with policies and recommending appropriate changes.* Because it is responsible for the development of pricing policies, including basic contract terms and conditions for price concessions, pricing should also monitor the process of ensuring compliance with policies as well as the relevance of the policies themselves. When a large proportion of contracts are exceptions to the current policies, either the process for exception or the policies must be revisited.

- *Monitoring the effectiveness and profitability of contracts.* Once contracts are enacted, the pricing function should have the ability to follow up and determine the degree to which the customer has fulfilled its contractual obligations. Performance-based discounts, provided at the time of sale as opposed to the end of a contractual period, should be monitored carefully to ensure that the basis for discounts (either market share or unit sales) has been achieved, that the assumptions for the contract were valid, and that the contract was warranted

- *Monitoring the competitive pricing environment.* Dr. Louis Pasteur said, "Chance favors the prepared mind." The effectiveness of any pricing plan is affected more by competitive pricing actions than any other outside influence. Customers often use competitive prices as benchmarks of appropriateness of prices and as bargaining chips in negotiations. It is vital that the pricing function have complete knowledge of competitive pricing and marketing activities. This competitive intelligence effort can be conducted by persons within the pricing function or through close work with another department. However, some aspects of competitive intelligence should be managed by the pricing function, especially the development and maintenance of competitive price files and databases. The pricing function should have files or databases of list prices, discount prices, terms and conditions of sale, pricing histories, and detailed documentation of the pricing actions of all major competitors.

- *Coordinating any pricing research that is performed.* The pricing function must be fully in the loop when marketing research involving *any* aspect of pricing is conducted. Because many methods of marketing research misstate the role or importance of price in decision making, it is crucial that personnel from the pricing function advise marketing research personnel on research that may affect pricing decisions or the firm's view of prices in the marketplace.

- *Establishing pricing strategies for new products.* When new products are about to be launched, the pricing function should have the primary responsibility for establishing the pricing strategy for the product. Working in conjunction with product management teams, the pricing function must ensure that the pricing strategy is consistent with corporate pricing policies and the marketing strategy for the new product. It is also important to determine—before decisions are made—the degree to which the pricing of a new product may affect the pricing and success of products already marketed.

- *Developing and enforcing pricing policies.* Pricing policies, which are the guidelines used to make individual pricing decisions, are among the most important elements of an overall corporate pricing strategy. The policies guide the firm's pricing decisions to ensure their consistency with overall strategy. The pricing function should have primary responsibility for establishing and recommending the policies and for their enforcement. The function should participate in all decisions that lead to exceptions to policy and monitor the effectiveness of the policies on an ongoing basis. This monitoring serves two purposes: to ensure compliance and to reevaluate the current policies to determine the need for changes.

- *Conducting internal outreach programs in pricing.* Many individuals working in functions with regular customer contact see profitable and effective pricing as an impediment to sales and marketing goals. The most effective pricing functions work with field personnel to help them understand the importance of profitable pricing policies and the ways in which sales and marketing personnel can help the firm achieve the most profitable prices. This includes conducting or sponsoring workshops on understanding and selling value, managing competition, and understanding their customers' business.

To achieve this deep understanding of the internal and external environments in which pricing operates, personnel in the pricing function must either perform specific tasks or interact on a regular basis with a variety of other functions that perform those tasks. Depending on the firm, some tasks, such as monitoring competitors or performing pricing research, are handled by other departments, but personnel from the pricing function are, and must be, involved fully in these areas.

REFERENCES

1. Bonoma TV. Major sales: Who really does the buying? *Harvard Bus Rev.* 1982; 60(May-June):111-19.

Chapter 13

The Process
for New Product Pricing

*Pricing is the moment of truth—all of marketing comes to
focus in the pricing decision.*
—Raymond Corey

Regardless of the industry, setting the price for a new product
is a difficult task, filled with uncertainty and risk. Despite the
many types of research and the plethora of information that may be
available to the pricer, one is never sure that the price is right. There
is, in our experience, little that we can do to eliminate the uncertainty and allow us to set the "optimal" price, but there are steps
that we can take to minimize risk and, at the very least, increase the
likelihood of a proper decision. Chapters 4 through 10 of this book
detail the elements of pharmaceutical pricing, issues that must be
addressed when setting and managing prices. When incorporated
into a comprehensive process for pricing analysis and decision
making, these elements provide the best way to ensure that the
pricing decision is fully informed and well-reasoned. These issues
are summarized in Figure 13.1.

Pricing is a process, not an event, and our recommended
approach to pricing new pharmaceutical products so that they
produce maximum value to the firm consists of a series of analyses

FIGURE 13.1 Factors to Consider for New Product Pricing

COMPETITION
• What are the current competitive alternatives? • Are new competitors anticipated? • Do competitors have a history of responding to the pricing actions of others? • What steps might competitors who feel threatened by this new product take?
DISEASE AND PATIENT CHARACTERISTICS
• Will the symptoms or severity of the disorder affect price sensitivity? • What is the position of the disease on the "radar screen" of the payer, provider, or public? • What is the potential for patients to view the drug positively (i.e., as offering relief of symptoms, disease reversal, or cure)? • How likely are patients to protest the price? • Is the patient population likely to have trouble affording this new product? • Alternatively, could affordability be a key feature of this product?
VALUE OF THERAPY
• What does this disorder cost the health care system and society? • What is the potential to reduce this cost with the new product? • What information will be needed to document and demonstrate any savings? • What is the potential of this product to increase costs but improve outcomes? • How satisfied is the market with current therapies?
DECISION-MAKING PROCESS
• What role does price play in the decision to prescribe, dispense, consume, or purchase drugs in this category? • How likely are prescribers to receive negative feedback on the cost of the drug?

REIMBURSEMENT ENVIRONMENT
• How is this product reimbursed?   • Who stands to make or lose money with the new product?   • Are there any elements of reimbursement in this area that are out of the ordinary?
COMPANY NEEDS AND ABILITIES
• How vital is this new product to the future of the company or to a current franchise?   • Will the pricing of this product complicate, or be complicated by, the pricing of other company products?   • What would be the cost to the company of a pricing mistake for this product?   • Is senior management prepared to address controversy if the price is seen by the public as too high?   • Will senior management supply the necessary financial support to make an innovative approach to pricing successful?   • What is more important to the firm, the first or fifth year of sales?   • If you make a pricing mistake, would you rather price too high or too low?
PUBLIC POLICY
• What is the likelihood that the price of this product will attract the attention of the press or of legislators?

and reports that follow a product through its development and into launch. Undertaken as soon as a new product candidate enters the research pipeline, the pricing process helps firms better understand the commercial potential and ability of the compound so that the product can be launched successfully.

Each step of the process requires the cooperation of two or more functional areas, and their work and recommendations should be fully documented. In addition to providing an ongoing record of activities, issues, decisions, and rationales that have influenced the pricing of the product, this documentation can help the firm learn from its mistakes and repeat its successes.

THE PROCESS

The process used to price new products involves ten steps, as summarized in Figure 13.2. Each step is fully described below. At the end of this chapter, you will find several exhibits that are referred to in the text. We have developed these decision-making tools to support the new product pricing process.

Step 1. Estimate Initial Price

The process begins when a new product candidate has been identified. Upon notification of the new product and the specific indications for which it will be developed, pricing and marketing research should collect the information necessary to complete the first section of a document that we call a *pricing plan*. The content of the first section of the pricing plan is the completed *Checklist for the Basic Pricing Model* (see Exhibit A), on which is recorded specific information used to generate an initial price range.

Also covered in the checklist are reimbursement specifics for the disease area and factors that must be considered for every product. Section One of the pricing plan is used to establish the initial price ranges and record pricing assumptions for the product. It is essential that the assumptions used for the development of initial price ranges are recorded in the pricing plan, which will be a living document that is reviewed and updated as new information becomes available.

At this point, the document should be reviewed by members of the pricing, new product planning, and marketing research departments, as well as any individuals whose input is valuable or who may find the information in the document to be of use. The pricing plan should be maintained in and by the pricing department.

FIGURE 13.2 Overview of New Product Pricing Process

Event/Activity	Responsibility	Price Plan Output
Drug Candidate & Indications Identified		
1. Estimate Initial Price	Pricing Marketing Research	**SECTION ONE**
2. Develop Financial Model of Disorder(s)	Health Economics	Report to Pricing and New Product Planning
3. Identify Economic Leverage Points	Health Economics Pricing Marketing Research	Report to Clinical Research
4. Determine Initial Price Ranges and Critical Success Factors	Pricing New Product Planning Marketing Research	**Update SECTION ONE**
5. Test Clinical Assumptions	Clinical Research	Report to New Product Planning
6. Refine Price Ranges	Pricing Product Marketing Marketing Research	**SECTION TWO**
7. Test Price and Value Propositions	Pricing Marketing Research Product Marketing Outside Supplier	Report to Pricing and Product Marketing
8. Develop Pricing Strategy	Pricing Product Marketing Marketing Research	Initial Recommendation to Senior Management
9. Decide Final Price	Pricing Product Marketing Senior Management	**SECTION THREE**
10. Develop Contracting Tactics	Pricing Product Marketing	**SECTION FOUR**
Ongoing Price Management	Pricing Product Management	**PRICE PLAN UPDATES**

EXHIBIT A
SAMPLE CHECKLIST FOR BASIC PRICING MODEL

INDICATION: _____
❏ Mild ❏ Moderate ❏ Severe
(Note: Separate evaluations must be completed for each level of the indication.)

PART 1: Disease State and Product Background
(To be completed by new product planning, pricing, marketing research, and others with relevant knowledge of disorder)

Name: _____
Department: _____
Background/Knowledge of Indication: _____

For the indication listed above, please check the boxes that are most descriptive.

Description of disease state:
❏ Acute/Symptomatic   ❏ Chronic/Symptomatic
❏ Chronic/Asymptomatic

Time from diagnosis to mortality:
❏ Less than 6 months   ❏ 6 months to 2 years
❏ 2 to 5 years   ❏ 5 to 9 years
❏ 10 or more years/not fatal

Period of disease progression to end state:
❏ Less than 6 months   ❏ 6 months to 2 years
❏ 2 to 5 years   ❏ 5 to 9 years
❏ 10 or more years/not progressive

Treatment duration:
❏ 1 day/dose   ❏ Less than 1 year
❏ 1 to 2 years   ❏ More than 2 years

Severity of disease (impact on survival or functional status):
❏ Critical ❏ Severe ❏ Moderate ❏ Mild

Product will be used to:
❏ Treat disease/symptoms
❏ Prevent disease or disease progression

Product will be used:
❏ On an acute/episodic basis
❏ As chronic therapy

PART 2: Environmental Factors
(To be completed by pricing)

For medications used in this disorder, what is the current payer mix?

Private Third Party	_____%
Medicaid	_____%
Medicare	_____%
Cash	_____%

For nonpharmaceutical treatments, what is the payer mix?

Private Third Party	_____%
Medicaid	_____%
Medicare	_____%
Cash	_____%

Does this drug candidate have the potential to shift the payer mix? If so, how?

_____
_____
_____
_____
_____

To what degree will each of the following factors affect the pricing decision? (A 7 indicates that special attention should be paid to a factor, while a 1 indicates that a factor can be reasonably ignored in reaching the final pricing decision.)

Factor	Not Important	Highly Critical	Rationale for Score
Current or anticipated competition	1 2 3 4 5 6 7		
Disease characteristics	1 2 3 4 5 6 7		
Patient characteristics or considerations	1 2 3 4 5 6 7		
Social and economic value of therapy	1 2 3 4 5 6 7		
Clinician decision-making considerations	1 2 3 4 5 6 7		
Reimbursement environment	1 2 3 4 5 6 7		
Importance of product to company	1 2 3 4 5 6 7		
Willingness of company to support special issues	1 2 3 4 5 6 7		
Potential for public policy or public relations problems	1 2 3 4 5 6 7		

Are there any other special considerations or critical issues that must be addressed?

_____

_____

_____

_____

_____

Step 2. Develop Financial Model of the Disorder(s)

A financial model of the disease helps fine-tune pricing assumptions and provides critical input into the clinical development process to ensure that the clinical protocols are designed to extract the greatest commercial potential from the product. The *Checklist for the Financial Model of Indication(s)* (see Exhibit B) is completed by the knowledgeable individuals, usually from the health economics department with assistance from pricing, marketing research, and other departments. Separate checklists should be prepared for each indication and dosage level if the product is likely to be used for more than one indication and/or at different dosage levels for the same indication (e.g., mild, moderate, and severe). Copies of the completed checklist are maintained by the pricing department.

The checklist provides a greater understanding of the costs associated with the disorder and identifies areas and types of cost where the product has the greatest potential to generate cost savings for payers and patients. For example, if a disorder currently requires a significant amount of laboratory testing, a new product that can reduce or eliminate the need for tests offers the potential for savings and thus provides flexibility for pricing. Similarly, some indications are well treated, but the incidence of side effects is sufficiently high to warrant special attention. In such cases, to achieve differentiation and command a premium over current choices, a new drug must reduce side effects.

EXHIBIT B
SAMPLE DATA FORM FOR FINANCIAL MODEL
OF INDICATION(S)

(To be assembled by health economics with input from pricing, new product planning, and marketing research)

INDICATION: _____

❏ Mild   ❏ Moderate   ❏ Severe

(Note: Separate evaluations must be completed for each level of the indication.)

- Which entities bear the current costs of treatment for this indication? (e.g., hospitals, patients, Medicare, HMOs)
- What is the current mix of costs associated with this disorder? (e.g., direct/indirect, drug/inpatient/MD/other)
- Which of these are the major sources of cost?
- Are these costs usually episodic (short term), or are they born over a long period of time?
- What is the potential for the current drug (candidate) to affect these major sources of cost?

EXAMPLE: BASIC FINANCIAL INFORMATION FOR DVT PROPHYLAXIS

Treatment Event*	Warfarin	Heparin	Enoxaparin
Major Bleed	$100,476	$173,042	$114,431
Proximal DVT	$69,700	$66,912	$27,880
Distal DVT	$163,400	$45,580	$17,200
Minor Bleed	$13,041	$10,773	$15,498
Nonfatal PE	$175,770	$123,690	$6,510
Total	$522,387	$419,997	$181,519

*Based on treating complications only in 1,000 patients Step 3. Identify Economic Leverage Points

The financial model of the disorder is a basic first-level pharma-coeconomics model used to identify the *economic leverage points* that will allow the product to drive value into the marketplace and the firm to capture value with higher prices. These leverage points should be reflected in clinical trial protocols that include the endpoints identified. The firm should then monitor the progress of the product and its success in achieving the commercially relevant endpoints. Failure to achieve these endpoints would indicate a reduction of the commercial potential of the product.

Step 4. Determine Initial Price Ranges and Critical Success Factors

After the financial model is complete and the economic leverage points have been identified, an analysis will be performed and a report prepared to incorporate this new knowledge into the pricing process. The leverage points identified by health economics—the critical success factors—will enable the product to be differentiated and command higher premiums. These factors, together with financial and economic information gathered in the process of identifying them, will be used to refine the initial pricing assumptions. (A more complete discussion of the pricing of products with multiple indications is presented later in this chapter.)

Should the product have the potential for use in multiple indications, those with the greatest pricing potential (which is determined by multiplying highest price by quantity) should be identified and given priority.

Once this information is gathered and incorporated into Section One of the price plan, senior managers should sign a cover sheet, indicating that the document is official and complete.

Step 5. Test Clinical Assumptions

In most cases, no further work can be done until information on the product's clinical performance becomes available. During this step, the clinical studies will be used to gather safety and efficacy data. This data will be measured against the product's critical success factors.

Step 6. Refine Price Ranges

After results from initial trials have been determined, the price ranges used for planning must be revisited. Pricing, product marketing, and marketing research will develop a plan to complete the pricing process based on Section One of the price plan and the information gathered in clinical trials. During this step, Section Two will be produced. Section Two of the price plan is a detailed list of the steps that must be taken to achieve a final price recommendation, including:

- Refining and updating assumptions for prices used to date
- Assessing the product's success (or failure) in meeting the critical success factors determined earlier
- Identifying key gaps in information (What additional information is needed to ensure a good decision?)
- Defining any changes in the factors addressed in the basic pricing checklist.

In addition to this information, Section Two will include the pricing research plan, which will list—and justify—the kinds and amount of pricing research that will be needed to develop complete pricing recommendations. Research audiences, methods, and desired information will be listed in this document, together with the likely product profile(s) that will be tested. As with Section One, this section, when completed, should be signed by the appropriate managers and maintained in and by the pricing department.

Step 7. Test Price and Value Propositions

Pricing research, if it is to be performed, is now undertaken. The objectives of the research should be to:

- Determine the role that price plays in the decision(s) to prescribe, consume, dispense, or purchase the product
- Determine what steps, if any, need to be taken to ensure adequate reimbursement for the product
- Identify the groups or individuals for whom special programs or other activities would be undertaken to ensure the firm's ability to capture fully the value of the new product in the price charged.

In addition, any pharmacoeconomic work that has been done so far should be examined for guidance in further pricing analysis. Ideally, the results of economic studies should be used in developing the product profiles that will be used in pricing research.

Step 8. Develop Pricing Strategy

The information collected thus far will provide essential guidance in developing the pricing strategy. Developing pricing strategy statements is more than just an exercise in creativity. The strategy statement guides all pricing actions, both initial and subsequent. Far too often, a price is set and then left to be "managed" by others. The result is often that the original strategic idea is lost. The pricing strategy statement helps to prevent this from happening.

The pricing strategy should be developed in concert with the overall marketing strategy for the product. The strategy involves more than simply selecting a price. Rather, it should include specific statements indicating how the marketing and pricing strategies are related, what actions would be taken to ensure the success of the strategy, and what events might indicate the need for a change in the strategy.

Of necessity, each product requires a unique pricing strategy that reflects marketing and pricing research, additional competitive and payer analysis, and pharmacoeconomic information gathered for the specific indication. The following example illustrates a pricing strategy statement for one type of product:

> The price of Panacea™ has been set to communicate the high value of the product. The communication of this value will be supported with the publication and dissemination of the results of the pharmacoeconomic study conducted by major universities that demonstrated Panacea's ability to reduce the cost of treatment by over $20,000 after taking its price into account. This price will be maintained, and no discounts or other special considerations will be offered, unless and until a similar or better product enters the market at a price at least 15% below the price of Panacea and captures at least 25% of the market. (See Exhibit C for additional examples.)

Step 9. Decide Final Price

Deciding the final price involves selecting prices to charge for each form of the product in accordance with the pricing strategy. Final price(s) are included in Section Three of the pricing plan, which will serve as a record of the final pricing decision. In addition to a complete price list of all product forms, Section Three includes a statement describing the strategy and the critical assumptions and information that drove the development of the strategy. This information will include highlights of the findings of marketing and

EXHIBIT C
SAMPLE PRICING STRATEGY STATEMENTS

For a Unique New Technology

The price of Panacea™ has been set to communicate the high value of the product. The communication of this value will be supported with the publication and dissemination of the results of the pharmacoeconomic study conducted by major universities that demonstrated Panacea's ability to reduce the cost of treatment by over $20,000 after taking its price into account. This price will be maintained, and no discounts or other special considerations will be offered, unless and until a similar or better product enters the market at a price at least 15% below the price of Panacea and captures at least 15% of the market.

For a "Me Too" Product

Because Alsomab™ does not provide significant new advantages over the market leaders, and the company has chosen not to provide heavy promotional support, a lower price will be used as a principal appeal for Alsomab. Alsomab's price will be set at 15% below that of Primotec™, the market leader. Contracts with managed care and GPO groups will reflect a greater level of discount: between 20% and 30% below the net price offered by Primotec. We will meet or beat any competitive price to gain or retain sales.

For a Major, But Not Leading, Product

The price of Gudinuff™ will be set to be consistent with our marketing strategy, which is to be among the top three products in the market. To retain this position, the retail price of Gudinuff will be within 3% to 5% of the market share leader, and contract prices will not be more than 5% below those of either of the two leading products. Senior management must be consulted if the price falls below that charged to Gorilla Care, our largest MCO customer.

For a Market Leader

PrimoPen™ will be priced above any and all competitors. Our price will be at least 20% higher than any competitor in all markets. PrimoPen™ will not be sold at prices equal to or below those of any direct competitor, including A, B, C, and D. Customers who insist that the price be lower than or equal to a competitive offering will be informed of this policy and provided the opportunity to purchase PrimoPen™ at the prices we quote and no less. A competitive price offering will not be matched or beaten and a competitor's list price higher than ours will not be tolerated unless our leadership role in the market deteriorates significantly and our share falls below 40%.

economic studies that support the decision and a series of analyses that examine the likely impact of setting prices both higher and lower than the final recommended price. This allows decision makers to understand the implications and trade-offs involved in the selection of those specific prices.

Again, Section Three will be signed off by the senior managers whose authority is necessary for the approval of the final prices.

Step 10. Develop Contracting Tactics

Entering into contracts with large buyers should not be considered an automatic activity with each new product. Contracts should be negotiated and agreed to only when their execution is in the best interests of the product and the firm. When undertaken, contracts should be developed that complement the pricing strategy. Contracts should be written and price concessions made *only* when absolutely necessary to achieving marketing goals—and all contracts should be consistent with the pricing strategy.

Ongoing Price Management

Winston Churchill once said, "Plans are nothing, planning is everything," and so it is with pricing. Regardless of the research performed, the analyses conducted, and the thought and work put into the development of a pricing strategy, changes in the external or internal environment may necessitate a change in pricing strategy. The assumptions and information that drove the strategy must be revalidated periodically. Should major changes occur in the market or in the firm, the strategy must be reconsidered.

PRICING AND PRODUCT DIFFERENTIATION FOR THE SAME MOLECULE

The pricing of pharmaceuticals is complex, risky, and difficult. In situations that are more complex than usual, the task can be quite daunting. Among the most difficult pricing situations is one where the firm is faced with multiple opportunities for a single agent. Although the problems in this area are not restricted to price, the pricing decision in this situation can determine which indications are pursued and the ultimate development plan for the product. When there are disparate indications that can capture different levels of value, the ability to price the product to capture those differences in value can be quite restricted. To our knowledge, it is not possible to vary the price charged for a pharmaceutical product for different uses without altering the brand or the form to bring about an actual product difference. Some firms have established, and received approval for, different brands of the same compound targeted to different indications. However, when the doses are essentially the same, the firms have been unable or unwilling to discriminate in price.

What can be done in this situation? The greater the difference between the products used for each indication, the greater the ability of the firm to set and maintain different prices. Differences in brand, formulation, and daily dose can provide some ability to vary price for the same molecule. These differences, with a summary of their pricing implications, are listed in Figure 13.3.

Each basis for differentiation for a compound brings unique levels of ability to set and maintain price differentials. Differences in formulation provide the greatest potential for pricing discrimination, while marketing distinct brands of the same compound for separate indications may provide some differential, especially if there is a separate dosage regimen for each indication. The level of differentiation ultimately determines the level of defensible price discrimination. As noted in the figure, unique brand identities, distinct product formulations, and different dosing regimens, or a combination of these options, may allow pharmaceutical manufacturers to charge differential prices for the same compound in unique indications.

Brand Identity

Several manufacturers have marketed two separate brands of the same molecular entity but for different indications, including Wellbutrin SR® and Zyban® from GlaxoSmithKline, which are used for depression and smoking cessation, and Eli Lilly's Prozac for depression and Sarafem® for premenstrual dysphoric disorder. In both cases, the products were available at the same strengths in the same form. For example, Wellbutrin SR was available in 150mg tablets in 60 tablet quantities, as was Zyban. In both the Lilly Prozac

FIGURE 13.3 Basis for Price Differentiation for a Product with Multiple Indications

BRAND IDENTITY	DOSING REGIMEN	PRODUCT FORMULATION	IMPLICATIONS FOR DIFFERENTIAL PRICING
Same	Same	Same	Impossible to price differently
	Different	Same	Difficult but not impossible, depending on dosage relationship
	Same	Different	Less difficulty in setting differentials, but challenges are likely
	Different	Different	Easy to accomplish, depending on formulation differences
Different	Same	Same	Minor price differences maintainable
	Different	Same	Difficult but not impossible, depending on dosage relationship
	Same	Different	Less difficulty in setting differentials, and challenges are less likely than with the same brand
	Different	Different	Ideal for price differentiation

case and the Glaxo Wellbutrin SR case, the extension into unique brands occurred at prices in parity to the initial brand.

In these cases, the same manufacturer controlled the price of each brand. Situations have occurred in pharmaceutical markets where different brands of the same compound have been available from different manufacturers targeting different indications. Amgen's Epogen and Ortho's Procrit had the same indications, but Epogen was targeted for anemia associated with dialysis and Procrit for anemia associated with chemotherapy. In this case, Amgen attempted to create a different price for its product but was ultimately unsuccessful.

Product Formulation

Genuine formulation changes are a completely different matter from mere changes in brand name. Janssen's Risperdal was an oral formulation of an atypical antipsychotic. Recently, Janssen launched Risperdal Consta®, an intramuscular injection of risperidone for depot delivery of the antipsychotic. This enables Risperdal to be used in noncompliant patients. Janssen's per milligram price for Risperdal Consta was set at a significant premium over the price for the oral formulation—more than 100% greater.

GlaxoSmithKline's Imitrex® (sumatriptan) migraine therapy is available in multiple forms: injectable, nasal spray, and oral. Each form has a different per milligram price. Both per milligram and per dose, prices of Imitrex injectable are greater than the prices of Imitrex nasal spray, which are greater than the prices for Imitrex oral.

Dosage/Dosing Regimen

Pharmaceutical manufacturers have often sought to change the dosing regimen through line extensions. Historically, this has involved an extended-release product that moves dosing from oral

216

daily dosage form to oral weekly dosing. Eli Lilly changed the dosage regimen for Prozac from daily to weekly, launching Prozac Weekly at a per milligram premium to Prozac 20mg capsules. Per day prices, however, were roughly at parity to the Prozac 20mg capsules. Similar to Lilly, Merck extended its Fosamax® product from a daily oral dose to a weekly dose. The Fosamax 70mg weekly dose was launched at a parity price to the daily dose.

Combination Strategies

Firms can achieve price differentiation for the same molecule through a combination of changes in brand name, formulation, and dosing. For example, the two Merck brands of finasteride, Proscar® (for the treatment of benign prostatic hypertrophy) and Propecia (for the treatment of male pattern baldness), were launched at different strengths for the conditions, Proscar at 5mg orally and Propecia at 1mg orally. Propecia was launched at a sizable premium over Proscar on a per milligram basis.

BUILDING THE MARKET

Pharmaceutical marketing history shows that price differentiation between two indications for the same chemical compound is achievable. However, history also demonstrates that markets are more willing to accept price differentiation when the final branded products are markedly different. Differences in brand names alone are unlikely to generate defensible price differences. Those firms with the greatest success in establishing and defending price differences launched unique brands with unique dosing and formulations. In these situations, although the parent compound was the same, the end result was hardly comparable across brands. Therefore, a company with a chemical compound that has potential multiple disparate indications should determine the market it desires and then develop a strategy to achieve the goals it has set. This strategy should be based on three issues: timing, resources, and market opportunity.

Timing

Ideally, when marketing a chemical compound for multiple indications with multiple price points, a firm should launch the compound for one indication first and launch it for subsequent indications later. Parallel timelines with unique beginning and ending dates are developed using information from the approval process for Brand A, such as lowest effective dose and highest safe dose. The trials for Brand B can then be structured to demonstrate that Brand B is clearly distinguished from Brand A and to justify a different price. However, if the approval process for Brand B has progressed significantly beyond the ability to modify formulations or dosing, then the goal becomes to make the best of the situation.

The relationship between development timelines and product strategy is summarized in Figure 13.4. As the figure shows, the further the second brand has progressed in clinical development at the point of approval for the first brand, the more restricted a company's strategic choices become.

Resources

A strategy that employs multiple approval timelines must weigh anticipated market opportunity against available resources. Clinical trials are costly and risky.

Market Opportunity

It is important to understand the market opportunity for each available indication. This includes forecasted unit sales and anticipated

FIGURE 13.4 EFFECT OF TIMING
ON STRATEGIC OPTIONS

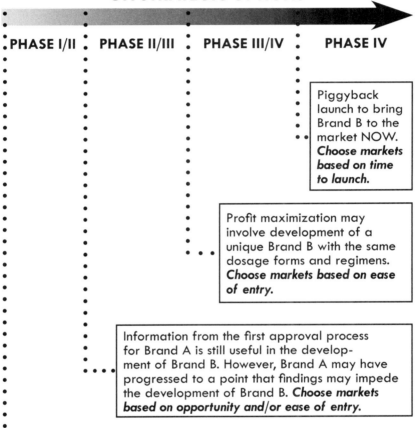

PHASE I/II   PHASE II/III   PHASE III/IV   PHASE IV

> Piggyback launch to bring Brand B to the market NOW. *Choose markets based on time to launch.*

> Profit maximization may involve development of a unique Brand B with the same dosage forms and regimens. *Choose markets based on ease of entry.*

> Information from the first approval process for Brand A is still useful in the development of Brand B. However, Brand A may have progressed to a point that findings may impede the development of Brand B. *Choose markets based on opportunity and/or ease of entry.*

> Information from the first approval process for Brand A, such as lowest effective dose and highest safe dose, can be used to structure the trails for the second approval process so that Brand B can have a level of distinction from Brand A that allows price differntiation. *Choose markets based on opportunity.*

competition. No forecast is 100% accurate, but, as long as steps are taken to ensure the accuracy of assumptions used in the model, forecasts can be extremely useful decision-making tools. In this light, a forecasted market opportunity for different indications can help a manufacturer choose the appropriate options for the approval process.

CASE STUDIES

The following cases illustrate some of the factors that influence a manufacturer's ability to obtain different prices for a single compound that has been approved for different indications.

Prozac and Sarafem

Eli Lilly launched its drug for depression, Prozac, in January 1988. The drug reached its peak sales in December 2000 with $2.8 billion. In August 2001, total sales decreased due to the launch of generic fluoxetine. Before Prozac went generic, Lilly adopted two different strategies to attain more earnings. The first strategy was to launch the same active ingredient, fluoxetine, in the same dosage and formulation for a different indication. In August 2000, Lilly launched Sarafem for premenstrual dysphoric disorder (PMDD). Sarafem was launched at a parity price to Prozac. The second strategy was to launch a line extension with an extended-release form of Prozac called Prozac Weekly™ in March 2001. Prozac Weekly was priced at a premium on a per milligram basis, but the per-day price is equal to the price charged for Prozac 20mg.

The dollar sales for Sarafem and Prozac Weekly are very similar. Prozac Weekly was priced at a premium on a per milligram basis. Through a different formulation and a different brand name, Lilly was able to achieve a different price for the same active ingredient.

Wellbutrin and Zyban

The same situation is found with GlaxoSmithKline's Wellbutrin for depression and Zyban for smoking cessation. Wellbutrin was launched in December 1985. A sustained-release version for twice-a-day dosing was launched as a line extension in 1996; a second line extension, an extended-release version for once-a-day dosing, was launched in 2003. The generic form of bupropion was launched in November 1999. In June 1997, GSK launched a second brand with the same ingredient. Zyban is indicated for smoking cessation and was launched at the same dosage and the same price as Wellbutrin SR. Both drugs were available in 150mg tablets in 60 tablet quantities. As soon as GSK came out with a new formulation for bupropion in a once-daily form, it was sold at a premium per milligram price as Wellbutrin XL.

Both these cases show that justifying a price premium for one indication over another takes more than just a different brand name. A good negative example for this is the active ingredient epoetin alfa (EPO). As mentioned previously, EPO is sold by two different companies for the same indication but for two different patient groups: Amgen's Epogen for anemia associated with dialysis and Ortho's Procrit for anemia associated with chemotherapy. Amgen attempted to price its drug differently from Procrit, but this price differential was unsustainable and the subject of a license violation lawsuit between Amgen and Ortho.

Proscar and Propecia

If simply having a different brand name does not allow the company to defend a price difference, the previously mentioned case of Proscar and Propecia shows that a different dosage seems to be sufficient to sustain a price premium. This may eliminate the need to invest in a more expensive change in formulation.

Proscar was launched in March 1997 for benign prostatic hypertrophy. Since then, its sales have been rising continuously. In January 1998, just 9 months after the launch of Proscar, Merck introduced Propecia for male pattern baldness. The company managed to market the same ingredient, finasteride, under two different brand names at two different dosage strengths. Under the name Proscar the company sells a 5mg tablet, while under the name Propecia it sells a 1mg tablet at a premium per milligram price. Proscar's price in 2003 was $86.26 AWP for 30 tablets of 5mg strength. For the same number of tablets with 1mg active ingredient, Propecia's price was $54.69 AWP. In the German market, the prices of the two drugs are closer to each other on a per tablet basis, making the premium for Propecia even higher.

The sales of both drugs grew at a steady pace. More than half of the total finasteride sales in 2003 dollars were the result of Proscar prescriptions. But a substantial amount, about one third, came from Propecia sales. At a similar price Propecia had 5 times less active ingredient. Just by changing the dosage, Merck was able to charge a premium price for Propecia.

These cases demonstrate that achieving different prices for different indications is possible, but it requires product differentiation—and the greater the product differentiation, the greater the potential for differentiation in price.

Chapter 14

Generic Markets

Generic-drug companies usually have lower research and development costs (relative to sales) than the big pharmaceutical houses. Perhaps the biggest drawback to this business are the legal costs that generic companies often encounter when challenging well-entrenched branded drugs.
—Forbes Magazine

Since the early 1980s, all states have passed laws that allow for, or even require, generic substitution by pharmacists. These laws were euphemistically referred to as "drug product selection" rules. Prior to the promulgation of these laws, generic substitution in most states required that the prescription be written for the generic name of the compound. After the passage of the generic substitution laws, most states would legally force the brand to be dispensed only if the physician specifically noted on the prescription "brand medically necessary," "do not substitute," or DAW (dispense as written). Over time, the numbers of prescriptions that prevent substitution have declined to the point of irrelevance in the marketplace.

With the advent of managed care, prescribers who sought to block generic substitution were challenged to support their decisions. Most plans simply forced prescribers to submit and allow substitution. At the same time, payers put financial incentives in place to promote generic substitution, offering pharmacists higher dispensing fees and even bonuses for generic substitution. Some major pharmacy chains also pay bonuses to staff pharmacists for achieving or exceeding a specific rate of generic use and have made generic substitution rates a performance criterion by which management of the pharmacy is judged.

As more pharmacies and pharmacy systems automated the processing of prescriptions, online adjudication of prescriptions became possible, and generic substitution itself became automated. The system is practically at the point where generic substitution is unconscious, occurring without any real consideration by prescribers or pharmacists. The system can be said to "suck" generics into itself, to the point that their mere availability is enough to generate, even guarantee, their use. In recent years, this has become problematic because, as discussed later, some generic products have actually come to market at prices higher than those of the branded drug, causing payers to lose money because of the automated nature of the system.

However, rather than conceding defeat prematurely, pricing professionals should take a moment to assess the situation rationally. Yes, a branded product cannot beat its generic competitor on price; the generics industry is structured so that products can be sold as close to cost as possible. Yes, the prescription and distribution systems are set up in a way to encourage and financially incentivize the use of generics. But…the impact of a generic entry on the entire category should not be overstated and should not unduly influence pricing decisions.

GENERIC PRICING PRINCIPLES AND BEHAVIOR

The pricing of generic drugs takes place at several levels, which complicates any analysis of the segment. Manufacturer prices are driven by one set of principles and objectives, while the pricing activities of wholesalers and retailers are driven by different forces.

Each, however, is important in understanding the way the market works.

Generic Manufacturers

Upon approval of a generic product, the first manufacturer to announce an AWP essentially establishes that figure for all other generics. Once the first AWP is announced, others appear to copy it. In recent years, the AWP for generics is typically 10% less than for the branded product, although larger differences of about 20% have been observed. The actual prices charged by generic manufacturers are lower than the AWP—usually much lower. Most manufacturers meet competitive offers, making generic prices very similar within a molecular entity, regardless of manufacturer. The prices eventually settle out quite low relative to the brand.

The principal driver of the actual prices charged by generic manufacturers is the number of competing generic products. Because the main mode of competition among generic manufacturers is price, it is essential that a manufacturer stay price competitive. Manufacturers must match (or nearly match) every competitive offer. Thus, they are at the mercy of their competitors when it comes to price. When a manufacturer has exclusivity with its generic product due to specific patent issues (as with Schwarz Pharma and omeprazole) or to the 180-day exclusivity awarded for a successful patent challenge (as in the case of Barr and fluoxetine), the manufacturer will set and maintain a price (WAC) that is high, usually within 25% of the brand price. When a second competitor is present, it is likely that the price will remain high because both recognize that they earn more money by maintaining the higher prices. Entry of a third competitor into a generic market usually guarantees that the price will erode quickly.

The value of the 180-day period of exclusivity in competition among generics is illustrated by Barr's experience with fluoxetine (Prozac). During Barr's 180-day exclusivity period for 20mg fluoxetine, the company had $400 million in sales of the product. After Barr's exclusivity expired and it was forced to compete with other suppliers, Barr's net sales in the next 6 months dropped to $4 million. This was due to a combination of price erosion (about 95%) and unit losses to competitors.

The effect of competition from multiple suppliers can be seen in two extreme cases of very rapid price erosion: fluconazole (Diflucan®) and lisinopril (Prinivil/Zestril). On the first day of the availability of generic fluconazole, there were reportedly up to 12 manufacturers with approved products, and the price eroded by a reported 95% within 8 hours of availability of a generic. The anticipated price erosion for lisinopril was so high that at least one manufacturer simply chose to provide its product free of charge to customers who bought other products. Often firms will pre-book sales with competitive price guarantees to ensure they will at least be able to move out the product they are producing.

It is important to understand that the business imperative for a generic manufacturer is to operate its production facility at full capacity. Unit sales are the key to effective business management for generic firms because more complete use of the fixed costs of their manufacturing facilities reduces the overall costs of production for all products. Theirs is a business driven by cost accounting and production capacity, not market share. The strategy of running at capacity both enables and requires them to out-compete branded firms when it comes to price. Selling at or even below cost makes no long-term sense for a branded manufacturer, but it could provide a clear strategic advantage to a generic firm.

Unit sales are so important that generic manufacturers will match competitive offers, through pre-booking and other actions, even before they have product to sell. The rapid erosion of prices in this market has been termed "price rot" by distributors, whose main worry is buying before the prices hit the bottom. Generic manufacturers protect their customers from this by making retro-active price adjustments. Commonly, for the first month or more of a product's availability from multiple sources, the initial invoices lack "true" prices. Generic manufacturers handle the transaction by simply waiting until the "price rot" has bottomed out before sending a "trued up" invoice.

It is indisputable that a generic competitor can devastate its branded predecessor. Twenty years ago, a generic would take 10% to 25% of the sales of a brand in its first year. Now a brand can lose as much as 90% of its business to generics in the first month or two of generic availability—primarily because of automated generic substitution, the generic industry's ability and willingness to sell at or near cost, and the profit potential reimbursement provides retail pharmacies. Figure 14.1 illustrates the difficulty a branded product faces when a generic competitor enters the market.

Wholesalers and Distributors

Wholesalers and distributors are the most common customers of generic firms. Although some large chains do purchase directly from some generic manufacturers, most rely on some level of intermediary. Distributors' objectives for generics are twofold: to get the lowest price and to get the most consistent supply. All things being equal, distributors and other parties further along the distribution chain would prefer to purchase and sell the same manufacturer's product. This simplifies inventory, ordering, and customer relations.

Most distributors will pass the bulk of the savings from generics on to their own customers. Many will wait until "trued" invoices are received from manufacturers before sending their own invoices to customers, while others will make adjustments after the fact through credit memos and other means. They do not, however, charge all customers the same prices. Wholesalers, especially full-line whole-salers, will offer their best customers the lowest prices. Their "best"

FIGURE 14.1 Pricing Behavior of Generic Products

Product	Date of First Generic	Brand Price (AWP per dose) at Expiration	AWP of 1st Generic Relative to Brand
Zestril 2.5mg	Jul-02	$0.71	90%
Zestril 5mg	Jul-02	$1.07	90%
Zestril 10mg	Jul-02	$1.11	90%
Zestril 20mg	Jul-02	$1.18	90%
Zestril 30mg	Jul-02	$1.68	90%
Zestril 40mg	Jul-02	$1.73	90%
Prozac 10mg cap	Jan-02	$2.89	95%
Prozac 20mg cap	Jan-02	$2.96	90%
Vasotec 2.5mg	Aug-00	$0.89	90%
Vasotec 5mg	Aug-00	$1.13	90%
Vasotec 10mg	Aug-00	$1.19	90%
Vasotec 20mg	Aug-00	$1.69	90%
Diflucan 50mg	Jul-04	$6.53	85%
Diflucan 100mg	Jul-04	$9.78	86%
Diflucan 200mg	Jul-04	$16.00	90%
Paxil 10mg	Sept-03	$2.81	83%
Paxil 20mg	Sept-03	$2.94	83%

Source: Analy$ource and Federal Supply Schedule, February, 2009

# Generics in 1st Month	Federal MAC Price	Actual Current Generic Cost Per Dose	Current Brand WAC Per Dose	Generic Price as a % of Brand Price
8	$0.08	$0.02	$1.07	2%
9	$0.05	$0.02	$1.28	2%
9	$0.07	$0.03	$1.32	2%
9	$0.08	$0.05	$1.42	4%
8	$0.16	$0.08	$2.00	4%
9	$0.15	$0.07	$2.07	3%
1	$0.14	$0.07	$5.12	1%
1	$0.15	$0.08	$5.25	2%
4	$0.05	$0.44	$0.50	88%
5	$0.06	$0.49	$0.58	84%
5	$0.07	$0.57	$0.64	89%
5	$0.09	$0.79	$0.91	87%
2	n/a	$5.17	$6.36	81%
4	n/a	$8.12	$9.99	81%
4	n/a	$13.30	$16.34	81%
1	$0.34	$2.08	$88.57	2%
1	$0.36	$2.17	$92.42	28%

customers are often those who participate in an "autosub" program, an agreement to accept whatever generic manufacturer's product the wholesaler uses to fill an order. Because wholesalers would prefer to maintain a consistent offering, they will try to ensure a continuous supply from one manufacturer. The manufacturer can accomplish this by charging different prices for the same product to the same wholesaler, providing a discount for products included in autosub programs. These pricing differentials are accomplished through rebates.

As with branded products sold through contracts, wholesalers are also involved with chargebacks for generic drugs, but these chargebacks for generics are paid based on manufacturer contracts with retailers, rather than hospitals or their buying groups.

Retail Pharmacies

More than any other party in the flow of generic drugs, retail pharmacies work to "buy low and sell high." Initial retail pricing is based, to date, on the AWP set for the generic. The AWP is usually set at a slight discount to the brand, but for private third-party payers and some Medicaid programs, a greater deduction from AWP is taken for generics than for brands after reimbursement is calculated. For example, a pharmacy may sign a contract with a PBM that reimburses brands at *AWP − 17% + $2.25 dispensing fee* and generics at *AWP − 40% + $4.25 dispensing fee*. Because price erosion for generics is so rapid and deep, there is seldom *any* relationship between retail prices to pharmacies' customers and pharmacies' own costs for generic drugs. Price fluctuation for generics can be so large and so common that Snopes.com, an Internet Web site for "urban legends," devoted a page to documenting these large discrepancies in price, including fluoxetine, which, in a single metropolitan area, could cost as little as $9.69/month or as much as $92.24/month.

At some point, many payers will establish a MAC price (maximum allowable cost) for a specific generic. This results in a substantial reduction in reimbursement for the generic product, but, even then, generics remain a profitable line of business for retail pharmacies, almost always more profitable than if pharmacies had dispensed the brand until a MAC price is established.

Once a MAC price has been set, the immense profits from generic substitution are limited, but most MAC prices still allow pharmacists a healthy profit margin. Currently, the federal MAC price for an albuterol inhaler is $16, while the current acquisition price is less than $4. The federal MAC for fluoxetine is $25.20 per 100, but pharmacists can purchase it for approximately $3.50 per 100. Although most PBMs will set MAC prices lower than the government, the prices are still higher than a pharmacist's acquisition cost, and, with the added dispensing fee that is often used to promote generic substitution, dispensing generics remains a profitable line of business for retail pharmacies.

Potential changes to the reimbursement for generics, including moving to "AMP" pricing, which is under consideration by Congress as this book goes to press, could have profound implications for retail pharmacies when it comes to generics. Should an AMP- or ASP-based reimbursement scheme take effect, many retail pharmacies would see their businesses become unprofitable and, unfortunately for their customers, find it necessary to close.

Payers

Because of the substantial potential savings to payers from the use of generics, virtually all mandate generic substitution for branded products. Most payers are aware of the profit potential for retailers from generics, and many would argue that the extra profit is built into the system to encourage generic substitution. There is so much money to be saved by encouraging generic utilization that, even in cases where the payer is "losing" money when paying for a sole-source generic product (e.g., generic Prilosec), many payers do not try to reverse the system.

As mentioned previously, the basis for reimbursement of generics is usually different from brands. A typical branded pharmaceutical may be reimbursed by a payer at *AWP – 17% plus a dispensing fee of $2.50*. That same plan would reimburse a generic prescription at *AWP – 40%* plus a fee that is sometimes higher than that for the brand.

Effect of Generics on the Drug Class

To date, except in some fairly unique cases, when a brand loses patent protection in the US market, the generics will take most of the unit sales in a short period of time because of automatic substitution and generic incentives and mandates. However, for the most part, other brands in the same class with different molecular makeups remain relatively unaffected. Generics, in general, devastate the sales *only* of the originator brand.

There is a misconception that the entrance of a generic into a market will affect the shares and use of other products in the category as well. We have not found this to be true in most cases. The misconception probably stems from a misinterpretation of prescription share data. We do find the new prescription (NRx) share of other products will drop in the first few months of generic availability for a competing compound, but this is a data anomaly based on the way prescriptions must be recorded. Most new generic prescriptions are, in fact, refills of branded products that are now filled with a generic. Because a "new" product—the generic—is being used, a new prescription must be generated. This artificially increases the number of "new" prescriptions for the compound and reduces the NRx share of other products in the category. Examination of the total prescription shares (TRx) will show no effect on other products. A review of the total prescription data will show that any bump in prescription share for the generic is not there or is only temporary. In fact, the total share of sustained-release diltiazem *decreased* after promotion for the product ceased. Examinations of

FIGURE 14.2 Statin Market Through 2007

Effect of Simvastatin on Cholesterol Market through 2007

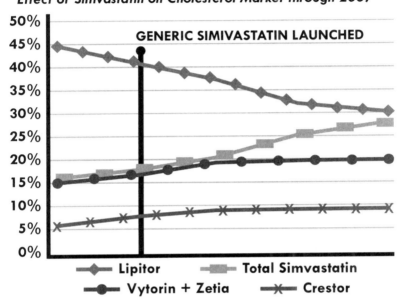

Source: IMS Health, IMS Dataview™, [1/06-12/07]

other markets show similar results: generic drugs compete with their own molecule and not across the category.

These and other examinations of market shares within a market before and after a brand loses exclusivity show that market shares tend to follow their pre-generic trend after generics enter. When lisinopril and enalapril generics launched in the angiotensin converting enzyme (ACE) inhibitor market, the remaining single-source agents held their shares.

It remains to be seen whether this tendency of generics not to affect other brands continues. Many arguments can be made that certain forces will eventually change this dynamic, but these forces, particularly very active interventions by payers and physicians prescribing more of a product after it loses patent than before, have been building for a decade and little has happened yet. The generics most recently entering the market have made the problem for payers somewhat worse because they have used the 180-day period of exclusivity as their "window of opportunity"—the only time when they can generate very high profits. This has resulted in *increased* costs for payers.

When a generic for Prilosec (omeprazole) entered the market, it was the most expensive proton pump inhibitor (PPI) on the market for the payer. The PPI market had traditionally been a competitive one, and managed care organizations (MCOs) and Medicaid had been receiving discounts and rebates on virtually all of the brands. The generic version set a price very close to that of Prilosec and provided no discounts. Payers' spending on PPIs went up because the generic cost to the plan was so much more after accounting for rebates and patient co-pays. And because payers, both public and private, had set in place automatic substitution systems which drove the use of the generic omeprazole, they were initially helpless to stop the spending increase.

Since then, the prices of the generic omeprazoles have dropped to a great extent because several other suppliers have entered the market. Before those new omeprazoles became available, however, some private PBMs actually required prior authorization for the generic and placed it on the third formulary tier while encouraging the use of branded PPIs. Only recently have managed care plans attempted, through letters to members, to get patients to request generic omeprazole in lieu of branded PPIs. But this situation could repeat itself with other generics in the future, changing the very nature of substitution.

Are Generics Turning a Page?

More recently, the availability of generic simvastatin (Zocor) has greatly affected the statin market. The share of Lipitor (atorvastatin) has decreased in the face of lower cost alternatives—not precipitously, but certainly enough to notice. And in subsequent months the share of other products in the class has declined while the TRx share of generic simvastatin has continued to increase. This, to our knowledge, is the first and only case of a class-wide effect of generics. As can be seen from Figure 14.2, Zocor prescriptions were increasing rapidly prior to the launch of the generics because of Merck's heavy promotion. This growth continued after the generics entered the market.

Lipitor lost a substantial amount of business to the generic—the first time we have seen this kind of cross-molecule effect. It has since affected the other entrants in the market, with both Crestor and Vytorin seeing their shares flattening out. It is important to point out that the other generic entities in this market, lovastatin, fluvastatin, and pravastatin, all continued to lose share during this period, which indicates the effect was unique to simvastatin.

Managed care plans marshaled their forces to move patients to generic simvastatin and slowly began to move all or most other agents to third tier, resulting in further share gains for the generic as patients, who aren't particularly fond of statins (see the discussion of negative goods in Chapter 1), opted to spend less.

Does this mark a change in managed care's ability to "move share" to generics, or is it just that the stakes were so high and the risks so low in this product category? Did the more than $15 billion in annual statin sales, combined with the relative ease of moving patients from Lipitor to generic simvastatin with few risks of negative consequences, make this a special case? This remains to be seen.

Still, for products with some level of differentiation that is recognized by the market, it is unlikely that the availability of generics in the same category will have any meaningful effect on the ability to price. As always, the key is differentiation.

Chapter 15

Pharmaceutical Contracting Basics

with Jack Mycka

Con•tract: An agreement between two or more parties,
especially one that is written and enforceable by law.
—American Heritage® Dictionary
of the English Language, 4th ed.

The dictionary definition we cited above belies the complexity of contracting in our business. First, in a pharmaceutical context, contracting is not an endpoint but a pricing tactic designed as a means to an end. Contracts are not agreements to purchase certain quantities of product at certain prices. Rather, they are largely "contracts of sale," that is, they are an offer of terms (e.g., discounts, rebates) in exchange for performance (e.g., formulary listing, market share achievement). Second, the dictionary definition focuses on enforceability, a concept that is somewhat irrelevant in contracts between pharmaceutical marketers and their customers. A manufacturer cannot *force* its customer to take delivery of product. All it can do is not pay the promised rebate if the customer does not perform as promised. Third, the terms of the agreement may be somewhat obscure because contracting is usually linked to reimbursement status, and customer perception of the price of a medication will vary significantly depending on reimbursement.

Let's focus on the part of the definition that definitely does apply to our business. A contract is an agreement, and agreements are built upon mutually beneficial terms. Contracting must benefit both the marketers of pharmaceuticals and their customers. If the deal offered does not work for both of the parties involved, then it is likely doomed to failure from the start. This means that marketers must carefully consider the implications and outcomes (both intended and unintended) of a contract not only for themselves but also for the "other side." And to complicate matters, the other side may not be just one party; contracts can involve the needs of payers, prescribers, patients, and others. Taking the time to understand the motivations and goals of each of these groups greatly increases the chances of entering into a successful contracting arrangement. Motivations are not just important in getting the parties to agree to a deal and "sign on the dotted line." They are even more important *after* the deal is signed—in the implementation stage. Only after signing does the real work of achieving those potential benefits to both parties begin.

The other common point with our simple dictionary definition is that single word, "law." Pharmaceutical contracting is a regulated activity in the US and many other places, including some where it is not permitted. While marketers are allowed a significant degree of freedom, they had better understand—and obey—contracting rules and laws. This may be a challenge because contracting practices are constantly changing due to the interaction between marketers, payers, prescribers, and consumers of prescription pharmaceuticals. Because understanding the intricacies of compliance is usually not within the scope of the marketers' responsibilities, it is essential that they obtain advice from experts in these areas.

In this chapter, we will focus on some of the complexities that characterize pharmaceutical contracting as a pricing tactic, including why and when we use contracts, who we contract with, and how we structure contracts. We will focus primarily on the US, although we will touch on contracting outside the US and draw a few distinctions in methods and use.

WHY CONTRACT?

Given the lack of certainty, negative profit implications, and administrative expenses involved in a pharmaceutical contract, why would a marketer even consider contracting as a tactic? The first answer is often a negative one—self-defense against government regulation ("Provide us with a discount, or we will limit your ability to market your product!") or punitive reimbursement status ("Give me a rebate, or I'll make it more difficult for prescribers and patients to gain access to your products!"). It may also be a case of historical inertia ("We've always contracted before."), competitive pressure ("Our competitor is doing it. So we should, too."), and salesmanship ("If I give a discount, my customer says she'll be my friend.").

In reality, marketers should consider contracting only when it supports the overall goals of the company and the brand(s) in question and when the contracting effort is likely to be rewarded with returns, either through positive gains in performance or avoidance of losses that might occur if a contract is not undertaken. The contract must fit within an overall pricing and reimbursement strategy, which in turn should support both brand and corporate goals. While this "higher standard" seems self-evident, it is often not the basis on which the decision to contract is made. Contracting by this standard requires a marketer to have a thorough and realistic understanding of the market and, sometimes, to challenge the conventional wisdom of the organization that employs him or her.

In the simplest terms, any marketer considering contracting should examine the net revenue implications of any actions before offering any deal. If a deal cannot be reasonably expected to achieve a positive break-even point based on the actions of the individual client (or the client's potential competitors), then it probably should not be offered. While this might seem like a high internal hurdle for contract offers to overcome, it is entirely reasonable. Because marketers generally work for for-profit companies, any reduction in that profit should be intently scrutinized. (Of course, this also assumes that the same rigorous, market-focused standard was applied when the original price of the product was set, and unfortunately this is not always the case. Similarly, it implies that the terms of the contract will be rigorously managed. Without proper management, contracts can make losses even easier to see.)

Marketers must remember to consider net revenue within the context of the product life cycle. For example, if a product is about to lose its patent protection and generic competition is expected, then the net revenue requirements are different than for a product with no generic competition on the horizon. The contracting policy must also be viewed from both macro and micro perspectives, building on the fact that the macro market is made up of a multitude of micro customers (payers, physicians, pharmacists, and patients).

But, as we said before, contracts are based on mutual benefit. It's not just about the marketer's needs. In many cases, especially in competitive markets and with nongovernment customers, the contracting objective is a collaborative agreement designed to promote the mutually agreed upon goals of the marketer and the contracted customer. Understanding the goals of these customers may be more difficult. As customers, health care technology, and the delivery of care evolve, the business models that support the health care system also change. Understanding the motivations of the various parties to the contracting transaction increases the chance of successful implementation, and without successful implementation the entire contracting effort is a waste of resources. So, let's consider who we're contracting with and what's motivating them.

WHO PAYS FOR DRUGS?

To determine the customer a marketer might offer a contract to, we need to start with who pays for pharmaceutical products in the US (or in any other health care system). It's an essential question because the entity paying the bill is the one most interested in lowering that bill. However, the disjointed nature of the US payment system often obscures who the actual bill payer is. For instance, the patient is usually the ultimate "bill payer" but almost always through an indirect route. The insurance premiums (offset with benefit payments made by an employer) or taxes that patients and nonpatients alike pay subsidize reimbursement for drugs and other health care services. Patients end up paying for the majority of drugs in the US, but indirectly, through co-pays or other out-of-pocket mechanisms. When drugs are self-administered (as oral solid pills/capsules or self-administered injectables), they are usually reimbursed through the patients' pharmacy benefit. This benefit is set up by an employer or government agency and administered through a payer, such as a pharmacy benefit manager (PBM), health maintenance organization (HMO), or state Medicaid program.

These same payers are also the source of the money spent for drugs administered in the hospital or physician's office through the medical (rather than pharmacy) benefit, but, in this case, the "bill payer" is different. The classic example is the hospital as "bill payer" for inpatient drugs. In this case, the payer (e.g., the insurer or Medicare) does not reimburse separately for drugs. Drug costs are aggregated with many other hospital services and supplies and paid for with a single payment negotiated by the hospital with the payer for the applicable DRG (diagnosis-related group). The "bill payer" for the drugs is not the insurer or Medicare, but the hospital. Therefore, the hospital is interested in purchasing the drugs at the lowest possible price so that any savings will increase the profitability of the fixed DRG payment received from the insurer. Although acquisition cost is an important factor in this situation, clinical factors always take precedence in a hospital's decision to use a drug. However, hospital pharmacy directors are aware that if they *act* as if acquisition cost, rather than value, is of the utmost importance, they are likely to get a better price on most products. This difference between the recognition of value and cost, which is discussed in detail in Chapter 10, is at the heart of setting pharmaceutical prices.

To control drug budgets (and to accomplish other operational and quality objectives as well), payers establish formularies. These are lists of drugs, usually selected by an interdisciplinary Pharmacy & Therapeutics (P&T) Committee, that payers prefer physicians use with their patients. These lists are based on a therapy's efficacy, safety, and cost within the context of other therapeutic options. If there are multiple drug alternatives to treat the same patient, payers will often contract with marketers to obtain a price incentive (in the form of a discount or rebate through a contract) in exchange for preferential formulary status. This formulary preference is reinforced by mechanisms, such as lower co-pays and/or utilization edits[2] and controls, that support the preferred product and discourage use of its competitors. These mechanisms are designed to ensure that proper medications are used for patients and that the payer is able to maximize the value (and potentially minimize the cost) of the therapy chosen. The contract is built around the trade-offs that payers, patients, physicians, and marketers make in these situations.

---

[2] A utilization edit occurs when a claims processing system flags a prescription. The edit may be triggered by economic factors (e.g., therapeutic duplication) and also by clinical factors (e.g., drug interactions, dosage levels). For instance, the edit triggers a request for prior authorization or possibly denial of the claim.

Potential Commercial Contract Customers

Marketers must be able to tell when the opportunity value of a contract appears reasonable, when it does not, and how this applies to various potential contract customers. Their assessment should not be based solely on the customer type or "class of trade," though, because while this does indicate the customer's ability to perform on the contracted terms, these abilities vary greatly even within a single customer type. Instead, the effective marketer should consider the contract situation at a deeper level, looking at the payer's plan design, control mechanisms available, and the payer's ability and willingness to exercise these mechanisms in a given therapeutic category.

What follows is a short description of ten major customer types in the US. This list is not all inclusive, and it changes as customers evolve and new methods of managing care develop. For instance, Medicare PDPs did not exist before 2006, and just a few years ago, if specialty pharmacy providers appeared on this list at all, their description would have been quite different.

- *Hospitals/Integrated Delivery Networks (IDNs).* Hospitals usually focus on the delivery of acute care to patients for a relatively short period of time. Most hospitals also have outpatient care facilities, and many of them are part of an integrated delivery network or system in which a number of facilities collaborate to deliver a continuum of care to a community or region. Most of the 6,000 hospitals in the US are not-for-profit entities, although there are major exceptions.
- *Group Purchasing Organizations (GPOs).* GPOs are designed to bring together the purchasing power of their individual members (which

might be hospitals, physician offices, or other entities) to negotiate better pricing for their members as a group. GPOs also provide other consolidated clinical and administrative services to members that are designed to help increase efficiency and/or reduce costs.

*   *Pharmacy Benefit Managers (PBMs).* PBMs manage the pharmacy benefit (drug carve out) for employers, health insurance plans, unions, and other clients and usually emphasize their size in contract negotiations. Through their clinical expertise, they recommend therapies to their clients that balance safety, efficacy, and cost. They enforce the approved recommendations through formularies, electronic claims processing, and other preference methods, while also negotiating rebate contracts with marketers. Drug therapies are delivered through their retail pharmacy networks, mail-order services, and specialty pharmacy operations.

*   *Health Insurance Plans.* Insurance plans such as health maintenance organizations (HMOs) manage both the medical and pharmacy benefit for employers, unions, and other clients. They make clinical recommendations, directly apply them to their members through formulary control mechanisms, and negotiate contracts with marketers. HMOs vary from PBMs in that their responsibility for all medical spending on enrolled patients makes them much more likely to look beyond the impact of a drug therapy on the pharmacy budget to its effect on their total budgets.

- *Medicare Preferred Drug Plans (PDPs).* The Medicare Modernization Act of 2003 established Medicare Part D as a new option for Medicare patients to obtain pharmacy benefit coverage. Implemented in 2006, these plans are offered by numerous commercial insurers, including most major HMOs and PBMs. These insurers are encouraged to provide coverage through formularies and to reduce costs by negotiating rebates from marketers. Rebates offered to these entities are excluded from consideration in the calculation of government-mandated pricing, which we will discuss later in this chapter.
- *Specialty Pharmacy Providers.* SPPs provide specialized delivery of drugs and associated care to patients with specific maladies that are treated by injectable biologic drugs. These products commonly represent a high risk to the pharmacy budget because of their high acquisition costs. SPPs presently are more likely to negotiate with marketers to receive payment for services related to the administration of care (e.g., case management, data) rather than direct rebates or discounts. SPP is currently the fastest growing area of pharmacy. As the number of therapies of this type and the frequency of their use has expanded, the opportunity for SPPs to play an important role in care and cost management has expanded exponentially.
- *Clinics/Physician Offices.* Certain therapies (especially oncology) require patients' drug therapy to be administered to them in an outpatient facility. These clinics actually purchase

drugs for their own inventory, i.e., prior to the delivery of care. Marketers will often attempt to contract directly with these offices and offer pricing incentives in exchange for certain performance in terms of market share or some other criterion.

- *Trade (Wholesale/Retail).* Most drugs in the US are sold by the marketer to a wholesaler for further distribution to a retail pharmacy or other end pharmacy customer. In some cases (e.g., with generically available products), these customers exercise significant control over which product will be dispensed based simply on their decisions about which products they will stock. Trade customers also play a key role in the initial distribution of a new product. Marketers will often seek to contract with these entities.
- *Long-Term Care (LTC).* Nursing homes provide long-term care for patients. Drugs administered in LTC are usually obtained from pharmacy providers who specialize in this area. Marketers will often seek to negotiate contracts with these entities to obtain preferred positioning for their products in these facilities.
- *Home Health Care.* When patients are discharged from acute and subacute care facilities but still require specialized care in their homes, that care is usually delivered by nurses working for home health agencies. In some cases, where home health agencies can influence the choice of drug therapy for patients, marketers will attempt to contract with them.

While it is tempting for marketers to set contracting policy based on the customer type—especially as they are legally prohibited from discriminating between customers—simply segmenting by customer type doesn't provide enough useful information for marketers. The maxim, "If you've seen one HMO, then you've seen one HMO," actually applies to each of these customer types. A subsegmentation that looks at customer abilities, mechanisms, willingness and ability to apply controls, and performance experience is needed to determine when, how, why, and with whom contracts should be considered and reconsidered. The ability to use controls to influence product selections and product use varies both by payer type and within a single payer type. Further control mechanisms and their application are constantly evolving. All of these factors should be considered in setting contracting policy and considering individual contracting decisions.

HOW ARE MOST CONTRACTS STRUCTURED?

The grand symphony that is pharmaceutical contracting broadly consists of a few thematic areas with a multitude of variations on these themes. The most basic difference is the form of the pricing incentive. These are typically either discounts (up-front reductions in price) or rebates (retrospective payments made after the initial sale occurs). Usually customers prefer discounts if they are available because discounts mean less working capital must be consumed in the transaction. Customers, such as hospitals and clinics, who take product into their pharmacy inventory are often offered discounts as pricing incentives. Marketers, on the other hand, usually prefer rebates because they allow for measurement of customer performance before paying under these agreements. Customers who never take possession of product (e.g., HMOs, PBMs) but deliver drugs through a retail pharmacy network also prefer rebates because they are not able to take advantage of discounts.

The use of rebates in a contract does not imply that the marketer makes no payments at all until the customer meets the defined performance criteria. It is standard practice, especially within highly competitive drug classes, for *base* rebates to be offered in exchange for formulary status or other actions with *additional* rebates tied to other criteria. For instance, if the base requirement is formulary position with additional rebates for attaining certain volume or share benchmarks, then the base rebate is paid as long as the formulary position is maintained, even if sales and market share are declining and additional rebates are withheld. Other specific contracting terms you may encounter include:

- *Performance Rebate.* This type of rebate is tied to achievement of a specified performance target. For instance, upon achievement of a 50% market share, a 10% rebate will be paid, and an additional 1% rebate will be paid for each additional 2% increase in market share.
- *Price Protection.* The customer is guaranteed a fixed price for a fixed period of time, thereby mitigating the effect of any general list price increases.
- *Administrative/Service Fees.* Marketers pay customers such as PBMs, GPOs, and SPPs fees for specific actions undertaken by these entities. They are sometimes fixed amounts but can also be a percentage of contracted sales.
- *Most Favored Nations.* This contract clause states that if a more favorable price is offered to another customer, the marketer will also extend that same price to the "favored customer." This assures customers that they will receive the best commercial price offered by the manufacturer.

GOVERNMENT CONTRACTS IN THE US

Although marketers can choose whether or not to contract with commercial customers, they must contract with certain government customers. Just because marketers *must* contract with government customers does not mean that these customers should not be thought of as key segments to be pursued. On the contrary, these customers purchase significant amounts of product, and other factors, such as the prominent physician teaching programs that require rotation of interns thru the VA hospital system, can make these customers attractive for marketers to pursue.

Each unit sold to these customers is subject to mandatory pricing incentives, so the break-even point associated with achieving positive net revenue must be examined at a deeper level. Contracts with different government entities will also have different requirements, as described below.

State Medicaid Programs

Medicaid rebates, which originated with the OBRA 90 legislation, cover a mixed federal and state program developed to provide care for the poorest segment of the US population. All of its relevant pricing calculations are based on average manufacturer's price (or AMP), which approximates the average price charged for all sales to retail pharmacy. It requires that branded manufacturers pay the states a rebate of 15.1% of AMP or the "best price" (i.e., lowest commercial price)—whichever is greater—plus a penalty for any price increases taken above the Consumer Price Index (CPI) since the product was launched. Generic manufacturers pay a flat rebate of 11% of AMP.

In the past few years, state Medicaid programs have begun to exercise controls over product use by imposing formularies called preferred drug lists (PDLs). If a drug is not listed on the PDL, prescriptions will require prior authorization and/or be subject to other controls. In exchange for this preferential formulary treatment on the PDL, states request supplemental rebates, above those mandated by law. Some states have banded together to administer these programs through PBM/GPO hybrid "purchasing pools."

Public Health Service (PHS) and Disproportionate Share Hospitals (DSH)

Under section 340B of OBRA 90, special pricing must be offered to qualifying hospitals that deliver a large portion of their care to indigent patients. These facilities may access a discount price equivalent to the Medicaid price (with a time lag due to the need for a an up-front discount price versus a retrospective rebate) for outpatient drugs if the facilities:

- Are owned and operated by state or local government
- Provide a high volume of care (above 11.7%) to indigent patients
- Purchase for outpatient pharmacy outside other purchasing arrangements (e.g., GPO contracts). Outpatient is defined as "administered to patients up until the time of admission" and therefore includes the Emergency Department, although billing limitations sometimes prevent implementation in the ED.

Marketers may voluntarily extend lower prices to the facilities' inpatient purchases, and these are exempt from best price calculations. Many eligible institutions are large, urban teaching hospitals. Marketers may also choose to offer lower-than-mandated prices to PHS/DSH eligible institutions or to extend these prices to include inpatient purchases.

Federal Supply Schedule (FSS)

Federal government entities are eligible for special pricing defined in the Federal Supply Schedule. In November 1992, the Veterans Health Care Act (VHCA) mandated FSS prices could be no higher than non-FAMP (non-Federal AMP) minus 24.6%, which is the federal ceiling price (FCP) without commercial discounts or rebates. This base level is approximately *WAC − 26%*. A price lower than non-FAMP could be established, based on "comparable customer" discounts in place or negotiation between the marketer and the VA. FSS contracts typically last for seven years. Allowable price increases are governed within the terms of the agreement.

FSS customers fall under two categories. FSS1 covers the "Big Four" (Veterans Affairs, Department of Defense, Indian Health Service, Coast Guard), who account for the majority of federal sales. FSS2 covers the "other than" entities—all eligible entities other than the Big Four. Manufacturers may elect to cover both of these schedules with a single price or to create separate "dual" pricing for the two schedules.

Average Selling Price (ASP) and Medicare Part B

ASP was introduced under the Medicare Modernization Act of 2003 as a new price basis for reimbursing drugs administered under Medicare Part B. The basic concept is that ASP will be calculated quarterly based on the total commercial sales garnered for a product divided by the number of units sold. The reimbursement rate is then set based on the ASP (presently 106% of the ASP for outpatient drugs and 105% for inpatient).

The programs mentioned above do not include all of the government programs that mandate discounts and/or rebates. For instance, if a marketer sells a drug for HIV/AIDS, then the pricing required for AIDS Drug Assistance Programs (ADAPs) will be a key consideration. Navigating the murky waters of government contracts and pricing is not for amateurs or the faint of heart. This is another area where the marketing generalist should seek the counsel of experts more familiar with the terms, conditions, and practices of government contracting.

CONTRACTING OUTSIDE THE US

As with many other aspects of pharmaceutical pricing outside the US, contracting practices are similar to those used in the US in some countries and radically different, or even prohibited, in others. The basic difference can often be attributed to the single-payer environment that exists in many countries in contrast to the multitude of payers participating in the US system.

When the government is the sole payer, the reimbursement negotiation with that country's regulatory authority is somewhat similar to the contracting process used with a US payer, with the critical difference being that this payer has monopolistic negotiating power. For instance, in France, even after a product has received clinical clearance, it cannot be marketed until pricing and reimbursement negotiations have been successfully concluded. This process always includes a government-approved price and sometimes an additional agreement that, if sales exceed a certain level, the marketer will be subject to penalties or "claw backs." These penalties can range from rebates paid to the government to forced price cuts and a cessation of marketing activities.

Presently in the UK, however, prices are freely set by marketers but profits are regulated. Tenders with National Health Service (NHS) hospitals and Primary Care Trusts in the UK are very similar to contracting with US hospitals. This type of supply contract for hospital products—typically awarded through publicly regulated, competitive bidding processes and seeking heavily discounted prices—is the most common form of contracting in ex-US markets.

Another relatively new contracting mechanism outside the US is the risk-sharing agreement. In this type of arrangement, the marketer agrees to guarantee some level of outcome with the product and if it is not achieved to refund part (or all) of the purchase price. These agreements attempt to balance the price granted by a monopolistic payer (often on a provisional basis for a limited period of time) and the value that the payer expects to receive from the therapy in clinical practice beyond a trial. More on this concept will be discussed in Chapter 16.

The variations in contracting practices between US and ex-US systems and their applicability (or even legality) in specific situations are substantial. General rules that apply in all situations are very rare. The difficulties in understanding the pricing, reimbursement, and contracting intricacies of a single market can be exponentially multiplied when applied to the number of markets in the developed world, and they only compound when we consider practices in less developed countries. So, let the marketer proceed with caution.

WHEN TO CONSIDER CONTRACTING?

The simple answer to the question above is that contracting should always be considered; however, it should NOT always be done. The fit of contracting as a tactic within an overall pricing strategy is an essential element to consider in the US and increasingly elsewhere. In every case, the local laws, customs, and payer motivations need to be considered, and this is a constantly changing labyrinth to navigate. The good news for marketers is that, as mentioned earlier, as long as they keep the overall goals of the company and the brand(s) in question and the likelihood of the contracting efforts being rewarded with returns in mind, they should be able to make informed decisions on when and where contracting is appropriate and mutually beneficial.

Chapter 16

International Pharmaceutical Pricing
with Renato Dellamano and Jack Mycka

Structure creates behavior.
—Unknown

The way a health system is regulated—or not regulated—determines the way it works. This also applies to the pharmaceutical market, one of the most regulated markets in the world, and it is particularly true for pharmaceutical pricing. The way health systems operate, how they are funded, and how they make decisions heavily affect drug pricing processes, the timelines related to these processes, and, obviously, the price level at which the same product will sell in different countries. But what we said earlier about MCOs—when you know one MCO, you know one MCO—also applies to specific health systems. Although they share many characteristics, they also have distinctive mechanisms that manufacturers must take into account when setting pricing strategies.

Our goal in this chapter is not to acquaint you with the regulations of every health system in the world, but to underscore the importance of understanding the differences between health systems and appreciating the impact that these differences have on pharmaceutical pricing. We will be examining the most important mechanisms used in the ex-US environments to control pharmaceutical pricing and to make pricing and reimbursement decisions. In the process, we will flag some of the critical areas that pharmaceutical and biotech companies commonly tend to undervalue or to focus on only when it is probably too late to remedy mistakes. We will not focus here on the role of pharmacoeconomics—not because the topic is not important, but because the subject has been far too often overemphasized or demonized, with little benefit for the science and for those who want to understand pharmaceutical pricing.

Everyone in the pharmaceutical industry knows (or should know) that the pricing freedom enjoyed for new products in the US is the exception to the worldwide rule. But free pricing versus controlled pricing is not the only difference between the US and ex-US health systems that is relevant to pharmaceutical pricing. Consider the following examples of what makes pharmaceutical pricing a different exercise in ex-US environments:

- Regulations in ex-US systems make increasing drug prices an extremely difficult exercise—an almost impossible one in many countries. For instance, in Japan, increasing prices of pharmaceuticals is formally forbidden by national law and can be punished as a criminal offense.
- In many countries, authorities can cut the prices of reimbursed pharmaceuticals if spending in local health care budgets exceeds the planned levels. Italy and Spain are two "top 10" pharmaceutical markets in which governments recently cut prices in an ever-increasing struggle to control drug budgets.
- In other countries, like France and Belgium,

products that have been reimbursed for a certain number of years can face mandatory price cuts—irrespective of their patent status—simply because they have been reimbursed for a relatively long time.

- In innumerable countries, local pharmaceutical prices for a given product are tied to prices set for the same product in other countries, thus making global pricing coordination a vital and extremely difficult exercise.

- Last but not least, in some health systems, pricing and reimbursement authorities not only set prices for new products but also impose sales caps. In other words, they define maximum sales targets for individual products. If these targets are exceeded, penalties for the "guilty" company can be hefty, ranging from mandatory rebates to the imposition of temporary or permanent price cuts. France was the first large country to introduce these so-called "price-volume" agreements, but other countries (e.g., Italy) have joined in linking pricing and reimbursement negotiations to specific maximum sales thresholds.

The first step in appreciating how pharmaceutical pricing and reimbursement work in most ex-US systems is recognizing that national authorities in these countries have the power to set prices, grant formulary placement and status, define the care that will be provided, and ensure the actual delivery of care through physicians' prescribing guidelines. This is truly a different world from the US market. In this chapter, we will try to provide an overview of this different and intricate environment as it relates to pharmaceutical pricing so that you can better understand emerging trends in the maze of the global health care systems.

MULTIPLE PAYERS VERSUS NATIONAL PAYER MONOPSONIES

Consumers, physicians, and pharmaceutical companies in the US are accustomed to a multiple payer environment. In this environment, private and public third-party payer organizations coexist and, at least to some extent, compete to retain existing customers and win new ones. Competition in the payer environment is totally absent in most ex-US health systems. They are instead characterized by the presence of monopsonistic national payers. In a monopsonistic national payer system, the system is funded through taxes. Everyone entitled to health care coverage is enrolled in the national health scheme and is obliged to pay health insurance contributions according to national laws. Patients have no real opportunity to select an alternative third-party payer.

From the perspective of a pharmaceutical manufacturer, a national payer monopsony normally means that there will be only one national formulary in that specific country and, in controlled pharmaceutical pricing systems, one national authority that will set or negotiate prices according to the local pharmaceutical pricing regulations.

The National Health Service (NHS) in the UK is the prototype of the single, government-run, comprehensive national health system typical of many European and non-European countries, including Belgium, Finland, France, Italy, Portugal, Spain, Sweden, and Japan. This type of system delivers universal coverage through a single, government-run health care system. In other countries (e.g., Germany, the Netherlands, and Switzerland) a slightly different model can be found, with several public payers sharing the responsibility for funding and managing reimbursement of pharmaceuticals and other health services.

Canada is a unique example of a "multiple payer" country. The autonomous health systems run by the Canadian provinces or territories provide universal coverage and coexist with private insurance companies, which provide supplementary coverage for products and services not included in the public plans.

The operation of national health systems is evolving. Recently, national payers have learned to network, sharing information and best practices directed at handling common, thorny issues. For instance, in December 2004, the Canadian government contracted with the British National Institute for Health Care and Clinical Excellence (NICE)[3] to review the Canadian health technology assessment process—the key step in Canada to accessing provincial formularies. In the spring of 2006, NICE, the French *Haute Autorité de Santé* (HAT), and the German *Institut für Qualität und Wirtschaftlichkeit im Gesundheitwesen* (IQWiG) began meeting regularly to share information on their latest decisions, to compare processes and methodologies, and, possibly, to standardize them. Last, but not least, the European Commission's Directorate-General Health and Consumer Protection is funding the Pharmaceutical Pricing and Reimbursement Information (PPRI) project, which is aimed at creating a pan-European database of pricing and reimbursement systems. This will allow the various national payers throughout the European Union to access each other's pricing and reimbursement information through a common intranet platform. The PPRI project started in April 2005, with completion originally planned for the end of 2007, although as of this writing it has not been completed.

As these examples suggest, national payers not only have a strong monopsonistic power, but they are growing more deter-

---

[3]   NICE is authorized by the UK NHS to evaluate the cost-effectiveness of health technologies reimbursed in England and Wales and provide guidance for their use. Since January 2002, the Scottish Medicine Consortium (SMC) performs a similar function for Scotland.

mined and clever in using it. Moreover, national payers in different countries are increasingly benchmarking each other's reimbursement processes and decisions. National reimbursement decisions may now have international implications. In this type of environment, a clear understanding of the issues at hand and how they are evolving is critical to successful pharmaceutical pricing.

Clearly, the potential negotiating power of a monopsonistic national authority that can decide whether a product will be listed on its formulary and at what price is different from the negotiating power of even the largest commercial MCO in the US. On the other hand, it may well be that competition among multiple payers and PBMs might be more efficient at extracting lower prices from manufacturers than a state monopsony. The question is suggestive but, as yet, unresolved.

FIGURE 16.1 Countries with Multiple and National Formularies

Multiple Formularies	Single National Formularies
Brazil	Australia
Canada	Austria
United States	Belgium
	Denmark
	Finland
	France
	Germany
	Greece
	Italy
	Netherlands
	New Zealand
	Portugal
	Spain
	Sweden
	Switzerland
	United Kingdom

While politicians and health economists struggle to find sensible (and documented) answers to the "efficiency" question, governments in most ex-US markets persist in their strong belief that national payer monopsonies are still the way to go, especially because these monopsonies can theoretically control prescribing and drug use decisions as well as pharmaceutical prices. At the same time, while the national monopsonies continue, pharmaceutical and biotech companies must also pay close attention to the potential internationalization of drug and technology assessment processes. National payers around the world have already started exchanging information, comparing results and methodologies, and sharing best practices. Companies that do not coordinate their international pricing and reimbursement strategies and cannot consistently demonstrate their products' value risk failing at both the individual country level and on a much larger, international scale.

MULTIPLE DRUG FORMULARIES VERSUS SINGLE NATIONAL DRUG FORMULARIES

As Figure 16.1 suggests, more countries tend to use the single national formulary approach than multiple drug formularies. Interestingly, the dominance of the "national formulary" model is independent of the administrative form of the payer systems,[4] as evidenced by the fact that national formularies and reimbursement lists can also be found in health systems with more than one national payer—at least formally.

Pricing and reimbursement on the national formulary are closely related processes and are indeed the very same process in

---

[4] In some countries (e.g., Austria, the Netherlands, and Switzerland) patients can enroll with one of several authorized payers, depending on their place of residency, profession, or preferences. However, coverage standards are set at the national level and subject to public regulations, as are premiums, and payers cannot discriminate among enrollees or refuse enrollment.

some countries, i.e., listing of a new product can happen only after its price has been approved. The monopsonistic or semi-monopsonistic centralized reimbursement decisions made by national authorities usually take the form of listing (or not listing) a product on a national reimbursement list or formulary. Moreover, in many countries, reimbursement decisions and price negotiations involve the very same (or closely related) national committees.

National payers are the only entities deciding whether a new product will be listed on national formularies, and they can also decide at any time to reverse course and revise the national formularies. In fact, periodic and/or exceptional formulary revisions—at the individual product level or for entire therapeutic classes—are the rule rather than exception in virtually all pharmaceutical markets worldwide.

Finally, it is worth noting that the presence of one unique national formulary not only limits manufacturers' bargaining power in pricing negotiations but also limits physicians' and patients' choices because patients' limited ability to pay may pose insurmountable hurdles for the adoption of nonreimbursed therapies.

Let's use France as an example as it has one of the most comprehensive national formularies in the developed world. The local institution in charge of conducting reimbursement assessments and reviews is the *Commission de la Transparence* (Transparency Commission). The Transparency Commission evaluates all new approvals, including newly approved indications, dose strengths, and presentations of existing products, and periodically reviews the status of all reimbursed products. For new products, the Transparency Commission assigns a rating to both the medical condition treated by the product—the *service médical rendu* (SMR)—and to the incremental value brought by the new product in relation to existing treatments, in each of its approved indications—the so-called *amélioration du service médical rendu* (ASMR). The ASMR rating determines how prices will be set for a new product (or for its new presentations/indications) and, to a large extent, how the new product's price will relate to the prices of other therapies already reimbursed for the same indication(s). For products already reimbursed, the Transparency Commission will typically reevaluate the ASMR rating, considering new clinical evidence for the product or the introduction of other therapies for the same indications. Italy, Spain, and Sweden also periodically revise the reimbursement status of individual products and/or whole therapeutic classes.

Normally, the "value" of a given product is always a key factor in determining its reimbursement status. However, in most systems based on national formularies, the therapeutic value of the product is just one of several factors in listing decisions. Budgetary considerations, the manufacturer's contribution to the national economy (in terms of jobs, exports, and R&D expenditure), and even the historical relationship between the manufacturer and the national health authorities may affect listing decisions and, most importantly, the price at which the product will be reimbursed. And this assessment process is applied continually, not just to new products at the time of their approval. Formularies are subject to periodic reviews, so a current product may find its formulary status changed or its price revised...or it may be delisted outright...or the entire therapeutic class may be delisted!

Sometimes drug manufacturers themselves trigger a reimbursement revision by introducing product line extensions. In several countries, pricing and reimbursement authorities systematically review the reimbursement status of the whole brand every time the company obtains approval for a new indication, a new formulation, or even just a new package size. Needless to say, review of a product's reimbursement status normally signals price revisions, which are much more likely to be price cuts than increases. Therefore, the possible benefits of making any changes in an existing reimbursable brand should always be measured against the risks of triggering restrictions to its overall reimbursement status and/or a price cut. This is just one example of the importance of creating a pricing strategy early in the product development process.

Because reimbursement is no longer a one-time decision in most systems, but rather the subject of ongoing reassessment, pharmaceutical and biotech companies should verify the adequacy of their global and local organizational structures to meet the new, highly dynamic international payer environment. Demonstrating value and coordinating pricing and reimbursement strategies at launch is no longer enough because new pricing and reimbursement challenges may arise at any point in a product's life cycle. Effective price management must become an ongoing process, beginning long before commercialization and lasting throughout the product's commercial life.

MULTIPLE HEALTH PROVIDERS VERSUS NATIONAL HEALTH SERVICES

In most developed countries, national health systems control the majority of inpatient and outpatient services, directly providing health services from prevention to diagnosis and treatment, covering the whole continuum of care from primary through secondary and tertiary care. This means that most physicians in these countries are either state employees, belonging to the same health services whose authorities make pricing and reimbursement decisions, or are subject to mandatory and regulated service contracts with these health systems. This is particularly true in the primary care area; there is some room for private health service providers in specialty care, at least in some countries. As a result, public health systems in most of Europe are empowered to control physicians' prescribing behaviors closely. Some systems can even set budgets for the individual doctor.

Germany is the most highly controlling country in Europe in this respect, with detailed budgets set by region and by individual physician for both general practitioners and specialists. The health system determines an average prescribing cost per patient per year, and physicians exceeding their targets are subject to mandatory auditing of their clinical practice. If they overspend their budgets by more than 25%, doctors may have to pay back some portion of the excess. German physicians are also obliged to prescribe according to treatment guidelines set at the national level. Other countries with some form of strict prescribing controls and treatment guidelines include Austria, France, Italy, the Netherlands, Spain, and the UK.

It is critical to note that the ability of individual national systems to implement these controls is highly variable and depends on the efficiency of the health system at the local level. Regionalizing national health systems (i.e., decentralizing the management of health budgets and health service provision from the national to the regional level) tends to increase controls on prescribing and health spending; on the other hand, this may actually exacerbate regional differences in efficiency within the same country. Italy, Spain, Sweden, and the UK have decentralized management and budgetary responsibilities for their national health systems.

In addition, in most of Europe, the management of claims databases is not nearly as developed as it is in the United States, thus making the implementation of prescribing control measures more difficult. Still, the most efficient health systems (which are not necessarily the most effective in terms of patient care) constantly monitor drug consumption and expenditures to identify areas of potential misuse and overuse.

Typically, these systems determine rate of use with the ATC/DDD system, which is maintained by the Oslo-based World Health Organization Collaborating Center for Drug Statistics Methodology. The Anatomical Therapeutic Chemical (ATC) tool—popular in many countries, including Canada and most of Europe—classifies drugs, while the Defined Daily Doses (DDDs) tool reports medication use in a given territory per unit of time per inhabitant (or patient, if adequate epidemiological data is available). DDDs can be used to compare alternative treatment costs for a given condition and to set maximum reimbursement prices in the context of therapeutic reference pricing schemes. (We will discuss therapeutic, as well as international, reference pricing later in this chapter.) ATC/DDD-based drug utilization studies can also be used by national payers after launch to monitor the potential "overuse" of expensive therapies. Prices of drugs found to be "overused" can be cut, and treatment guidelines may be implemented to ensure appropriate use of the products. Many systems provide regular feedback to doctors, analyzing their prescribing activity and benchmarking it against that of other physicians. Similarly, if physician budgets are used, a physician's personal budget will be analyzed and benchmarked against other physicians' budgets.

In this context, it is worth mentioning that, unlike in the US, off-label use of approved medicines is formally illegal in most ex-US systems. For example, in Germany, off-label use of specific medicines in patients and indications for which there is no suitable approved therapy must be explicitly approved by the Federal Health Committee (GBA). Doctors found to be prescribing off-label must justify their actions to their *Krankenkasse* (the regional health care provider and payer). If the prescription is deemed inappropriate, they may have to repay the related expenses.

Pharmaceutical and biotech companies should never forget that pricing and reimbursement procedures in most of Europe also imply negotiating what specific prescribing guidelines or restrictions will apply to the individual product or to its therapeutic class. The monopsonistic nature of these national health systems allows them to negotiate prices, while their effectiveness in implementing prescribing guidelines and controls allows them to enforce the conditions they negotiate or impose on drug manufacturers.

Irrespective of their effectiveness in implementing controls, health systems will always tend to negotiate or impose specific conditions on the use of a new product, especially expensive therapies. This means that the clinical data submitted during the regulatory approval process must be especially compelling. Many pricing and reimbursement failures are often rooted in a clinical development strategy that produces data sufficient to obtain regulatory approval but insufficient to obtain appropriate use criteria or reimbursement in the desired patient subgroups.

FREE PRICING VERSUS CONTROLLED PRICING

The most obvious difference between the vast majority of ex-US health systems and the US health system is the pricing freedom that manufacturers enjoy in the US when setting prices for new products. The only countries in Europe that allow pharmaceutical manufacturers to set prices for their products freely are Germany and the UK, and, even in these countries, the freedom exists only under certain circumstances and carries certain caveats. What might be less obvious, however, is that the biggest impact of controlled pricing is not on the initial prices set for new products, but rather on price management over the product's life cycle. This is because it is extremely difficult to raise prices after launch in most of the "controlled price" countries.

The creativity of the various national health authorities in inventing rules and methods to control pharmaceutical prices is almost infinite. Therapeutic and international reference pricing, monitoring of drug consumption, price-volume contracts, price freezes, and mandatory price cuts for products exceeding a certain sales growth rate are all popular methods applied in ex-US health systems. Whatever the method, the end result is always the same: an assault on profitability. Managing global pricing strategies to ensure profitability requires an increasing level of sophistication and knowledge of the international payer environment.

No individual controlled-price health system is exactly the same as another, except for two characteristics:

- The philosophy behind the systems—i.e., the belief that a centralized monopsonistic body is

better positioned to negotiate or set fair prices for pharmaceuticals than free market forces, thus protecting consumers from the "excessive power" of drug manufacturers
• The use of price controls to manage pharmaceutical budgets and keep the growth of drug expenditures in check.

To illustrate this, let's compare how pricing is controlled in Japan, the second largest pharmaceutical market in the world.

In Japan, prices of new products reimbursed by the National Health Insurance (NHI) are set by the Ministry of Health, Labor and Welfare (the *Korosho*). Two methods can be used to set new product prices: comparative price and cost-plus. Under the comparative pricing method, which applies to products deemed comparable to existing therapeutic options, the new drug is priced at parity—on a daily treatment cost basis—to the relevant comparator. Premiums may be added on top of the "comparative" price to reward therapeutic value and innovation. Recently, the possibility of garnering premium prices has been extended to products approved for pediatric indications. Under the cost-plus approach, which applies only to products deemed to have no suitable comparators, the price of the new drug is set based on factors including manufacturing and distribution costs plus an appropriate profit margin. No premiums are available for products priced according to the cost-plus method.

New product prices are set at the NHI level, i.e., at the level officially reimbursed by the NHI. Regardless of what price-setting method was used, these prices are benchmarked against an international reference price. Japan uses public prices, as published in national drug directories, from four countries: France, Germany, the UK, and the US. If the initial pricing calculation is significantly above or below the international average, the price is adjusted downwards or upwards to bridge the gap, at least partially.

With regard to the pricing of marketed products, we observed earlier in this chapter that increasing pharmaceutical prices is explicitly forbidden by law in Japan. But beyond forbidding price increases, Japan is also famous for implementing periodic price cuts. In April 2006, an average cut of 6.7% was imposed on most products.

There are two kinds of price cuts in Japan: "regular" and "exceptional." They are normally implemented simultaneously every two years. The "regular" price cuts reflect the level of discounting offered by manufacturers when selling to their customers and are aimed at keeping reimbursement prices paid by the NHI as close as possible to real market prices. This is necessary because of one of the unique characteristics of the Japanese health system.

Unlike the US system, which allows physician dispensing only in specialty care, Japanese doctors may both prescribe and dispense medicines. They sell medicines at the official reimbursement price, but purchase them at a significant discount. The greater the discount on a given medicine, the greater the profit (or *yakkasa*) the doctor makes and the higher the financial incentive to prescribe the product. Although the Japanese government does not want to abolish this practice (known as *bungyo*) altogether, it has systematically targeted the distortions derived from it by gradually reducing the so-called "allowable discount range" to just 2%. If average discounts (measured as a percentage of the NHI price) on a given reimbursed product are found to be greater than the "allowable range," NHI prices for the product are cut by the same percentage, minus the "allowable range" of 2%.

This relationship between discounting and price cuts is important to pharmaceutical marketers. As several proprietary studies conducted over the years have failed to show any real relationship between the level of discounting—and the subsequent *yakkasa* or profit—and a product's market share, the value of discounting to marketers is questionable. Discounting as a tool to gain market share will work only in the short term, if it works at all. The imposed price cuts, however, which are directly proportional to the discounts, will affect profitability forever. So, marketers would be wise to think twice before entering a "discounting war" in Japan.

"Exceptional" price cuts in Japan are driven by the volume of a product's sales and its sales growth rate. Larger products achieving faster growth are hit hardest. Because of the prohibition on increases in pharmaceutical prices, all price cuts in Japan are, by definition, permanent, even after sales have slowed. The concept that prices of larger and faster-growing products should be cut is not unique to Japan; France and Italy are other remarkable examples of "top 10" pharmaceutical markets where "excessive" success may result in temporary or permanent price cuts.

Thus, controlled pricing, as practiced in Japan and other countries, means that pharmaceutical companies face an uphill battle in pricing and must struggle simply to maintain their profitability. But is the situation any better in the "free" pricing environments outside of the US?

Throughout Europe, there are only two countries—the UK and Germany—that, in principle, grant pharmaceutical manufacturers relative freedom to set prices of their products. However, even these two countries do not allow total pricing freedom.

In the UK, the profitability of pharmaceutical companies selling branded products reimbursed by the NHS is controlled under the Pharmaceutical Pricing Regulation Scheme (PPRS). The PPRS is the result of periodic negotiations between the Department of Health (DoH) and the Association of the British Pharmaceutical Industry (ABPI). Under the PPRS, a target return on capital (ROC) is defined for all pharmaceutical and biotech companies selling to the NHS. In this context, companies can freely set prices of new products, provided their overall profitability remains within the allowed limits. Companies exceeding the allowable ROC must either pay back the "excessive" profits or take price cuts on their NHS products until they fall again within the allowed profitability limits.

Companies whose profits are significantly lower than the

allowed target (less than 40% of the allowed ROC, under the current agreement) can apply for price increases until the overall profitability on their products sold to the NHS reaches a certain limit (65% of the allowed ROC, under the agreement which expires at the end of 2009).

Companies can also adjust UK prices of marketed products through a mechanism called "modulation." This means that companies can increase prices of certain NHS products if they proportionally decrease prices of other NHS products in their portfolio, ensuring that the overall impact on the NHS is neutral.

In addition, when the PPRS is renewed, the DoH typically imposes generalized price cuts across the whole portfolio of products reimbursed by the NHS. In January 2005, this generalized price cut was 7%. Companies are "free" to choose how to implement the price cut: they can lower prices of all products across the board, or they can redistribute the price cuts to only some of their products. What matters is that the overall result of the price modulation is in line with the imposed price cut.

Germany is the other notable example of pharmaceutical pricing "freedom" outside the US. Manufacturers can freely set launch prices of new products, and—in theory—they can also freely adjust prices of marketed products. However, to keep the drug budget under control, the government can impose price freezes and mandatory rebates. For example, the price freeze in place for the 2-year period from April 1, 2006, to March 2008 was imposed just 16 months after the previous freeze had been lifted. A mandatory 6% rebate was instituted at the same time on all patented medicines not subject to the therapeutic reference pricing scheme.

Apart from price freezes and mandatory rebates, Germany is also universally famous for its contentious therapeutic reference pricing system. Under this system, large groups of products, irrespective of their patent status, that are deemed therapeutically interchangeable are clustered in homogeneous reimbursement classes called "jumbo" groups. Examples of recently created jumbo groups—comprising off-patent as well as patented drugs—include statins, proton pump inhibitors, migraine products belonging to the "triptans" class (e.g., sumatriptan, naratriptan, almotriptan), and the ARB class of antihypertensives (e.g., losartan, irbesartan, eprosartan, and valsartan, plus their fixed combinations with diuretics). Under a therapeutic reference pricing scheme, the reimbursement level of all products included in a homogeneous group is capped. In other words, the *krankenkassen* will reimburse according to the reference price (or *festbetrag*) only—not the actual price of the individual products. Reference prices for each group are based on periodic surveys of selling prices (at the public price level) of all products in the group, including generics. In theory, German manufacturers are "free" to maintain prices of their products included in a reference group. However, because patients normally are required to pay the difference between a product's price and the reference price (something to which they are not accustomed and would rather not do), sales of products with prices significantly higher than the reference price tend to drop dramatically. For this reason, most companies choose to bring prices down to or just above the reference level, to avoid losing unit sales.

In a nutshell, outside of the US, there is an unwritten rule: all manufacturers are completely free to drop their prices, but taking a price increase is more fantasy than reality.

The pricing asymmetry prevalent in the controlled-price systems has an obvious impact on the gross profits generated over the life cycle of a product, even when ex-US launch prices are relatively high and not significantly different from those in the US. As a matter of fact, sales volume tends to be highest when a product reaches maturity, which is exactly the phase in a product's life cycle when price differentials between US and ex-US markets tend to be greatest.

This means that profits on drug sales in controlled-price environments may, over time, end up being less than half of what they would normally be in a truly free-pricing environment, where manufacturers would at least be able to recoup inflationary cost increases through price adjustments. The impact of this situation on a company's ability to fund R&D of new products is obvious, as is the profitability gap between companies with a large sales base in the US and those with a greater share of sales in regions like Europe or Japan. Several studies examining the relationship between pricing levels and pharmaceutical R&D in various nations have all found that price controls lead to reductions in R&D productivity and new drug development.

INTERNATIONAL AND THERAPEUTIC REFERENCE PRICING

In the context of pharmaceutical pricing, the term "reference pricing" often refers to two very distinct concepts of reference pricing that may coexist within the same health system: international (or cross-border) reference pricing and therapeutic reference pricing.

International Reference Pricing

Under international reference pricing, a country benchmarks its local price for a particular product against prices set for the same product in one or more other countries. International reference pricing is probably the most popular tool used in controlled-pricing systems. In the European Union, all but three countries (Denmark, Germany, and the UK) apply various forms of international reference pricing. Outside the EU, Japan, Canada, and Brazil are the largest pharmaceutical markets in which international price benchmarking is used to adjust and/or control local drug prices.

The one thing that all international reference pricing schemes have in common is that they are never the same. Countries may accord varying levels of importance to the international reference price in the overall price-setting process. Schemes may also vary according to:

- Which countries they include in the international reference (countries with similar population and/or per capita gross domestic product, countries geographically close, countries with the lowest prices in the region, similar languages, etc.)
- How many countries they include (from 1 to more than 15)
- What price is used for benchmarking (Canada, France, and Italy use ex-factory prices, while the Netherlands and Sweden use pharmacy purchase prices and Japan uses public prices.)
- How the reference is defined (e.g., the average price in the basket, the average of a certain number of the lowest prices in the basket, the median in the basket)
- What products are included in the international reference scheme (e.g., new products versus marketed products, all reimbursed pharmaceutical products versus all reimbursed pharmaceutical products sold through the retail pharmacy channel, or just any pharmaceutical product—including nonprescription and nonreimbursed drugs).

Needless to say, managing international pricing strategies requires knowing how to move in the international reference pricing maze. The appropriate initial price for a new product must be carefully chosen in light of this international coordination in price setting. The importance of international reference pricing is now more widely recognized, and "corridor-based" international pricing strategies have become the rule in the pharmaceutical industry rather than an exception. And there are ramifications for post-launch international pricing maintenance as well. A growing number of health systems monitor international prices after launch and may force price cuts if international prices in the reference countries drop. International price maintenance strategies are increasingly important to maintain profitability over the life of the product. Ongoing price management should not be left entirely in the hands of local affiliates.

It is important to note, however, that international reference pricing can also be an *opportunity* for drug manufacturers. Health systems may use international prices to order price cuts, but manufacturers can use them to justify price increases, at least in countries where regulations allow.

Therapeutic Reference Pricing

Therapeutic reference pricing is almost as popular as international reference pricing. Under therapeutic reference pricing, a health system sets a maximum reimbursement price for products in classes where there is opportunity for substitution with generics, less costly but therapeutically equivalent drugs, or less expensive therapeutic options. In other words, a branded product's price is essentially benchmarked against the prices of other therapeutic options in the given region. It is interesting to note that the first form of therapeutic reference pricing was actually implemented in the US, not Europe. Medicaid has used the Federal Upper Limit (FUL) or maximum allowable cost (MAC) system since the late 1970s, and it has since been adopted by most third-party payers in the US. European systems did not adopt therapeutic reference pricing until the early to mid-1990s. Germany was the first to implement it (the previously mentioned *festbetrag*), but only within groups of *generically* identical drugs. The extension of this system to *therapeutically* similar drugs is a later and purely European "innovation." In addition to Germany, Spain, Italy, and, more recently, France use therapeutic reference pricing.

Not surprisingly, every country tends to have its own version of therapeutic reference pricing. Systems may be distinguished by such factors as:

- Whether patented medicines are included (For example, Spain and Italy include off-patent products only, while Germany includes both off-patent and patented products.)
- Whether manufacturers are free to maintain prices higher than the reference
- How often reference prices are adjusted.

Most therapeutic reference pricing systems are similar, however, in that most create their homogeneous therapeutic groups by means of WHO's ATC/DDD system (or a slightly different version of it).

Developing a global pricing strategy for a new product requires an intimate knowledge of pricing and reimbursement rules in at least the most important countries where the product is to be launched. Factors perceived as secondary and typically considered as a boring duty of the regulatory affairs department—like the product's placement in the ATC classification—might play a major role in setting a product's reimbursement prices, at least in those countries applying therapeutic reference pricing. In large therapeutic classes, "me too" products and products with poorly documented clinical differentiation—even *patented* products—are at risk of being clustered with low-priced generics. This means that the clinical development strategy and approved product label must provide the desired positioning and the clinical differentiation needed for successful pricing and reimbursement negotiations.

LATEST DEVELOPMENTS: RISK SHARING THE EUROPEAN WAY

One of the most recent developments in the European pricing and reimbursement environment is the introduction of product-specific or therapy-class-specific "risk-sharing" agreements. Under these agreements, the price of a product (or a group of products) is set on a temporary basis only and is subject to review pending the availability of specified outcomes data. This approach is presently applied on an exceptional basis to therapies like orphan drugs and specialty products, especially in the oncology area. However, as news of this approach spreads, more payers may start experimenting with it.

An example of risk sharing is GlaxoSmithKline's deals with pricing and reimbursement authorities in two European countries. The negotiated prices for a new product were based on initial clinical data but will be renegotiated when more data becomes available from real-world observational studies. Interestingly, it seems that in these specific agreements, future prices may go *up* as well as down, depending on the results of the studies.

How this approach will be formally included in the context of existing regulations and the extent to which it will be used is still unknown. What is certain, though, is that the risk-sharing ball is rolling, and this may soon become the next "big thing" in national negotiations over pricing and reimbursement.

The concept of payers and manufacturers sharing the financial risks associated with product use is not entirely new. Drug manufacturers have previously offered free additional treatment to patients not achieving a satisfactory response with a given therapy within a certain time frame (e.g., Merck's program during the US launch of Proscar for treatment of benign prostatic hypertrophy). However, there are some substantial differences between these programs and the more recent risk-sharing deals seen in Europe.

In the Proscar case, the manufacturer *freely* decided to offer the deal, for a *limited* time, in the context of the product launch strategy. In addition, the manufacturer *freely* decided for how long the patient should be treated with purchased goods (ten months) and how much free treatment (two extra months) patients participating in the program would receive. In the European context, the deal is *imposed* by the national payer as a condition for including the product on the national drug formulary and will last until the payer decides that the deal is no longer necessary. Also, the level of financial risk sharing is *negotiated* between the national payer and the manufacturer. In other words, in Europe the manufacturer's freedom is limited to accepting the deal and thus obtaining reimbursement for the product or rejecting the deal and, in most instances, forgoing launch of the product in that country.

The most prominent example of this type of risk-sharing agreement was the February 2002 agreement between the UK Department of Health and five manufacturers of multiple sclerosis drugs, known as the Cost-Effective Provision of Disease-Modifying Therapies for People with Multiple Sclerosis. This program grew out of the January 2002 NICE appraisal of beta interferon (three different products) and glatiramer acetate for the treatment of MS. The appraisal was negative, and the NHS was advised not to reimburse either treatment except for patients who had already initiated therapy. However, NICE also invited the Department of Health to consider alternative strategies, "... with a view to acquiring any or all of the medicines appraised...in a manner that could be considered to be cost-effective." The risk-sharing agreement was the compromise that eventually allowed reimbursement of these products under the conditions specified in the deal. Under the terms of this agreement, manufacturers issued a "voluntary" price cut (ranging from 6% to 26%, depending on the product) to meet initial cost-effectiveness thresholds based on estimates of short- and long-term health outcomes derived from the limited clinical evidence then available. British MS patients could access these therapies only by participating in a ten-year observational study aimed at documenting short- and long-term health outcomes. Almost halfway through this ten-year deal, many British MS patients are still not enrolled in this observational study and therefore cannot access these disease-modifying therapies.

The most important implication of the deal for price was the further requirement that clinical outcomes in the prospective study were to be verified at two-year intervals to document the products' cost-effectiveness. If the cost-effectiveness ratios were worse than anticipated in the initial pharmacoeconomic model, then prices would be cut again. To date, no reassessment has taken place due to the difficulties in implementing the observational study. However, while the details of the implementation of this specific deal have not worked as planned, the precedent for further such agreements has been set.

Similar approaches are being explored in other countries. For example, in Italy prices of some products recently approved for certain oncological indications have been negotiated based on initial assumptions regarding response rates and duration of clinical remission. Future prices will depend on the outcomes of prospective observational studies that are expected to document "real-world" clinical outcomes. Similarly, in the Netherlands reimbursement applications for orphan drugs—typically approved on the basis of very limited clinical data—are being accepted on a provisional basis, postponing the full evaluation of the cost-effectiveness of the new products until there is enough clinical evidence to make a decision.

It remains to be seen whether all the clauses agreed upon in these approaches will actually be enforced. What is certain is that the financial risk taken by manufacturers is substantial. If the therapy does not deliver according to expectations, manufacturers may be required to pay back any "excessive" profits generated in the period before outcomes data became available. On the other hand—and with some caveats—this seems a reasonable way to obtain reimbursement, at least on a temporary basis, at prices and within timelines that would likely be unattainable with a more traditional approach.

If this type of agreement becomes more widely used, pharmaceutical and biotech companies must begin to consider acceptable deal structures at least as early in the clinical development process as Phase III planning. This reinforces the importance in the clinical development plan of factors such as the choice of clinical comparators (active comparators versus placebo), the kind of study design (superiority versus noninferiority), and the choice of clinical endpoints—an importance that has not been fully appreciated by pharmaceutical and biotech companies and has often led to major difficulties in achieving satisfactory pricing and reimbursement for new products. In the future, companies simply cannot afford to ignore these issues.

Clearly, this chapter was not designed to answer all possible questions with regard to international pharmaceutical pricing. An entire book would not be enough, and, given the speed at which the international pricing and reimbursement environment is developing, it would be outdated before it was in print.

If there is one key message to take away from this chapter, it is this: national health authorities around the world are not there just to foot the pharmaceutical bill. Instead, they have the overarching goal of ensuring that taxpayer money is properly used to fund cost-effective therapies, within given budgetary constraints, so that coverage can be offered to as many patients as possible. The array of methods these authorities use may vary, depending on the resources and health care priorities they are given by politicians in their respective countries, but their overarching goal is always the same.

Understanding this simple message alone can lead to myriad changes in how pharmaceutical companies do business. The way sales forecasts for new products are created; the design of clinical development plans; the timing and the methods used to develop international pricing, reimbursement, and market access strategies: all of these practices must be shaped by the reality of a regulated, global—but diverse—health care environment. The most advanced pharmaceutical and biotech companies have already made these changes. The others must follow suit, sooner rather than later, if they wish to succeed globally.

Chapter 17

The Future of
Pharmaceutical Pricing

*The [pharmaceutical] industry has not been successful
in halting the attacks, but on the other hand the attacks
to date have not had much effect on the industry in terms
of lessened prices or profits, or changes in operational
procedures. Whether this stand-off can continue under
current conditions and for how long is of course
the dominant issue at hand.*
—George Squibb

There is an old Arabic saying: "He who tells the future, even when correct, lies." Therein dwells the danger of prognostication. A reading of George Squibb's 1969 book chapter, quoted above, would have led many to believe that the end was near for the pharmaceutical industry.[1] Fortunately, for all of us, it is still here. But when, if ever, will the doomsayers' predictions come true? Twenty years ago, there were predictions that, in the very near future, MCOs would dictate virtually 100% of pharmaceutical product use and that they would use only the cheapest product. So what's happened? The principal result of managed care's entry into the US health care system was the dramatic increase in the use (and sales) of prescription medicines. According to J. D. Kleinke, noted health economist and entrepreneur, "One of the hallmarks of managed care in the United States has been the deliberately liberalized use of pharmaceuticals".[2] A funny thing happened on the way to the future.

Still, change is inevitable. Some changes in the pricing environment have taken place, and more will certainly occur. The advent of the Medicare Part D benefit has resulted in deep discounts to secure formulary placement, further widening the gap between list prices and actual selling prices. As I write this, the gap between list prices and selling prices is the subject of litigation at both the state and federal levels. The most certain result will be the end of AWP…and good riddance! Outside the US, we see that Germany has implemented reference pricing for several classes of drugs, Canada has used pharmacoeconomic arguments to deny reimbursement of many new agents, and the French and Japanese pricing authorities have forced price cuts and rebates for most drugs. In the US, we see that the cost of some new cancer agents has shot past $100,000 for a course of therapy. These are all major changes, coming from several different directions.

The pharmaceutical industry has done little of consequence in response to these and other changes. Prices are still often set based on the results of faulty assumptions and flawed marketing research. They are managed with little regard for the long-term future of the company, and they are defended with the same arguments that haven't worked for years. Fortunately for the industry, thus far the changes and challenges have been minor and rich research pipelines are still rewarded. But what new issues might change that?

Ten years ago, when the predecessor to this book was published, the prognostications I made were minor and almost inevitable. I predicted further consolidation of buyers, a narrowing of international price ranges, greater use of low price as a selling point, and continued demands for discounts. The one prediction that was only partially realized was the broadened use of pharmacoeconomics. In the mid-1990s the industry was abuzz over the prospect that pharmacoeconomics might help us identify, and justify, the right price for our products. For the most part, that has not occurred, despite the industry's substantial investment in pharmacoeconomics.

The response of participants in the US market to pharmacoeconomics hasn't changed much since then. Pharmacoeconomics is still not trusted or relied upon, especially if the companies themselves perform or sponsor the studies. Some foreign pricing authorities use pharmacoeconomics to justify their decisions not to cover new agents, and some costly products have been able to support their prices with economic data. Still, pharmacoeconomics has not proven to be the panacea many had predicted, unlocking the door to more profitable and value-oriented pricing. In fact, it is often used to slam the profit door shut by internal decision makers who believe they can sell product only with lower prices.

Part of the problem is the rigidity that has emerged among marketers, especially their insistence on the almost exclusive use of cost-utility analysis which, despite its inconsistencies and acknowledged flaws, has become the industry standard. This rigidity may make pharmacoeconomics easier, but it violates the very economic principles upon which the field was founded. The result is a lot of studies that have little practical use in the marketplace. As a noted economist recently said to me, "Pharmacoeconomics is like teenage sex. Everybody is doing it but nobody is doing it very well." This does not mean that pharmacoeconomics isn't useful or even necessary, but that, in its current form, it has failed to address the very issues it was designed to resolve.

THE $100,000 PRISONER'S DILEMMA

Perhaps the biggest question about pharmaceutical prices now and in the foreseeable future is, "How much higher can they go?" With new cancer therapies offering a few months of additional survival at a six-figure cost, many believe that it is only a matter of time before the government somehow intervenes and forces those prices lower. No one in the industry wants to see this happen, although many of its critics would be thrilled. The problem seems to be intractable because of game theory's classical prisoner's dilemma. In the prisoner's dilemma, two "prisoners" must decide whether to "betray" the other and escape punishment or "trust" the other's loyalty, refuse to talk, and be equally punished. You win only if you betray and the other player trusts. If the other player betrays too, you're both worse off. The best outcome is actually for each to "trust" the other; you both get punished but not as much. The dilemma is this: how do you know what the other player will do? Will he trust and pursue the greater "common good"? Or will he betray and tend to his own needs? Will individual pharmaceutical companies, in the face of potential government regulation, forgo a large amount of individual potential profit so that all can continue to enjoy moderate profit? Or will one company "betray" the rest, opting for the big profits and thereby triggering a payer reaction? There is every reason for the industry to show restraint in pricing because the consequences of government intervention would be devastating. At the same time, an individual firm that chooses to forgo the revenue and profits that can be earned through prices of this magnitude may arguably be failing in its obligations to stockholders. It will certainly be depriving its own research pipeline, which is the future of every firm.

And would the government intervene? There will probably be a lot of jawboning at high levels that are the equivalent of firing a shot across the bow of pharma, but, in the end, the response in the US will probably be through market mechanisms, rather than regulatory action. As we have seen in several non-US markets, the best way to rein in prices of this magnitude is to refuse to reimburse. When individual payers in the US believe the price is not reasonable, they can and will react by refusing to reimburse.

Payers are currently attempting to develop control mechanisms for high-cost products. The most common approach now is through patient cost sharing. A very high proportion of the Medicare Part D Prescription Drug Plan (PDP) formularies relegate high-cost biologicals and other categories to their fourth tier of coverage, requiring patient coinsurance of 20% to 40%. It is through this mechanism, in all likelihood, that those prices will eventually be brought down. These same methods will continue to be used for traditional pharmaceuticals as well.

This means that companies must pay much more attention to the management of their prices in the long term. They must stop pricing products in isolation (both from other products and from the rest of the market). They must see past what happens at launch. Currently, most firms have a "strategic pricing department" that recommends list prices and an account management or "managed markets" department that handles day-to-day pricing. There is often little in the way of continuity from "strategic pricing" to "strategic contracting," and the result tends to be wide price variation or a single-minded "no discounts" approach to pricing. Although each of these is a legitimate choice in some cases, no firm is served well by holding to a single approach.

Pricing is a process, not an event, and firms that fail to provide the attention and resources to pricing are costing themselves dearly. Pricing departments that report somewhere in the marketing services area of the firm tend to have no authority and only limited credibility and thus are not very effective. Those firms with pricing departments that report through their managed markets operations do not fare much better because these operations are usually advocates for the customer and not the corporation. This is not a criticism of the personnel within managed market operations, but a candid reflection on their orientation and the job they are expected to do—which is *not* the job of pricing. The pricing function must serve a different role, which it cannot accomplish if the compensation and evaluation of pricing personnel is determined by managers whose job it is to keep customers happy.

Someday most firms will realize that while pricing strategies are *really* hard to develop, they're also *really* important. Managing prices is at least as important as managing volume, cost, and the myriad other business aspects to which firms dedicate untold resources. The basic equation of *PRICE – COST X VOLUME = PROFIT* holds true, and price is the most powerful profit lever a firm can manage. Unfortunately, most firms have chosen to focus their attention on other aspects of the business and accept prices or pricing situations that are imposed by the market.

The future of pharmaceutical pricing is in the hands of the industry, as it always has been. If firms elect to continue their current practices, it is highly likely that prices will continue to be controversial and will be driven ever lower. If firms choose to manage their prices, the results will be different. Therefore, I have one prediction: the future of pharmaceutical pricing will be whatever the pharmaceutical industry allows it to be, through the actions and inactions of individual firms.

REFERENCES

1. Squibb G. Drug prices: The Achilles heel of the pharmaceutical industry. In: Keller BG, Smith MC, eds. Pharmaceutical marketing: An anthology and bibliography. Baltimore: Williams and Wilkins; 1969.
2. Kleinke JD. Just what the HMO ordered: The paradox of increasing drug costs. *Health Aff.* 2000; 19(2):79-91.

Index